HUMAN RIGHTS AND CORRUPTION IN BRAZIL

This book identifies two polarising concepts used by Brazilian mainstream sociology to explain the formation and identity of Brazil as a society: corruption and human rights.

As the 1988 Constitution is a milestone in the Brazilian transition to democracy and part of a broader movement of Brazil's integration into international law, the impact of international legal regimes on the attainment of human rights and the fight against corruption is analysed to evaluate the state of Brazilian democracy.

The book examines the outcomes of four specific international human rights regimes in Brazil, involving rights and policies related to:

- the right to food, the fight against hunger, and conditional cash transfer programmes;
- the right to health and the public healthcare system;
- the right to racial equality and affirmative action in superior education; and
- the right to recognition and the protection of Indigenous populations.

This approach is then applied to the examination of the international anti-corruption agenda. It focuses on Brazil's determination to deal with corruption against the backdrop of its worst democratic crisis of the last 35 years using meticulously researched case studies on the most prominent investigations, including *Mensalão* and *Lava Jato (Car Wash).* The book traces back to the origins of the international anti-corruption agenda and key legitimising efforts aimed at aligning the discourses with the developmental, good-governance trends, and delves into its repercussions within the Brazilian context, with a glance at their collateral effects in other parts of the world.

Thus, the core focus of the work revolves around human rights and the fight against corruption, shedding light on how democracy evolves or recedes over time under their influence.

Volume 4 in the Constitutionalism in Latin America and the Caribbean series

Constitutionalism in Latin America and the Caribbean

Series editors:

Richard Albert
Carlos Bernal
Catarina Santos Botelho

The *Constitutionalism in Latin America and the Caribbean* series publishes outstanding scholarship on the law and politics of the many varieties of constitutionalism in Latin America and the Caribbean. From single-jurisdiction and cross-national studies to inquiries into the relationship between constitutional and international law in multilevel legal orders in the region, the series welcomes submissions that identify, contextualise, illuminate, and theorise the origins, challenges, foundations, and future of constitutional law and politics in these understudied – but fascinating and important – parts of the world. Scholarship published in this series covers the range of methodologies in law and politics, including but not limited to comparative, doctrinal, empirical, historical, and theoretical perspectives. The series editors invite preliminary inquiries as well as full proposals for monographs and edited volumes in what aims to be the leading forum for the publication of exceptional public law scholarship on Latin America and the Caribbean.

Recent titles in this series:

Constitutional Erosion in Brazil: Progresses and Failures of a Constitutional Project
by Emilio Peduso Neder Meyer

Puerto Rico's Constitutional Paradox: Colonial Subordination, Democratic Tension and Promise of Progressive Transformation
by Jorge M Farinacci-Fernós

Constitutional Reasoning in Latin America and the Caribbean
edited by Johanna Fröhlich

Human Rights and Corruption in Brazil: Democracy at a Crossroads
by Lucas Delgado

Human Rights and Corruption in Brazil

Democracy at a Crossroads

Lucas Delgado

•HART•
OXFORD • LONDON • NEW YORK • NEW DELHI • SYDNEY

HART PUBLISHING
Bloomsbury Publishing Plc
Kemp House, Chawley Park, Cumnor Hill, Oxford, OX2 9PH, UK
1385 Broadway, New York, NY 10018, USA
Bloomsbury Publishing Ireland Limited, 29 Earlsfort Terrace, Dublin 2, D02 AY28, Ireland

HART PUBLISHING, the Hart/Stag logo, BLOOMSBURY and the Diana logo are trademarks of Bloomsbury Publishing Plc

First published in Great Britain 2025

A catalogue record for this book is available from the British Library.

Library of Congress Cataloging-in-Publication data

Names: Delgado, Lucas, author.

Title: Human rights and corruption in Brazil : democracy at a crossroads / Lucas Delgado.

Description: Oxford ; New York : Hart Publishing, 2025. | Includes bibliographical references and index. | Summary: "This book identifies 2 polarising concepts used by Brazilian sociology to explain the formation of Brazil as a society: corruption and human rights. The book examines the outcomes of international human rights regimes in Brazil, involving rights and policies related to: the right to food, the fight against hunger, and conditional cash transfer programmes; the right to health and the public healthcare system; the right to racial equality and affirmative action in superior education; and the right to recognition and the protection of indigenous populations. The book sheds light on how democracy evolves or recedes over time under their influence"—Provided by publisher.

Identifiers: LCCN 2024052799 (print) | LCCN 2024052800 (ebook) | ISBN 9781509981977 (hardback) | ISBN 9781509982011 (paperback) | ISBN 9781509981991 (Epub) | ISBN 9781509981984 (Ebook)

Subjects: LCSH: Human rights—Brazil. | Corruption—Law and legislation—Brazil. | Democracy—Brazil.

Classification: LCC KHD3003 .D45 2025 (print) | LCC KHD3003 (ebook) | DDC 345.81/02323—dc23/eng/20241106

LC record available at https://lccn.loc.gov/2024052799

LC ebook record available at https://lccn.loc.gov/2024052800

ISBN: HB: 978-1-50998-197-7
ePDF: 978-1-50998-198-4
ePub: 978-1-50998-199-1

Typeset by Compuscript Ltd, Shannon

For product safety related questions contact productsafety@bloomsbury.com

To find out more about our authors and books visit www.hartpublishing.co.uk. Here you will find extracts, author information, details of forthcoming events and the option to sign up for our newsletters.

To God, who worketh in us both the will and the doing of things.

To my mother, whose life epitomises what this book is all about.
To Loiane, Letícia and Miguel for being the reasons for everything I do.

FOREWORD

The book *Human Rights and Corruption in Brazil: Democracy at a Crossroads* discusses in depth an issue yet to be studied critically and, therefore, not fully understood: the role played by a legitimation discourse developed by American financial capitalism based on the fight, supposedly moral and legitimate, against corruption. As suggested by Lucas Delgado, the most recent outcome of such a strategy of imperialist dominion destroyed the incipient Brazilian dream of equality and sovereignty, broadly criminalised political activity and paved the way for the far right and fascism, without mentioning the relegation of Brazil from the position of the sixth biggest economy in the world to twelfth place.

The interventions in the name of the fight against corruption, led by the United States, but also championed by other superpowers of the Atlantic North, exemplify a broader movement according to which European imperialism from the nineteenth century, based on open and explicit 'racial racism', was progressively replaced by a slightly more subtle 'cultural racism'. Following this new trend, the 'white' is succeeded by the 'ascetic protestant' which changes the notion of a 'racial' backlog for a 'cultural' one, allowing the oppression of the same 'darker' peoples under the illusion of the end of racism.

The opposition between the 'flesh' and the 'spirit' has been the base of the Western social hierarchy for years. Dominance is associated with the 'spirit', as Kant proposed that capacities inherent to the intellect, morality and an aesthetic sensibility characterise the social class, the gender, or even the 'race' that ought to prevail as they embody these 'spiritual' dimensions. On the other hand, the oppressed must be convinced they do not have a 'spirit', but experience a life reduced to the body, a state of semi-bestiality, since animals, especially mammals, are regarded as those that share fleshly affections. This reduction to the dimension of the 'body' opens the path to the dehumanisation of the other. There is no place for empathy if these 'others' are considered 'less human' or 'dehumanised'. The difference in the reaction of Western Europe States and the United States to the refugee crisis in Ukraine, Libya or Gaza are an undeniable display of the argument presented here. The millions of Africans who die every day trying to cross the Mediterranean Sea or the sheer violence against civilians in Gaza, especially women and children, are perceived by average Americans and Europeans with far less outrage than the invasion of Ukraine, partially because they can see the Caucasian Ukrainian when they look at themselves in the mirror.

As the book well explores in its Introduction, the assimilation of the Brazilian as the sensual, the miscegenetic, as described by Freyre, or as the cordial, the passionate, and irrational, as argued by Holanda, is at the roots of the idea that patrimonialism is the defining characteristic of Brazilian politics and the State, found in Faoro. These accounts are reflections of the 'cultural racism' assimilation by local elites, educated in international universities, where elites, including 'cultural' elites, are formed. And it is precisely here that the false and cynical 'fight against corruption' discourse finds its dwelling, as a presumptive solution to problems deeply embedded in the formation of the society. The reality explored in this book, however, not only disputes that presumption but shows how the collateral damage of 'the fight against corruption' can be even more dramatic.

In fact, propelled by a democratic Constitution that embraced human rights, especially social and cultural rights, Brazil was experiencing a virtuous cycle as well depicted by Lucas Delgado in chapters 1 and 2 of his book, with arguments supported by solid empirical evidence regarding access to food and healthcare, ethnic minority access to higher education, and the protection of indigenous populations. These efforts to build a plural, vibrant, modern and economically dynamic society were paralysed due to a 'fight against corruption' saga, sponsored by the United States from top to bottom.

As documented in chapter 3, from its first steps to the detailed deployment of investigative methods and techniques during the *Car Wash* probe, American foreign policy and US Department of Justice leadership in the conception and execution of the anti-corruption international agenda is undeniable. Without a doubt, the 'fight against corruption' is one more façade to maintain in place the worldwide division of work, created in the post-War era, and according to which the Global South, represented by the Latin America, Africa and Asia, produces primary articles of little added value, like Brazilian soy, while the North has access to cutting-edge technology, financing their development with asymmetric international trades and the capture of the public budget.

Chapters 4 and 5 are a testimony to the deleterious effects of the anti-corruption saga not only on Brazil, but especially in Latin America, giving proof of its use as a tool of the new 'informal imperialism' we have already alluded to. This symbolic dominion renounces direct military and political intrusion to materialise itself in the form of a cultural command that legitimises economic exploitation based on the belief that the oppressed peoples are, indeed, inferior. American science, pop industry, and more recently, social media conglomerates manufacture ideals tailored to withdraw self-esteem from subordinate populations. Not without reason, in most of their media productions (movies, series, posts), Latin Americans are the criminals, the drug dealers, while the Anglo-Saxon is the man of law and justice.

Up until now, the world has been taught that the essential difference between the developed nations and the Global South is 'moral'. When it is said that corruption is episodic in developed countries while it is systemic in the Global South, and the oppressed themselves – including their main intellectuals and thinkers – believe it, then the domination is a given fact.

Without self-esteem, neither the individual nor society can defend themselves. The loss of self-esteem is the loss of the capability to control their own destiny. Denying a society its morality is to deny them what makes them human, and that is the part played by the international anti-corruption propaganda. Demonstrating how this idea has evolved since the constitutional transition to the most recent democratic crisis in Brazil is an effort of critical legal analysis that deserves attention and discussion not only in legal circles, but by everyone interested in understanding how law, politics and the economy are imbricated in our times. To understand the world we live in is one way to reverse the dehumanisation project. Whoever reads this book will understand the world better and, thus, invariably become more conscious of it and, therefore, human.

Professor Jessé Souza
Universidade Federal do ABC

ACKNOWLEDGEMENTS

This book is based on the doctoral thesis I submitted to The University of Manchester, entitled *Human Rights, Corruption, and Democracy in Brazil: How International Regimes Contributed to the Consolidation and Debacle of Brazilian Democracy*. As a key part of an enduring study that allowed me to attain the title of Doctor of Philosophy (Law PhD), I have to extend my gratitude to all my colleagues and professors who made that enterprise possible, and successful. Thus, I would like to thank Roberto Dalledone Machado, Carina Calábria and Guoshu Yang, with whom I had continuous and fruitful discussions. This work has also had so many inputs from my supervision meetings with John Haskell, as well as significant insights instigated by the acute mind of Chris Thornhill.

But if one asks me to identify whose existence was the most important in the writing of this book, I will undoubtedly point to Aloysa Rosa Delgado. She was a Brazilian woman born the youngest of five to a very poor family in a medium-sized urban town in the early 1940s. Brazil was experiencing the transition from a rural to an urban/industrial society, and in that process, the uneducated were relegated to the peripheries. Due to a flood, her family lost their home and belongings, living in a decommissioned railway carriage donated by the federal company so as not to end up on the streets. Childhood was not easy for her as she was not properly nurtured. For those who live with food insecurity, going to school is not an ordinary task. She dropped her studies in the second year of primary education, completing her literacy by her own informal means in the coming years. Her great companions were her twin brother, born minutes before her, and her piglet, Tantuim. As a teenager, with her older sisters working and her brother entering the Army, her family was able to move to a house in the vicinity of the city's prostitution district. That was not the best place to grow as a beautiful young woman, who had to deal with harassment and threats as routine, and so she got married at the age of 19 years old. Only four months after she had left her home, on a very rainy 9th of February 1962, a landslide demolished the little house where her parents, twin brother, sister-in-law and little nephew lived. They were all at home when the accident happened and died instantly. Every year, thousands of Brazilians who live in *favelas* and improvised housing on hills, mountain areas and similar landscapes lose their lives during the rainy season due to landslides. It is known as a kind of death that only poor people experience in Brazil. On that evening, it decimated the family of the young woman, who had the strength to move on and build a family despite the immense difficulties. She sacrificed every bit of her dream, and personal realisation, to provide a future for her children. By repaying every suffering, every act of violence, and every sorrow and pain with grace, love and unconditional support to everyone around her, she managed to raise a family of five children, 13 grandchildren, and two great-granddaughters. In her early eighties, she battled cancer with her relentless optimism and faith. She is an inspiration because her story renews my belief in the human being; she makes me believe that even surrounded by the worst conditions, suffocated by the roughest rocks, a flower can bloom. She gives me immense pride because I used to call her 'mom'.

I am also immensely grateful to my life partner, Loiane, who made my dreams and goals her own. I have never met someone so amazingly altruistic; I am so lucky to have her by my side. Letícia and Miguel are my fuel. The task of making such brilliant kids proud of me as a dad is really challenging and makes me want to be better every day, so I guess they have a big part in this as well.

Lucas Delgado

TABLE OF CONTENTS

LIST OF ABBREVIATIONS

CCT	Conditional Cash Transfer
CGU	Controladoria-Geral da União (Federal General Comptroller's Office)
CNJ	Conselho Nacional de Justiça (National Council of Justice)
COAF	Conselho de Controle de Atividades Financeiras (Council for Financial Activity Control)
DRCI	Departamento de Recuperação de Ativos e Cooperação Jurídica Internacional (International Mutual Legal Assistance and Assets Recovery Department)
ENCCLA	Estratégia Nacional de Combate a Corrupção e Lavagem de Dinheiro (National Strategy to Combat Corruption and Money Laundering)
FATF	Financial Action Task Force
GRECO	Group of States Against Corruption
IACHR	Inter-American Commission on Human Rights
IACtHR	Inter-American Court of Human Rights
IBGE	Instituto Brasileiro de Geografia e Estatística (Brazilian Institute of Geography and Statistics)
ICCPR	International Covenant on Civil and Political Rights
ICESCR	International Covenant on Economic, Social and Cultural Rights
ICHRP	International Council on Human Rights Policy
IPEA	Instituto de Pesquisa Econômica Aplicada (Institute of Applied Economic Research)
MDS	Ministério do Desenvolvimento Social e Combate à Fome (Ministry of Social Development and Fight Against Hunger)
MESICIC	Follow-Up Mechanism for the Implementation of the Inter-American Convention Against Corruption

MJSP	Ministério da Justiça e Segurança Pública (Ministry of Justice and Public Security)
MPF	Ministério Público Federal (Federal Prosecution Office)
OAS	Organization of American States
PAHO	Pan American Health Organization
STF	Supremo Tribunal Federal (Supreme Court)
SUS	Sistema Único de Saúde (Unified Healthcare System)
TCU	Tribunal de Contas da União (Federal Audit Court)
TI	Transparency International
TSE	Tribunal Superior Eleitoral (Electoral Superior Court)
UNCAC	United Nations Convention against Corruption
UNDP	United Nations Development Programme
UNODC	United Nations Office on Drugs and Crime
UNTOC	United Nations Convention against Transnational Organized Crime, and the Protocols Thereto
USAID	United States Agency of International Development

TABLE OF CASES

TABLE OF STATUTES

Introduction

Following a tendency launched worldwide by socio-populist urban gatherings such as 'Occupy Wall Street', thousands of millions of Brazilians took to the streets of Brazil in mid-2013. In the beginning, the protests were related to rises in public transport fares in big cities like São Paulo. Shortly after, a diffuse sense of discontentment led to larger demonstrations in which some were protesting for better education and public healthcare services, others against hegemonic media conglomerates' mass manipulation, while many were also calling for better representation and in opposition to the traditional political parties. The virtuous economic cycle initiated in the early 2000s was showing its first signs of exhaustion, the efforts in hosting two major worldwide sports events were not delivering the expected improvements in urban mobility infrastructure, and people shared a feeling that the best years were passing by, and life was not quite yet what Brazilian society had long desired. There was a sense of urgency as if an opportunity would be lost if there were no direct intervention.

For those who were watching the scenes on the news, it was difficult to discern what they were witnessing. The movement was not led by any of the traditional political parties. In fact, there was a fierce rejection of any partisan initiative at the centre of the mass manifestations, and the workers' unions were only marginally present. The perception of a spontaneous popular outburst was corroborated by a multi-layered agenda in which every claim seemed to be welcome. With time, some social movements identified with a liberal urban intelligentsia took responsibility for summoning mass gatherings in the most important cities. One of them, simply named *#vemprarua* (*#cometothestreets*), created an emotional video in which they used footage from a Johnnie Walker commercial.[1] The film shows the Sugar Loaf Mount – one of the most well-known landmarks of Rio de Janeiro – collapsing and a stone giant rising before the astonished and proud eyes of the population. The giant walks confidently into the sea and a subtitle provides the catchphrase: 'the giant is not dormant anymore'. The massive public rallies became routine in the following three years, but as time went by, they gained a patriotist aesthetic with a homogenous dominance of national symbols and colours of the Brazilian flag. The movements found heroes in young, bold law enforcement authorities who, with their decisions, cinematographic arrests, and packed press conferences following spectacular police operations, were shaking the political landscape and

[1] Dêivila Martins, 'Comercial Johnnie Walker O Gigante Acordou Rio de Janeiro Brasil' (YouTube, 1 July 2013), www.youtube.com/watch?v=Ja2CP0W3E6c.

bringing public authorities and influential businessmen to their knees.[2] Protesters had a common banner that seemed to encapsulate both the problem and the solution for all the nation's malaise: the fight against corruption. The commercial had a not very subtle reference to a verse of the national anthem that praises Brazil as a 'giant by its own nature', and the awakening was a metaphor for the decision of the Brazilian 'nation', the 'people', to voluntarily, autonomously, take the reins of their own destiny in their hands by going onto the streets to show their full and unconditional support for anti-corruption efforts.

The footage explores a contradiction that is very dear to Brazilian mainstream sociological thinking. Permanence and continuity are in contrast. The use of a geological structure to represent a 'country' or a 'society' invokes something immanent or inherited, that is in the state it is because it has always been there, immobile and incapable of change or movement. The collapse, and the rise of the giant figure, on the other hand, means rupture, revolution, and an unstoppable desire for the new. Most of the scholars who dedicated themselves to the task of describing how Brazil was 'formed' drew from a similar perspective.[3] Indeed, speaking of Brazilian society and culture, Holanda refers to a 'long and live tradition' that nurtures the Brazilian 'soul' inextricably connected to the Iberian Peninsula and, especially, Portugal.[4] In another passage, he comments on the political upheaval that took place in Pernambuco in 1817, and classifies the movement as 'exterior, epidermic', precisely because of how difficult it was to overcome the limits to 'political life' left as an inheritance of Portuguese colonisation.[5] Prado Jr also views Brazil in the context of a long and ongoing historical process stemming from the arrival of the Portuguese royal family in Brazil in 1808.[6] Later, Faoro says that from Dom João I to Getúlio Vargas, one socio-political structure resisted all transformations, challenges, and even the 'cross[ing] of the large ocean', and to explain the longevity of such form of power, he concludes that 'it is like this because it has always been'.[7] Ribeiro also underlines the idea that the Brazilian people have historically paid a 'terrible price' without producing the change they needed.[8] Fernandes goes a little further to claim that 'there is no definitive rupture with the past'.[9]

So, whether we look to authors who reflected upon the formation of Brazilian society in the first half of the twentieth century (Holanda, Prado Jr) or scholars who

[2] Editorial 'Moro é tratado como herói em manifestação em Brasília', *Estado de Minas* (Brasília, 13 March 2016), www.em.com.br/app/noticia/politica/2016/03/13/interna_politica,743045/moro-e-tratado-como-heroi-em-manifestacao-em-brasilia.shtml.

[3] Bernardo Ricupero, *Sete Lições sobre as Interpretações do Brasil*, 2th edn (Alameda, 2011) 24. The author shows that the objective to describe the 'formation' of Brazil is enunciated in the title or subtitle of the works of Caio Prado Jr and Gilberto Freyre and is present as an organising method for Sérgio Buarque de Holanda and Raymundo Faoro.

[4] Sérgio Buarque de Holanda, *Raízes do Brasil*, 27th edn (Companhia das Letras, 2015) 46.

[5] *Ibid* 103.

[6] Caio Prado Jr, *Formação do Brasil Contemporâneo: colônia* (Livraria Martins Editora, 1942) 6.

[7] Raymundo Faoro, *Os Donos do Poder: Formação do Patronato Político Brasileiro* (Globo, 1975) 819.

[8] Darcy Ribeiro, *O Povo Brasileiro: Formação e Sentido do Brasil*, 3rd edn (Global Editora, 2015) 21.

[9] Florestan Fernandes, *A Revolução Burguesa no Brasil* (Editora Guanabara, 1976) 202.

produced their work later (Faoro, Ribeiro, and Fernandes), the idea of a present that reflects a past that is impeditive of a better future is found in all of them.

An exception to that framework is Freyre. One of the pioneers in Brazilian historiography, he certainly points out the formative characteristics of Brazilian society, but not necessarily a need for change, rupture and revolution. His considerations about the Brazilian people are, in fact, deterministic, and the main traits of the 'new' Brazilian people have, in his view, contributed to the 'success' of the Portuguese colonisation enterprise.[10] Freyre's interpretation of Brazil is made up of antagonisms between the landlord and the slave, Christianity and African American cults, monogamy and sensuality, and so forth.[11] According to him, though, those contradictions were not detrimental to the surge of a new society; on the contrary, out of the synthesis of such contrasts came the singularity of the Brazilian people: miscegenation.[12] In his own words, in Brazil's formation, European culture was put in contact with the Indigenous culture, but that attrition was smoothed by 'the oil of African mediation'.[13] The result of such miscegenation is the idea of the Brazilian as physically and morally frail. The Brazilian would profess a 'lyric form of Christianity' and would be excessively prone to confraternisation, social mobility and 'moral tolerance'.[14]

As said, Freyre's work is predominantly descriptive, but it has had a profound influence on some of the works we have already alluded to. This moral malleability, and the absence of a clear-cut religious, political or social *ethos*, became the feedstock for some of the most influential Brazilian sociological work. For Holanda and Faoro, for instance, that is the 'cursed heritage' left by Iberic colonisation and that is what holds Brazil back from meeting its bright future. Holanda identifies the projection of the family – a classic Iberic institution around which the whole society orbits – over public affairs as the problem to be overcome. According to him, in Brazil's history, the private will has always prevailed over the impersonal order that characterises the bureaucratic State.[15] He coined the term 'cordial man' to describe the typical Brazilian, for whom personal bonds and affections dictate relationships, political preferences, business and State management despite the neutral and abstract assumption that shall govern the application of the law.[16] Faoro identifies a similar problem as the Brazilian drama, calling it 'patrimonialism' or 'capitalism politically oriented', that is the idea that 'the political community carries, commands, oversees public affairs as if they were their private businesses'.[17] For him, the State bureaucrat and the corrupt are one, so that

[10] Gilberto Freyre, *Casa Grande e Senzala: Formação da Família Brasileira sob o Regime da Economia Patriarcal*, 51st edn (Global Editora, 2021) 73.
[11] ibid 36.
[12] ibid 31.
[13] ibid 115.
[14] ibid 117.
[15] Holanda (n 4) 175.
[16] ibid 176.
[17] Faoro (n 7) 819.

'the strike against bureaucracy, as it hurts corruption, makes the nationalist string vibrate, the embryonic nationalism of Brazil'.[18] In other words, the 'corrupt essence' of the Brazilian people, inherited from the colonisation period and widespread in all areas of life, as described by Freyre, is the ultimate hurdle to development and prosperity. Corruption, in its multivariate forms, would be the sedative that has kept 'the giant dormant'.

The thread of thought presented here is developed by Souza who has already identified that Freyre's description of the results of miscegenation and correlated conceptual categories such as 'patrimonialism' and the 'cordial man' all belong to a similar account of Brazil's formation. He tries to demystify them, pointing to historical incoherences in Faoro's work[19] and debating how such ideas penetrated the Brazilian middle-class self-image.[20] Our purpose is slightly different, as while we acknowledge the importance and influence the works of Freyre, Holanda and Faoro have had on the mainstream understanding of Brazilian society's formation, vices and challenges, we want to establish that they are all conducive to the idea of different forms of corruption. Freyre's *pater familia*, who was the commander-in-chief of the religious, political and economic life of Latifundium, was polygamic and catholic, a lord of slaves who was sometimes sadistic, on other occasions sweet to them,[21] but above all corrupt in essence. Holanda's 'cordial man' is someone whose good manners towards all are a façade to cover personal affiliations and feelings, which govern his way to expand his 'personalism' to society.[22] The Brazilian 'cordial man' is, before anything else, a cynic, a hypocrite, corrupt. Faoro's 'bureaucratic estate' is nothing more than the projection of 'personalism' to the level of the State. The State bureaucrat is the one who 'steals and drains the sweat of the people', because in him public goals and personal interests are fused.[23] He is the embodiment of corruption in a public office.

Corruption – that is the very seminal element out of which Brazil was formed and the malaise to be rid of, the lingering tradition to be cut off, the permanent aspect that demands rupture.

Even adopting the same continuation/change, permanence/revolution dynamics, Prado Jr, Ribeiro, Fernandes and Souza belong to a different branch of Brazilian historiography. Prado Jr viewed all social structures studied by his counterparts – the Latifundium, the patriarchal family, and slavery – as subproducts of a 'vast commercial enterprise': the colony.[24] The foundational element that drove the formation of Brazilian society was not intrinsic to it, but extrinsic, related to the articulation of all social structures in favour of an exploitation system put

[18] ibid 200.

[19] Jessé Souza, *A Elite do Atraso: Da escravidão à Lava Jato* (Leya, 2017).

[20] Jessé Souza, *A Classe Média no Espelho: Sua História, Seus Sonhos e Ilusões, sua Realidade* (Estação Brasil, 2018).

[21] Freyre (n 10) 435.

[22] Holanda (n 4) 177.

[23] Faoro (n 7) 201.

[24] Prado Jr (n 6) 25.

in place by the coloniser. All activities in Brazil, from the relationship between landowners and slaves, and Portuguese and Indigenous populations, were in the service of the emerging market capitalists' colonial interests. The need for optimised production of agricultural and mineral goods of value in Europe is at the root of the 'sad human spectacle' of slavery,[25] which left behind a profound sense of racial discrimination. Ribeiro strongly rebukes Freyre's and Holanda's edulcorated views of the colonial period, pointing out that 'the original population of Brazil was drastically reduced by a genocide of alarming projections'.[26] Regarding the Afro-descendants, Ribeiro strongly says that although they were the ones who literally built Brazil from the ground up, our society has historically denied them 'any piece of land to sow and live, schools to educate their children or any order of assistance. It has given them only, and abundantly, discrimination and repression.'[27] Fernandes also refers to a process, intensified by independence, in which political power was assimilated by the oligarchal elites so that there would be no basic difference between the landowner and the citizen, or between dominant classes and civil society.[28] According to him, the articulation of the old aristocratic element with the legal-political aspirations of the new urban elite created a typical underdeveloped form of capitalism, still dependent on external demand, leading to a brutal social and regional concentration of wealth.[29] Out of that social construct would come the masses of black, poor, peripheric people: the 'ralé'. The 'ralé of new slaves' is also the focus of Souza's work, conceptualised by him as the black, brown and mixed race people in general, for whom the capitalist order that came about after the abolition of slavery and independence created only new forms of degradation. The state of abandonment only swapped places, from the crops in the countryside to the 'favelas' in the big cities.[30]

For these scholars, there is something inherited from the colonial period which Brazil has struggled to cut ties with. But it has nothing to do with corruption. It is an ongoing system of international exploitation, first colonialist, then imperialist, and finally neoliberal, that, being extremely profitable to national elites, creates a scenario of structural and systemic exclusion. Thus, inequality, disenfranchisement and deprivation would be the reminiscences to be fought against.

Human rights – to put aside all rhetoric subterfuge to sugarcoat slavery and indigenous genocide and recognise a history of their lack of access to most of the people. Exclusion in its crudest and most horrific form: that would be the Brazilian drama. The denial of basic human rights to huge portions of the population would be the legacy that has always been present, always lurking, always coming to haunt the attempts at emancipation.

[25] ibid 269.
[26] Ribeiro (n 8) 108.
[27] ibid 167.
[28] Fernandes (n 9) 40.
[29] ibid 210.
[30] Souza (n 19) 47.

The parallel between human rights and corruption in Brazil's most recent democratic cycle is what drives the whole endeavour forward. By the time the 2013 street protests began, there was a significant consensus that historic impunity and inefficiency in combating corruption had been an obstacle to democratic consolidation in Latin America, and that a holistic integrity system composed of strong and independent accountability institutions well aligned to international anti-corruption standards was key for Brazilian democracy to reach its ultimate stage of consolidation.[31] The images and emotions were very compelling in the sense that the fight against corruption had sparked the democratic flame in the Brazilian people's hearts. Specialist literature pointed in the same direction, and transnational agencies, such as Transparency International, were enthusiastic about such a remarkable societal and institutional engagement with their agenda. Compliance with international anti-corruption standards and democracy would be mutually reinforcing, and the demons of the past were about to be finally exorcised. Yet, a question was still to be answered: was that a sign that Brazilian democracy was maturing, or was it the beginning of the end?

The first chapter of this book articulates the two claims that encapsulate mainstream sociological interpretations of Brazil with the awakening of the last democratic cycle, initiated in the mid-1980s. It takes the reader through the discussion of how modern concepts of democracy respond to Brazilian sociology's historical claims for rupture against corruption or for the full embracing of human rights.

As we will see, as the 'electoral', 'minimalist' or 'low intensity' account of democracy settles for the mere presence of fair, free and competitive elections between concurring political forces from time to time, it suits the desires of those who advocate the anti-corruption cause. In other words, interpreters of Brazil who are for a rupture against a persistent culture of corruption see the 1988 Constitution arsenal of controlling agencies and oversight institutions as

[31] Mathew M Taylor, 'Corruption, Accountability Reforms, and Democracy in Brazil' in CH Blake and SD Morris (eds), *Corruption and Democracy in Latin America* (University of Pittsburgh Press, 2009); Timothy J Power and Mathew M Taylor, *Corruption and Democracy in Brazil. The Struggle for Accountability* (University of Notre Dame Press, 2011); Lindsay Carson and Mariana Mota Prado, 'Mapping Corruption and its Institutional Determinants in Brazil' (2014) SSRN Electronic Journal, https://papers.ssrn.com/sol3/papers.cfm?abstract_id=2497935; see also JC Calleros-Alarcón, *The Unfinished Transition to Democracy in Latin America* (Routledge, 2007); John Bailey, 'Corruption and Democratic Governability' in CH Blake and SD Morris (eds), *Corruption and Democracy in Latin America* (University of Pittsburgh Press, 2009); Stephen D Morris and Charles H Blake, 'Introduction: Political and Analytical Challenges of Corruption in Latin America' in SD Morris and CH Blake (eds), *Corruption and Democracy in Latin America* (University of Pittsburgh Press, 2009); Alfredo Rehren, 'The Crisis of The Democratic State' in CH Blake and SD Morris (eds), *Corruption and Democracy in Latin America* (University of Pittsburgh Press, 2009); Susan Rose-Ackerman and Bonnie J Palifka, 'Corruption, Organized Crime, and Money Laundering' in K Basu and T Cordella (eds), *Institutions, Governance and the Control of Corruption. International Economic Association Series* (Palgrave Macmillan, 2018); Barney Warf, *Global Corruption from a Geographic Perspective* (Springer, 2019).

important institutional advances to curb the problem,[32] and 'electoral' democracy as a supporting mechanism of vertical accountability. After all, universal suffrage would allow the population to hold representatives found corrupt by the judicial elites accountable, voting them out of office.[33] Although giving considerable weight to the right to vote, we argue that their vision of Brazilian democracy is still elitist and sceptical, as the exercise of vertical accountability by the 'people' on the ballot necessarily depends on the work of controlling agencies and prosecutorial authorities. Moreover, we will address the presence of influences, efforts and discourses originating in the international realm as driving forces behind the adoption of a whole vocabulary around the enhancement of the State's capacity to identify inefficiency bottlenecks, the need to map scenarios of imbalance between monopoly/discretion versus accountability, and the will to take the steps required to incrementally build an integrity system.

We will also explore how the urgency to resist the idea that the 1988 Constitution was just another chapter in the history of the preceding authoritarian regime made Brazilian constitutionalism fall into the trap of assimilating 'low intensity' democracy as full democracy, often referring to influences from international law as in 'opposition' to 'popular sovereignty', or as 'limitations' to the 'constituent power', missing an element that is formative of the constitutional moment itself.

Following the same logic, we will see that the claim for citizenship, enfranchisement and inclusion connects the turn to 'democracy' to a long process in which different democratic dimensions can be attained in multivariate ways and intensity. Democracy would present itself in different 'degrees':[34] be merely 'formal', advance to a 'participatory' intermediate level, or achieve inclusion to an extent that would make it 'social'.[35] Democracy could also manifest itself according to 'profiles' determined by trade-offs between its different dimensions that would make some prevail over others in different societies.[36] That mode of democracy, qualified by some basic human capabilities, faces the reality that human rights seldom become part of the legal political order through bottom-up

[32] Carson and Prado (n 31); Luciano da Ros and Matthew M Taylor, *Brazilian Politics on Trial. Corruption and Reform under Democracy* (Lynne Rienner Publishers, 2022).

[33] Emmanuel Nunes de Oliveira and José Álvaro Moisés, 'Corruption in the Perception of Brazilian Society: Persistence and Resilience' (2023) 29(2) *Revista do CESOP*; Letícia Barbabella, Miquel Pellicer and Eva Wegner, 'Court Performance and Citizen Attitudes Towards Fighting Corruption' (2022) 35 *Governance*.

[34] Guilhermo A O'Donnell, Jorge Vargas Cullel and Osvaldo Miguel Iazzetta, *The Quality of Democracy: theory and applications* (University of Notre Dame Press, 2004).

[35] Evelyne Huber, Dietrich Rueschemeyer and John D Stephens, 'The Paradoxes of Contemporary Democracy: Formal, Participatory, and Social Dimensions' (1997) 29(3) *Comparative Politics*.

[36] Larry Jay Diamond and Leonardo Morlino, 'The Quality of Democracy: An Overview' (2004) 15(4) *Journal of Democracy*; Hans-Joachim Lauth, 'The internal relationships of the dimensions of democracy: The relevance of trade-offs for measuring the quality of democracy' (2016) 37(5) *International Political Science Review*; David FJ Campbell, *Global Quality of Democracy as Innovation Enabler: Measuring Democracy for Success* (Springer International Publishing, 2019).

electoral representation processes, but are often championed by supranational organisations or multinational agencies, such as those promoting gender equality or environmental preservation.[37]

We will show that this was precisely the case in Brazil, where internationalists have always acknowledged that the constituent moment that preceded and immediately followed the enactment of the 1988 Constitution coincided with the insertion of Brazil into the international human rights movement, as proven by the signature and ratification of the main international human rights covenants and protocols.[38] Some argue that, after the enactment of Amendment 45 and the 2008 Supreme Court ruling in HC 87.585, Brazil moved to an imbricated hybrid dualism in which international law only integrates into the domestic legal system after a complex procedure that involves both the executive and legislative in a Presidential decree.[39] This ordinary ritual does not necessarily apply to human rights treaties. According to the Supreme Court's understanding, such treaties enjoy supra-legal status – above ordinary legislation and below the Constitution – until they pass the same procedure prescribed for Constitutional Amendments, in which case they integrate into the Brazilian 'block of constitutionality'.

Notwithstanding all these constitutional procedures to mediate the transition of international law into the Brazilian legal system, we will argue that Brazilian democracy has been incrementally influenced by a diffuse and subtle process of infiltration, in which international norms and mechanisms, discourses and agendas penetrate legal and judicial institutions and decisions without necessarily passing the constitutional procedure of international law internalisation. We identify the proliferation of issue-specific international legal regimes that invade, drive and influence decision-making through processes so dynamic and pluralist that the monist/dualist dichotomy becomes relatively irrelevant.[40] The penetration of international discourses and agendas into the Brazilian legal system seems to go beyond the reach of the legal constitutional procedures. International legal regimes can find porosities in the constitutional absorption procedure, finding informal ways to influence and produce legal and institutional developments.

[37] Hans-Joachim Lauth, *The Matrix of Democracy: A Three-Dimensional Approach to Measuring the Quality of Democracy and Regime Transformations* (2015).

[38] Antonio Trindade, 'Dilemas e desafios da Proteção Internacional dos Direitos Humanos no limiar do século XXI' (1997) 40 *Revista Brasileira de Política Internacional*; Flavia Piovesan, *Direitos Humanos e o Direito Constitucional Internacional* (Saraiva Educação SA, 2018).

[39] Juliano Zaiden Benvindo, *The Rule of Law in Brazil: The Legal Construction of Inequality* (Hart Publishing, 2022) 184.

[40] Nico Krisch, *Beyond Constitutionalism: The Pluralist Structure of Postnational Law* (Oxford University Press, 2010); Gunther Teubner, *Constitutional Fragments: Societal Constitutionalism and Globalization* (Oxford University Press, 2012), https://doi.org/10.1093/acprof:oso/9780199644674.001.0001; Martti Koskenniemi, 'Hegemonic Regimes' in MA Young (ed), *Regime Interaction in International Law: Facing Fragmentation* (Cambridge University Press, 2012).

One way or the other, a democracy underpinned by cutting-edge anti-corruption institutions or a democracy that entails human rights would have to face a legitimisation puzzle: democracy would not just be about elections, nor based solely on 'popular will', 'self-government' or 'people sovereignty', but would also refer to universalistic values, such as good governance or human rights.

In search of a better understanding of the relationship between democracy and these international influences, we have resorted to 'global constitutionalism' authors and theories. The prevailing debate in this body of literature refers to the transferability of 'constitutionalism' traits, such as representative deliberation bodies, or courts endowed with domestic legislation review powers, to supranational organisations like the European Union or the UN Security Council, to multinational agencies such as the World Trade Organization, or even to transnational organisations such as ICANN or FIFA.[41] The need to address the subject from this point of view stems from a concern about the 'legitimacy gap' between legislation imposed, and the binding decisions of such supranational organisations, and the 'people', the 'sovereign nations' that would be affected by them.[42] In this attachment to the idea that legitimacy only derives from effective 'popular participation', manifestations of 'self-government' of the 'people' have a striking similarity to the most orthodox idealisations of democracy. In fact, the disenchantment shown towards the expansion of international law and supranational organisations comes back to the apparent impossibility of projecting such idealisations about 'political participation' or 'democracy' onto the international realm.[43] By focusing only on the flux of national 'constitutionalism' influences on the international realm, these proposals lose sight of how strong and decisive international influences have been for the implementation of constitutional democracies worldwide. By 'breaking' the Habermasian idea that law only legitimises itself in the rationality of the communicative process provided by a democratic public sphere,[44] we find that there is no modern democracy that has been put into place or evolved without a decisive role played by international forces, mostly exteriorised under the idea of human rights.[45] In other words, not

[41] David Held, *Models of Democracy*, 3rd edn (Polity, 2006); Bardo Fassbender, *The United Nations Charter as the Constitution of the International Community* (Martinus Nijhoff Publishers, 2009); Gunther Teubner, 'Quod omnes tangit: Transnational Constitutions Without Democracy?' (2018) 45(S1) Journal of Law and Society.

[42] Neil Walker, 'Post-Constituent Constitutionalism? The Case of the European Union' in M Loughlin and N Walker (eds), *The Paradox of Constitutionalism: Constituent Power and Constitutional Form* (Oxford University Press, 2008); Samantha Besson, 'Human Rights as Transnational Constitutional Law' in AF Lang and A Wiener (eds), *Handbook on Global Constitutionalism* (Edward Elgar Publishing, 2017).

[43] Martti Koskenniemi, 'Constitutionalism as Mindset: Reflections on Kantian Themes About International Law and Globalization' (2006) 8(1) *Theoretical Inquiries in Law*; Michel Rosenfeld, 'Is global constitutionalism meaningful or desirable?' (2014) 25(1) *European Journal of International Law.*

[44] Krisch (n 40).

[45] Hauke Brunkhorst, *Critical Theory, Legal Theory, and the Evolution of Contemporary Society* (Continuum, 2012); Chris Thornhill, *The Sociology of Law and the Global Transformation of Democracy* (Cambridge University Press, 2018).

only is there no contemporary democracy in which domestic decision-making satisfies the same conditions of 'popular participation' required from international bodies, but also the idea that sovereign and fully stable democracies decided, in a second stage, autonomously to engage in supranational negotiations and comply with international consensus is historically inaccurate.[46] Mostly, contemporary democracy came about and has evolved ever since by a dialectical interplay of a national, participatory and popular aspiration and a universalist, cosmopolitan and international push for some worldwide consensus on ideas such as rights, governance, science, and even democracy itself.

We point out that some 'global constitutionalism' authors strike us with the reality that contemporary democracy and international legal regimes have been developed concomitantly in such an imbricated dynamic that it is impossible to historically or conceptually establish any causal relation between them. 'Global constitutionalism' theoretical references allow us to make the following claim: contemporary democracy has been founded on and consolidated by the constant mutual influence between a local, participatory electoral core and the influx of international content related to rights, governance and inclusion.

Chapters 2, 3 and 4 assess the results produced by different international regimes on Brazilian democracy, taking into consideration the twofold understanding of democracy set out in the first chapter. It means that after describing the main international legal instruments, declarations, and programmes related to the specific issue at hand, we move on to the legal and institutional unfolding of those initiatives in Brazil. In another step, we analyse the outcomes in terms of political enfranchisement and also in terms of inclusion in the form of access to/enjoyment of the rights under consideration.

The four international human rights regimes that compose our study are the right to food, the fight against extreme poverty and the implementation of conditional cash transfer programmes, the right to health and the Brazilian public healthcare system, the right to equality and the access of ethnic minorities to public universities, and the right to recognition and protection of the indigenous population.

The first two subjects are translated into the rights vocabulary by the 1988 Constitution as responses to historical deficits in Brazilian society. The 1988 Constitution elevates the eradication of poverty and reduction of inequalities to the status of objectives to be pursued by the democratic order it inaugurates (Article 3, III), and it sets out access to health as 'a right of all and a duty of the State' (Article 196). Therefore, although these constitutional semantics reflect

[46] James Tully, 'The Imperialism of Modern Constitutional Democracy' in M Loughlin and N Walker (eds), *The Paradox of Constitutionalism: Constituent Power and Constitutional Form* (Oxford University Press, 2008); Mathias Kumm, 'The Cosmopolitan Turn in Constitutionalism: On the Relationship between Constitutionalism in and beyond the State' in J Dunoff and J Trachtman (eds), *Ruling the World?: Constitutionalism, International Law, and Global Governance* (Cambridge University Press, 2009).

discourses and approaches also found in the international human rights movements related to these issues, they also represent the aforementioned historical claim for inclusion and citizenship enhancement in Brazil.

In these two cases, the universalist, cosmopolitan element of democracy would tend to cope well with the local, participatory factor, generating a bias risk in favour of our understanding of democracy as a political regime resultant of the relationship between international legal regimes, political engagement, citizenship enhancement and inclusion.

The last two subjects also have a seat in the constitutional order. Article 3, IV establishes as an objective the promotion of the well-being of all, 'without prejudice to race', and Article 4, VIII says that Brazilian international relations should follow the principle of 'repudiation to racism'. The whole of Chapter VIII of the 1988 Constitution is dedicated to the rights of the indigenous population to their 'social organization, customs, language, creeds, traditions, and to the land they traditionally occupy'. The historical record of slavery, violence and genocide against black and indigenous peoples in Brazil shows how difficult it has been to realise such rights. As they refer to issues that affect minorities, international organisations' declarations, shared best practices and international courts' decisions are often in a collision course of resistance from or, alternatively, negligence by the national, majoritarian political bodies of decision-making. The idea to address the access of ethnic minorities to higher education and indigenous peoples' recognition and protection is an intentional push for the opposite end of the spectrum in terms of majoritarian political support.

In chapter 2, we summarise the main international instruments related to the right to food and the fight against extreme poverty and famine, the right to health, the right to equality and the elimination of all forms of discrimination or prejudice, and the right to recognition and indigenous population's protection, and consider how they have influenced, produced and fostered the enactment of constitutional amendments, pieces of legislation, institutional practice, case law, and governmental policies in Brazil. Each section of chapter 2 has a concluding remark on the effects produced by the international agenda, the legal and institutional action it prompted or fuelled, and data collected on participation and inclusion. That is to say, in all four of our international human rights regimes, we analyse the outcomes both in terms of political enfranchisement and participation in elections, litigation before courts, access to public offices and positions of influence, and in terms of inclusion, rights to food, health, equality, and their recognition, fruition or enjoyment.

The analytical framework that underpins chapter 2 is also found in the following two chapters. But as they refer to the anti-corruption international regime, all the same steps are taken but from a different perspective. In chapter 3, we transition from human rights to criminal law by showing that, in several cases, international human rights propose imperatives regarding the criminalisation of acts and behaviour deemed as transnational violations of those rights. In those cases, the linkage between such criminalisation and human rights is a powerful way to rhetorically legitimise the expansion of criminal law by attaching it to such a successful international agenda. The international anti-corruption movement tried to hinge its discourse and exigencies on the idea that corruption invariably involves a human rights violation despite the absence of consistent data on the correlation between them.[47] However, that movement found its perfect harbour in the developmental *good governance* discourse. We address in more detail how few international anti-corruption initiatives had succeeded, from the approval of the 1977 Foreign Corrupt Practices Act in the United States to the 'cancer of corruption' speech, given by the World Bank President, James D Wolfensohn, in the 1996 World Bank/IMF annual meeting.[48] Then, we explore the expanding body of publications, articles, and even institutions portraying corruption as more than just a criminal offence, but as a transnational problem which nation-states were not prepared to combat efficiently, a matter of bad management that could be prevented by the adoption of the correct controlling institutions, and a cause in which society must engage to generate the expected results.[49] The mechanisms and direct influence that the international anti-corruption discourse had on Brazilian legislation and prosecutorial activity are also explored. In fact, Brazil went through three cycles of legal reform to implement the key trademarks of the international anti-corruption movement. The 'good governance' managerialist approach led to many legislative innovations in the early 1990s related to the implementation of 'efficiency' measures, such as Constitutional Amendment 19, the approval of an administrative improbity law, the enactment of a statute for public servants, and new public procurement legislation. Combating money laundering, public resources distortion and unchecked transnational flux of assets drove an institutional overhaul at the turn of the century, with the creation of the COAF (Council for Financial Activity Control), which is the Brazilian financial intelligence unit responsible to the FATF, CGU (Federal General Comptroller office), DRCI (International Mutual Legal Assistance and Assets Recovery Department) and ENCCLA (National Strategy to Combat Corruption and Money Laundering). And, finally, up-to-date, high-speed investigative methods and innovative forms of criminalisation underpinned the enactment of a new Anti-Money Laundering statute, a new Anti-Corruption law and a new Law Against Criminal Organizations at the beginning of the 2010s. Lastly, we examine the consensus in the specialist literature on expectations towards Brazil's alignment with international anti-corruption prescriptions, guidelines and discourses. In other words, we show how the adoption of strong

[47] Transparency International, 'Together Against Corruption: Transparency International Strategy 2020' (TI, 2015), TogetherAgainstCorruption_Strategy2020_EN.pdf (transparencycdn.org).

[48] Steven Sampson, 'The anti-corruption industry: from movement to institution' (2010) 11(2) *Global Crime*.

[49] Robert E Klitgaard, *Controlling Corruption* (University of California, 1988); World Bank Group, 'Helping Countries Combat Corruption: The Role of the World Bank' (1997), http://documents.worldbank.org/curated/en/799831538245192753/Helping-countries-combat-corruption-the-role-of-the-World-Bank; Susan Rose-Ackerman, *Corruption and Government: Causes, Consequences, and Reform* (Cambridge Unversity Press, 1999).

and independent accountability institutions, better equipped to carry on the fight against corruption, was depicted as the response to the historical social desire for the end of impunity and the promise that this was the missing piece of the puzzle in order for Brazilian democracy to complete its full cycle.

In chapter 4, we consider evidence of how the international anti-corruption agenda impacted the Brazilian political scenario. We intend to demonstrate how the strategic move to detach the fight against corruption from its criminological roots and to harbour it under a neoliberal legitimisation discourse acquired a strong grip on Brazilian democracy. The triumph of international anti-corruption standards came at the cost of core political traits of democracy. The coupling of the bold and reckless deployment of innovative investigatory methods provided by international anti-corruption law and best practices with the 'spectacularisation' of criminal prosecution shaped by the media and law enforcement authorities was the underlying cause of the interruption of a free and fairly elected presidential term and of a drastic and disruptive intervention in the 2018 general elections that impeded the frontrunner candidate's participation. Massive public campaigns made the loose definition of corruption adopted by Transparency International not only empty the Brazilian public sphere of any other political debate, but spread its effects to colonise and contaminate all the important human rights regimes addressed in the preceding chapters. We turn back to the human rights regimes discussed in chapter 2 to show how the obsession with the fight against corruption became the vocabulary of another cycle of exclusion and democratic impoverishment in Brazil.

Although the fight against corruption does not reside among the fundamental principles or objectives of the Brazilian Constitution, it stems from a long tradition in our historiography, becoming the lens through which Brazilian society prefers to envision policies adopted for the realisation of the rights provided by the Constitution. Therefore, we propose a broader discussion of the realistic possibilities of the success of the international anti-corruption movement. Data shows that not only does it not generate the promised virtuous developmental cycle, but it also often favours more unchecked corruption. Moreover, the detachment of corruption/anti-corruption from its criminological origins can pave the way for the engulfment of the political, participatory element of democracy. The thousands of millions of Brazilians that crowded streets and beaches wrapped in the Brazilian flag between 2013 and 2016 did not represent an autonomous outburst of citizenship after all. Their wholehearted engagement in the anti-corruption campaign had been planned, discussed and desired by technocrats in a UN meeting in Palermo, Merida, or even at the headquarters of an NGO in Berlin. The overall disenchantment with politics generated by massive media propaganda often empties the public sphere and favours the rise of national populist leaders only selectively committed to the anti-corruption agenda. The transition from the successful horizontal accountability of the institutions in combating corruption to the electoral vertical accountability advocated by Transparency International makes each citizen behave as a prosecutorial authority that uses the vote primarily to punish corruption according to a reality that one has little capacity to evaluate critically.[50] The public debate is absolutely dominated and captured by a corruption obsession that obscures every other relevant issue. Moreover, populists elected under the broad anti-corruption banner tend to address every policy through 'control', 'audit' and 'privilege cuts' discourses. In Brazil, the sequence of 'nit comb' operations to detect frauds and distortions in conditional cash transfer programmes superseded initiatives to better target those benefits or enlarge their coverage, generating a shrinking in public investment and an increase in the registration backlog until the Covid-19 pandemic struck. Local health councils were discouraged, and programmes were discontinued under the conspiracy allegation of 'ideological bias', 'political corruption' and public funds distortion discourse, with direct impact on primary assistance. The debate on ethnic quota policies has been encapsulated by the prevention of fraud by the identification commissions. The exploitation of mining in indigenous reserves became a priority because some political forces saw the reserves as an unnecessary hurdle to economic development and a disproportionate benefit to indigenous populations to the detriment of the majoritarian interest. Anti-corruption has not only dominated the political participatory element of democracy, but it has since aimed at the dismantlement of welfare state institutions, policies and programmes, leading to a cycle of exclusion related to the rights to food, healthcare, equality and recognition.

Chapter 5 is dedicated to the analysis of similar anti-corruption crusades in other parts of the world. Italy is well known for its pioneering anti-corruption push, having inspired the *Car Wash* operation in Brazil. Portugal witnessed similar levels of cinematographic prosecution activities with political repercussions in an operation which intertwined the threads of the *Car Wash* investigation. In Latin America, Peru and Ecuador were directly affected by the investigations in Brazil. We will also address how the specialist literature on the fight against corruption reacted to the traumatic events in all those countries, presenting a shy self-critique that, in fact, represents a reinforced faith in the virtuous cycle created by anti-corruption efforts. Lastly, we discuss those argumentative strategies and confront the empirical evidence on the possibilities of the fight against corruption becoming beneficial to democracy, development and human rights.

As we will see in the following pages, Brazilian democracy has been the object of a 'tug-of-war' between two different historical aspirations. For some, it is the regime of citizenship expansion, enfranchisement, access to human rights, and inclusion. For others, it has come as the chance to get rid of the 'cursed heritage' of Iberic colonisation – corruption. When democracy is at such a crossroads,

[50] International Council on Human Rights Policy, 'Integrating Human Rights in the Anti-Corruption Agenda: Challenges, Possibilities and Opportunities' (2010), https://ssrn.com/abstract=1705396.

discussions on what direction to take are necessary. This book is an attempt at signalling the way forward. If human rights regimes generated political engagement, making Brazilian society more plural and inclusive, contributing to democratic consolidation over the last 35 years, the triumph of the international anti-corruption regime sparked and fuelled a major political crisis, affecting democratic institutions (the presidential term) and procedures (barring a candidate from the 2018 general elections), contributing to the impoverishment of the public sphere and another cycle of exclusion.

1

Democracy and Political Legitimisation in Global Society

1.1. Introduction

On 5 October 1988, Ulysses Guimarães, President of the Constituent Assembly, gave a historic speech to introduce the Constitution that was being promulgated. He cursed tyranny, and started and ended by saying that 'the nation wants to change, the nation must change, the nation will change!' But what exactly did he mean when he so dramatically called for change? He said he had in his hands 'the statute of the man, the freedom, and the democracy'. In the same speech, he called corruption 'the termite of the republic' and outlined that, by that time, an 'outrageous 25% of the population were illiterate'. Seemingly, he understood that democracy would offer a response to all the changes the nation longed for, it would allow better oversight over public representatives and the end of corruption, and it would bring a solution for citizenship deficits such as illiteracy.

But after all, when the 1988 Constitution was enacted, was the transition to democracy in Brazil at the 'finish line' or at the 'starting point'? The answer depends on what one understands as 'democracy'.

Universal suffrage, with the extension of the right to vote to the illiterate, was enacted by a constitutional amendment approved in May 1985. Civil human rights such as freedom of manifestation, expression and thought were, in practice, exercised by different social movements before the new national constitutional assembly was installed in 1987, as shown by the massive gatherings during the '*Diretas-Já*' campaign. At the same time, social inequalities were so deep, and the levels of regional, ethnical and social exclusion so overwhelming, that Article 3 of that very same Constitution sets out as the nation's main objectives the consolidation of 'a free, just and solidary society', the eradication of 'poverty and substandard living conditions', the reduction of 'social and regional inequalities' and the promotion of 'the well-being of all'.

For those who believe that the great historical challenge to be addressed by 'the nation' is to fight corruption,[1] the controlling agencies and administrative oversight mechanisms provided by the 1988 Constitution were destined to produce a more efficient institutional web of corruption prevention and prosecution.

[1] eg Sérgio Buarque de Holanda, *Raízes do Brasil*, 27th edn (Companhia das Letras, 2015) and Raymundo Faoro, *Os Donos do Poder: Formação do Patronato Político Brasileiro* (Globo, 1975).

With greater social awareness of the problem, episodic competitive elections would allow constituents to use the power of the vote to distribute justice and punish corrupt representatives. For those who understand that profound social, economic and racial fractures are the hurdles to citizenship and emancipation, political participation and civil rights are important, but almost a luxury only accessible to a few.

In the followjng sections, we will show how the different sociological accounts of Brazilian society's formation relate to approaches found in twentieth-century theories of democracy and their impact on Brazilian constitutionalism.

We will first address how the claim for a rupture against 'the culture of corruption' seemingly copes well with a minimalist electoral form of democracy. We will argue that elitist accounts of democracy that tend to settle for power transfers between concurring political parties, as long as they are legitimised by free, fair, and periodic elections, share a tone of scepticism towards the possibilities of democracy in Brazil found in interpretations such as those offered by Holanda or Faoro. Furthermore, we will discuss how such elitist scepticism fed into accounts of the 1988 Constitution itself. As discussed below, 'electoral democracy' accommodates well the idea of the electorate as a complementary mechanism of accountability and control of government. The main driving mechanisms to move away from corruption, though, would be a web of high-performance accountability institutions fostered by international agencies, multinational financial aid organisations, and transnational NGOs, not necessarily reliant on means of popular participation. We will also approach how these ideas clash with Brazilian mainstream constitutionalism, as they build the constitutional identity upon the assimilation of democracy as a synonym for the manifestation of the 'constituent power', showing that the idea of 'rule by the people' suggested by the etymology of the word democracy (*demos* + *kratos*) still has a strong grip on how we approach the subject.

We will address how the Brazilian historical sociological claims for a substantial and inclusive form of democracy[2] confer an openness to international-universalist aspirations that pose a legitimation dilemma. The idea that democracy, as we know it today, is formed and evolves by legal constructs that are not necessarily responsive to mechanisms of popular consultation, involves a need to reconcile democratic legitimation with international influences and discourses, such as 'good governance' and human rights.

To solve that apparent contradiction, in the third section, we turn our attention to authors primarily dedicated to the comprehension of the phenomenon of law production and reproduction in the international, transnational, or even post-national landscape. We partially adopt Krisch's framework to place authors and their understanding of global governance regimes into two groups.[3] First, there are

[2] As seen in Darcy Ribeiro, *O Povo Brasileiro: Formação e Sentido do Brasil*, 3rd edn (Global Editora, 2015) and Florestan Fernandes, *A Revolução Burguesa no Brasil* (Editora Guanabara, 1976).

[3] Nico Krisch, *Beyond Constitutionalism: The Pluralist Structure of Postnational Law* (Oxford University Press, 2010) 13–17.

those whose work is related to the idea of *global constitutionalism*, who embrace the reality of regulatory regimes originating from international organisations and courts, but try to provide those imperatives with legitimacy by *transferring* concepts, institutions and procedures inherent to the national constitutional environment to the international or supranational ones. Second, other authors accept the proliferation and influence of a plurality of different law regimes, from equally diverse and multiple sources in the international, multinational, transnational, and even private sectors. Such mandates often overlap, contradict or reinforce each other, and do not depend on orthodox theories of legitimacy to impose and reproduce themselves, *breaking*, thus, the traditional description of law as the work of a monopolist nation-state centralised authority. We will address how those who are in the 'transfer' group insist on harbouring the legitimacy of international legal regimes in adaptations of notions such as 'self-government', 'sovereignty' and 'constituent power'. On the other hand, we will explore some of the proposals that 'break' with that pattern, and how they demystify the 'legitimisation gap', showing that modern democracy was formed by the conjunction of local and popular aspirations and universalist provisions. The idea of modern democracy being produced and developed by the incremental interaction between local/participatory political forces and universalist/cosmopolitan *ethos* is, then, advanced by showing that the arguments used to place democracy under siege across the world today refuse, deny and reject influences from global regimes. We will attempt to show that, by advocating the existence of a 'legitimisation gap' in international law decision-making bodies in 'defence' of democracy, this 'new' political trend becomes essentially anti-democratic. The challenge to demystify the 'legitimisation gap' will be carried out through a functionalist view of democracy in systems theory terms.

The last section discusses the Brazilian constitutional moment and how the influences drawn from the preceding discussions will guide the way forward. To determine whether Brazilian democracy is approaching its apex or definite decline – if it has advanced or receded – we will look at the Brazilian democratic experiment *telos* or profile, and how the two elements out of which democracy is founded and constituted have worked in that process and their relationship with mainstream accounts of Brazilian society formation and understanding.

1.2. Elitist Scepticism in Brazilian Mainstream Sociology, Theory of Democracy and Brazilian Constitutionalism

When Freyre and Holanda produced their work on the formation of Brazil and its society, democracy had not become a worldwide trend. Their masterpieces are from the early 1930s, when ideas such as eugenics and racial superiority were representative of a vanguardist intellectuality. Not without surprise, their hopes for democracy in Brazil were limited. Freyre thought that the sadistic relationship between the landowner and his slaves, with a mix of violence and sexual attraction, was mirrored in the relationship the Brazilian had with the State. For him, the bulk of the 'Brazilian people' had an intimate desire for 'a masculine government, boldly autocratic'.[4] Holanda believed Brazilian democracy had always been 'a sorry misunderstanding', which the rural aristocracy had imported and accommodated to its benefit. Proof of that would be the two main reformist movements experienced at that point in history, Independence and the Proclamation of the Republic, which were, in his view, intellectual and sentimental movements, welcomed by the masses with indifference or even hostility.[5] Even Faoro, an author from the post-war era, had a profound distrust of the Rousseanian 'popular sovereignty' ideal. According to him, the democratic order itself 'secreted' a government that was not determined by the majority, but by a minority that 'controls, perverts, and suffocates' the people.[6] Reflecting upon the reality of Brazilian society, he concludes that 'popular sovereignty' is sustained by the rural landowners, who become the 'people', because they speak on their behalf.[7]

Although discussing Brazilian democracy from a critical standpoint, both Holanda and Faoro show scepticism towards the chances for democracy to flourish in Brazil. More than that, for them, 'democracy' in Brazil is a political mode captured by what they identify as the problem to be overcome. Holanda believed that democracy was just a backdrop for the overflow of the rural elites' preferences and prejudices, and their sentiments. Faoro, similarly, believed that 'democracy' was a construct that allowed the factual exercise of power by the bureaucrat state, to the detriment of the people themselves.

According to that description, the main actors in Brazilian democracy are the elites who find ways of articulating themselves to fight for popular support and to reach power. Przeworski's definition of democracy shows a similar scepticism towards the possibility of democracy being conducive to rationality, representation or equality. He settles for a definition of democracy as a procedure of competition for votes, emphasising that it is the institutionalised periodicity of that competition under the same fair conditions that matters. The prevalence of that rule means that parties defeated in elections would be inclined to show compliance with the rules imposed by the winners. The prospect of winning under similar competitive circumstances in the next round would be the reason for the losers to keep 'playing the democratic game' without appealing to revolution, guns or cataclysm. That would sum up the advantage of democracy over other forms of decision-making, without any further implications in terms of legitimacy,

[4] Gilberto Freyre, *Casa Grande e Senzala: Formação da Família Brasileira sob o Regime da Economia Patriarcal*, 51st edn (Global Editora, 2021) 114.

[5] Holanda (n 1) 192.

[6] Faoro (n 1) 109.

[7] ibid 567.

meaning, values or purpose.[8] Huntington's assessment of the conjectures that led nations to adhere to democratic waves/counter-waves is also influenced by the factual possibility of power transfers through elections. He espouses the idea that periodical and institutionalised government transitions between rival political forces would be evidence of the competitiveness of the electoral system and that this would be enough to assign a regime as a democracy. He shares Przeworski's assumption that democracy can only be empirically verified by the occurrence of elections and the following chance that this procedure produces a change in who exercises power.[9]

Democracy as electoral competitiveness relies, thus, on a presumably value-free, objective, neutral and aseptic description of a political mode, characterised by one procedure to determine who governs – elections. Looking at those propositions through Sartori's eyes, *electoral democracy* is an effort to precisely depict democracy as it is, trimming the 'ethical fat'[10] from the classical philosophical idealisations of democracy.[11] Electoral democracy is an attempt to recalibrate the classical idea of democracy to make it suitable for a *polis* in which deliberation about every public affair in a single *agora* is no longer feasible, wiping from the concept subjective idealisations about the common good. It is a bitter solution for the task of making democratic ideals compatible with the large nation-state *polis* because it does so by relegating 'the people', and 'the nation', to a secondary supportive role. It is a conceptual framework that resembles Faoro's and Holanda's lack of trust in the possibilities of democracy in Brazil.

For those who envision corruption as the ultimate obstacle to democracy in Brazil, the unprecedented levels of autonomy granted to the Public Prosecutors' Offices, and the status given to the Federal Audit Court (*Tribunal de Contas da União*), were clear signs that the 1988 Constitution was heading towards an expanding web of accountability institutions and control agencies necessary to purge corruption from Brazilian government.[12] The new Constitution announced an arrangement in which a multi-institutional anti-corruption approach would be coupled with *periodic*, *free* and *competitive elections* that would 'provide the governed one of the most effective instruments of control over those who govern',[13] and give constituents the capacity to 'help reduce corruption' by 'voting corrupt

[8] Adam Przeworski, 'Minimalist Conception of Democracy: A Defense' in I Shapiro and C Hacker-Cordon (eds), *Democracy's Value* (Cambridge University Press, 1999) 15–16.

[9] Samuel P Huntington, *The Third Wave: Democratization in the Late Twentieth Century* (University of Oklahoma Press, 1993); Adam Przeworski, *Crisis of Democracy* (Cambridge University Press, 2019) 16.

[10] The expression is used by Susan Marks, *The Riddle of All Constitutions: International Law, Democracy, and the Critique of Ideology* (Oxford University Press, 2003) 50.

[11] Giovanni Sartori, *The Theory of Democracy Revisited* (Chatham House Publishers, 1987).

[12] Lindsay Carson and Mariana Mota Prado, 'Brazilian Anti-Corruption Legislation and its Enforcement: Potential Lessons for Institutional Design' (2014) SSRN Electronic Journal, https://ssrn.com/abstract=2497936.

[13] Emmanuel Nunes de Oliveira and José Álvaro Moisés, 'Corruption in the Perception of Brazilian Society: Persistence and Resilience' (2023) 29(2) *Revista do CESOP* 273.

candidates out of office'.[14] Although believing in the power of elections to produce change, for its proponents, agency, citizenship, and participation would be mediated by the work of an emergent technocracy, represented by non-compromised, politically neutral, interest-free judicial/quasi-judicial actors who, through prosecution, would show the electorate the way out of the grip of corruption. This is, in essence, still an elitist, sceptical and minimalist account of democracy, as the real decisive change would be between the controlling elites. The traditional rural oligarchies, represented by Freyre's *pater familia*, Holanda's slaveowner or Faoro's state bureaucrat would merely be replaced by an urban intelligentsia in strategic prosecution and judicial roles, with the people relegated to the task of giving support to their initiatives, especially through voting.

Elitist scepticism is strongly resisted in Brazilian mainstream constitutionalism. In attempting to describe the Brazilian constituent moment, Cavalcanti affirms that constitutional narratives are part of the Constitution and that 'the way a country understands its own Constitution has profound effects on the system's legitimacy'.[15] If that is the case, it is possible to assert that the prevailing idea of democracy and power legitimisation in Brazilian constitutionalism was forged by the need to rebuke sceptical views that describe the mid-1980s constituent moment as a process of continuity, and the 1988 Constitution as an elitist pact. The transition from an autocratic regime to democracy in Brazil is often depicted as a moment of manifestation of a 'constituent power' consubstantiated in broad popular political participation.[16] For some, the 1988 Constitution fits the legitimate constitutional tradition of the country, as a product of the 'constituent power of the sovereign nation', as it came into being through a constituent assembly freely elected, made up of representatives of the national will, legitimised by the democratic principle.[17] The idea of democracy in Brazil is conducive to a historical moment of societal mobilisation epitomised by the enactment of a new Constitution, often seen as the 'crowning moment of the transition from the authoritarian regime towards democracy'.[18] The mutual reinforcement between the two ideas makes the 1988 Constitution appear democratic because it originated in the manifestation of this 'constituent power', and the 'constituent power' is assimilated as a stamp of legitimacy because it was democratic. According to Barroso, 'the debate around the entitlement to the constituent power is a discussion about the legitimacy of power', and the 'theory of democracy fixed itself in the conception of sovereignty of the people'.[19] The idea that shapes mainstream Brazilian constitutional theory is that democracy is a consequence of 'people's

[14] Letícia Barbabella, Miquel Pellicer and Eva Wegner, 'Court Performance and Citizen Attitudes Towards Fighting Corruption' (2022) 35 *Governance* 718.

[15] Ana Beatriz VR Cavalcanti, 'Brazil in comparative perspective: the legacy of the founding, and the future of constitutional development' (2019) 6(1) *Revista de Investigações Constitucionais* 25–28.

[16] José Afonso da Silva, *Curso de Direito Constitucional Positivo*, 25th edn (Malheiros, 2005).

[17] Paulo Bonavides, *Curso de Direito Constitucional*, 15th edn (Malheiros, 2004) 168–69.

[18] Cláudio PS Neto and Daniel Sarmento, *Direito Constitucional* (Fórum, 2012) 147.

[19] Luís Roberto Barroso, *Curso de Direito Constitucional Contemporâneo* (Saraiva, 2019) 127–29.

constituent sovereignty'. It is a mix of the reminiscence of that ancient Greek imagery and Sieyès's representation of the French Revolution's aspirations to cut ties with an '*ancien régime*' and build a different society from scratch, which would require the manifestation of a prompting force that was autonomous, unconditioned, free, *ex nihilo*.[20] Not without reason, Paixão provokes the following question as a defining point for how one sees the 1988 Constitution and the democratic cycle that it symbolises:

> The new Constitution inaugurates a new time in the social and political life of the country or is it only a moment of passage within the regime initiated in 1964? To put it simply: the new Constitution means rupture with the military regime or is it a document of transition?[21]

Permanence or rupture, continuity or a new beginning. The presence of this dichotomy presents itself again in Brazilian history. The prevailing understanding of democracy in Brazil is intertwined with the process that culminated with the promulgation of the 1988 Constitution. The Constitution is considered legitimate since it was produced democratically, in the same way that the period that followed is described as democratic because its legitimacy stems from that Constitution. That construct is jeopardised if the Constitution is depicted as a pact between dominant forces, or as a 'gentleman's agreement' between members of the armed forces that were at the head of the incumbent regime, and traditional oligarchs. Barbosa identifies this 'elitist continuity tradition' in speeches given by the leader of the opposition party and the Supreme Court Chief Justice in which they welcomed the upcoming constituent assembly as a moment of 'transition', 'without rupture or trauma', that ended the 'revolutionary cycle'.[22] Attempts to understate popular participation during the constituent work also take the form of criticism of its unsystematic and chaotic methods, or point to the inevitable intermediation of political leaders in arriving at the constitutional text, as done on multiple occasions by former constituent member, Supreme Court Justice and Minister of Defence, Nelson Jobim.[23] In Brazilian constitutional theory, Ferreira Filho stands for the idea that, since the constituent assembly was summoned by Constitutional Amendment 26 in 1985, the 1988 Constitution comes from a reforming device present in the 1967 Constitution. According to his account, there was never a 'revolutionary rupture', so those who hold a different view are not technically sound, trying to rhetorically strengthen the new Constitution.[24]

[20] José Joaquim Gomes Canotilho, *Direito constitucional e teoria da constituição* (Almedina, 2013) 72.

[21] Cristiano Paixão, 'Direito, política, autoritarismo e democracia no Brasil: da Revolução de 30 à promulgação da Constituição da República de 1988' (2011) 13(26) *Araucaria*, https://revistascientificas.us.es/index.php/araucaria/article/view/1379, 162.

[22] Leonardo Augusto de Andrade Barbosa, *História constitucional brasileira: mudança constitucional, autoritarismo e democracia no Brasil pós-1964* (Centro de Documentação e Informação, Edições Câmara, 2012) 190–205.

[23] ibid 209.

[24] Manoel Gonçalves Ferreira Filho, *Curso de Direito Constitucional* (Saraiva, 2012) 49–50.

Those views not only undermine the bond between the 1988 Constitution and democracy, as said, but they also ascribe themselves to that same tone of scepticism towards the possibilities of democracy shown by Holanda or Faoro. They tend to trace a parallel between popular participation, social mobilisation and irrationality, disorder, lobbying, interest bargains, and so on, in a way that makes democratic procedures seem secondary. In this view, people, their associations, religious groups and public opinion mediators have a say in constitution-making only to provide the outcome with enough legitimacy for it to stand. However, the main constitutional framework remains a result of manoeuvres, negotiations and concessions made by powerful minorities that dominated the debate in the constituent assembly.

The development of the constitutional democracy concept in Brazil was, thus, intentionally driven to the opposite path. As seen, sceptical elitists portray popular participation in the Brazilian constituent assembly procedures as – in effect – a concession made by elites. Elections would have such a relative weight in democracy that the fact the constituent assembly was freely elected, and that other means of participation were granted to society during the Brazilian constituent moment, would be almost irrelevant to them. All the evidence of popular mobilisation and participation would be overshadowed by the arrangements made by party leaders during the 1988 Constitution-making process.

As a reaction to a constitutional narrative that reflects such disaffection with democracy, a considerable number of the Brazilian constitutionalists decided to make the democratic character of the constituent assembly the source of legitimacy of the new Constitution. Benvindo acknowledges that the 'clash of narratives' on the constituent assembly had a strong impact on the idea of the rule of law in Brazil. He concludes that participatory constitutional practice does not follow from the participatory character of the formation of the Constitution.[25] Although Benvindo does not believe that the two concurrent versions of the Brazilian constitutional moment are mutually exclusive, he aligns with most Brazilian constitutionalist scholars in the sense that the unprecedented levels of popular engagement and participation in the production of the 1988 Constitution were an unequivocal sign of an aspiration for a rupture with authoritarianism and a turn to democracy. Silva says that Constitutional Amendment 26, from 1985, was a political act and not a technical legal resource because it did not intend to preserve the 1967 Constitution, but to destroy it.[26] Likewise, Barbosa relativises the importance of the fact the constituent assembly was summoned by an amendment to the previous Constitution, emphasising that 'the constituent process represented a moment of rupture, and was underpinned by a singular performative sense, the idea of an active people, main role actor'.[27] Neto and Sarmento argue that the

[25] Juliano Zaiden Benvindo, *The Rule of Law in Brazil: The Legal Construction of Inequality* (Hart Publishing, 2022) 77.
[26] Silva (n 16) 87.
[27] Barbosa (n 22) 45.

1988 Constitution 'was an authentic manifestation of popular sovereignty, which does not need, to exteriorize itself, of a violent revolution'.[28] The prevalent idea of democracy in Brazil is linked back to the constituent moment that preceded the enactment of the 1988 Constitution, often described as more than just the occurrence of elections for the constituent assembly, but as a moment of singular social mobilisation, ideological effervescence, and political participation through different channels and means.

To avoid elitist scepticist views of Brazilian democracy that describe it as just one more display of a typical Brazilian lack of compliance with rigid concepts, of soft morality, sentimentalism, patrimonialism or, for all previous words, corruption, 'democracy' in Brazil is a concept very much identified with the classic conceptions of 'popular sovereignty', 'self-government' and 'general will'.

For those who align with the thought that corruption is the interpretive key to unlocking Brazilian sociological formation and the political order's main traits, the 1988 Constitution brought ambiguous signs. On one hand, it appeared to be just another manoeuvre, under the illusion of popular participation, to maintain power in the hands of those who always had it. In other aspects, it improved the institutional framework of control, accountability, prevention and repression of corruption, which was received as a reason for hope that accountability institutions would be progressively incremented in their competencies and resources, and that the population would engage with their actions in a virtuous cycle.[29]

This coupling between the institutional effort to end corruption and the popular mobilisation toward the subject is not produced intrinsically. At the very least hypothesis, it has not been solely manufactured within Brazilian policies but inspired by foreign initiatives. That is to say that much of the so-called 'Brazilian integrity system' design was incorporated due to foreign policy influences, and not by the force of an idealised collective will. Lauth, Buhlmann et al, Diamond et al, and Campbell expand democracy theory to understand it in broader terms. Instead of focusing on specific institutional/legal requirements for democracy, their departure point is the shared idea that democracy has three basic dimensions: freedom, equality and control.[30] Diamond et al posit that eight dimensions of democracy, for instance, could be encapsulated in the aforementioned three: aside from freedom and equality, the remaining aspects highlighted are the rule of law, vertical accountability, horizontal accountability, and responsiveness, all

[28] Neto and Sarmento (n 18) 138.

[29] Ezequiel A Gonzalez-Ocantos et al, *Prosecutors, Voters, and the Criminalization of Corruption in Latin America: The Case of Lava Jato* (Cambridge University Press, 2023) 156.

[30] Marc Buhlmann et al, 'The Democracy Barometer: A New Instrument to Measure the Quality of Democracy and its Potential for Comparative Research' (2011) 11(4) *European Political Science* 521–22; Lauth, Hans-Joachim Lauth, 'The internal relationships of the dimensions of democracy: The relevance of trade-offs for measuring the quality of democracy' (2016) 37(5) *International Political Science Review* 608–09; David FJ Campbell, *Global Quality of Democracy as Innovation Enabler: Measuring Democracy for Success* (Springer International Publishing, 2019).

tautologically related to the generic idea of control.[31] Buhlmann's Democracy Barometer, for instance, denotes as functions of democracy the presence of rule of law guarantees, such as judicial independence, the existence of mechanisms for mutual checks on power, measures for public administration transparency, the fight against corruption, and minorities' representation in decision-making forums.[32] Those contributions open the very concept of democracy to inputs that have no intrinsic link to elections. They transcend the ideas of 'self-government', 'popular sovereignty' and the 'rule of the people' to incorporate elements of democracy not necessarily dependent on or established by elections, votes or suffrage.

On the contrary, in these theoretical and empirical endeavours, there are signs of expansion of the concept of democracy to the incorporation of agendas, institutional settings and governance goals that are seldom produced by majoritarian deliberation (elections, plebiscites or popular referendum). In fact, many of those dimensions or indicators of the quality of democracy were historically pushed forward by international forces. According to Rodriguez-Garavito, a great part of the constitutional, institutional and legal reforms adopted in Latin America aiming at strengthening the rule of law were decisively influenced by the 'institutional turn' of the Washington Consensus, promoted by agencies such as the US Agency for International Development (USAID), the World Bank and the Inter-American Development Bank (IADB).[33] Santiso adds that those 'efficiency/good governance' and 'rule of law' packages involved, in practice, the enactment of new legislation and institutional arrangements that would promote judicial independence in the region aiming at empowering the judiciary.[34] Largely, the adherence by developing countries to such accountability mechanisms and institutional arrangements to grant the judiciary independence to scrutinise measures adopted by the other branches of government was a matter of compliance with international standards. The internalisation of those packages was a demonstration of susceptibility to the interventions of multinational organisations and transnational propaganda, rather than a choice of 'popular will' or a display of 'self-government'.

Albeit important to the development of the Brazilian system of accountability and the combating of corruption, the idea that Brazilian democracy would need elements of institutional and legal design developed abroad is inimical to Brazilian mainstream constitutionalism as it strongly leans on popular participation as its source of legitimacy. In other words, a concept of 'democracy' that

[31] Larry Jay Diamond and Leonardo Morlino, 'The Quality of Democracy: An Overview' (2004) 15(4) *Journal of Democracy*.

[32] Buhlmann et al (n 30).

[33] César Rodriguez-Garavito, 'Toward a Sociology of the Global Rule of Law Field: Neoliberalism, Neoconstitutionalism, and the Struggle over Judicial Reform in Latin America' in Garth B and Y Dezalay (eds), *Lawyers and the Rule of Law in an Era of Globalization* (Routledge, 2011) 159.

[34] Carlos Santiso, 'Economic reform and judicial governance in Brazil: Balancing independence with accountability' (2003) 10(4) *Democratization*, www.tandfonline.com/action/showCitFormats?doi=10.1080%2F13510340312331294077.

entails universalist/cosmopolitan consensus not obtained through manifestations of 'popular will' has been either overlooked or strongly resisted in Brazilian constitutionalism.

It appears to be decisive, though, for the 'anti-corruptioners', as they understood that incremental steps to further the seminal 'integrity system' found in the 1988 Constitution were the only way to eliminate corruption. Electoral democracy elitism and scepticism fit well with the combination of vertical and horizontal accountability championed by anti-corruption advocates, but their cause depended on reforms strong on 'state efficiency', 'good governance' and 'transparency' sponsored by transnational discourses and initiatives. For them, the Constitution that Ulysses Guimarães held aloft after his historic speech in the October of 1988 was not the rupture long waited, but a window of opportunity to exorcise the ghosts of immorality, patrimonialism and corruption that haunted Brazilian society and the Constitution itself.

As we will see in the next section, the claim for inclusion and human rights does not lead to many different legitimacy dilemmas.

1.3. The Brazilian Constitutional Transition as a Turn to a Regime of Rights: Democracy Shall Not Live of Popular Will Alone

There is a branch of Brazilian sociology that does not see historical democratic shortcomings as an incapacity to overcome corruption but as a lack of attention to the structural racist, social and economic barriers that deprive most of the population of basic human rights. Prado Jr believed that the surge of an authentic Brazilian society would depend on the inclusion of a social element that was not organic to the function of the colony, a great mass of 'unqualified, useless, and unadapted individuals' that had no jobs, and no rights during the Imperial and the Old Republic periods.[35] Writing as a witness to the decline of the military dictatorship and signs of openness of the regime, Fernandes argued for what he called a 'democracy of broadened participation' in which all the dispossessed, exploited and oppressed would be mobilised, a condition for 'the democratic republic to cease to be a fiction'.[36] Ribeiro believed that one could only speak of democracy in Brazil under minimal conditions of social and racial equality, absent even after the enactment of the new Constitution. For him, 'there is either democracy for all or democracy for nobody because to the oppression against the black, doomed to the condition of a fighter for their freedom, corresponds the opprobrium for the white, relegated to the role of oppressor within their own society.'[37]

[35] Caio Prado Jr, *Formação do Brasil Contemporâneo: colônia* (Livraria Martins Editora, 1942) 279.
[36] Florestan Fernandes, *Brasil em Compasso de Espera* (Editora Hucitec, 1980) 31.
[37] Darcy Ribeiro, *O Povo Brasileiro: Formação e Sentido do Brasil*, 3rd edn (Global Editora, 2015) 171.

As we have seen, the claim here is for a qualified form of 'democracy' that 'electoral elitism' is incapable of fulfilling. There is an undeniable aspect of inclusion, access and fruition of rights to these accounts of Brazilian sociological origins. For these authors, the answer to the question we proposed at the beginning of this chapter is obvious: the Brazilian 1988 Constitution was just the starting point to a historical process of enfranchisement and social emancipation. Thus, although free, fair and periodic elections with universal suffrage – which are the landmarks of electoralism – had been present in the Brazilian legal system even before the 1988 Constitution, they would be just the bare minimum for a polity to be assigned as a democracy.

O'Donnell and others are very aware of the difficulties in drawing the internal and external boundaries of the requirements of a democracy. In other words, they find it difficult to determine what civil and political rights embody the essence of democracy and what social and economic rights inflate the concept of democracy with ideological desires and wishes.[38] Their attempt to categorise them caused them to consider that thresholds cannot be found in the kinds of rights that belong or do not belong to the concept of democracy, but are probably encountered in a search for the extent to which all of them are effectively realised within a society. That change of focus made them abandon the democratic/undemocratic dichotomy to consider 'different degrees of democraticness'.[39] Similarly, the asymmetries in the way different democratic principles are perceived in different realities made Beetham affirm that 'democracy is not an all-or-nothing affair, but a matter of the degree to which the basic principles are realized: a comparative rather than an absolute judgment'.[40] O'Donnell and others explicitly say that the premise of their analytical model 'is that the quality of democracy in given countries may be gauged by its different degrees of democraticness along several dimensions'.[41]

In other words, if a regime does not feature free, competitive and regular elections with civil rights related to freedom of the press, association and manifestation, then it cannot be considered a democracy at all. That does not mean that there are no asymmetries in the levels of attainment of these minimum requirements, nor that they are enough to characterise a consolidated one. Campbell incorporates in his Democracy Ranking sub-dimensions such as gender equality, income equality, human development and non-political development, assessed through indicators as varied as the Gini Index, life expectancy at birth, school enrolment and CO2 emissions.[42]

Gender equality and environmental agendas are iconic examples of issues pushed forward by multinational agencies and international forums. Gender

[38] Guilhermo A O'Donnell, Jorge Vargas Cullel and Osvaldo Miguel Iazzetta, *The Quality of Democracy: theory and applications* (University of Notre Dame Press, 2004) 53.

[39] ibid 64.

[40] David Beetham, *Democracy and Human Rights* (Wiley, 1999) 69.

[41] O'Donnell et al (n 38) 21.

[42] Campbell (n 30) 40.

equality efforts, for instance, took shape in the 1970s in the United Nations with the adoption of the Convention on the Elimination of All Forms of Discrimination Against Women (CEDAW) and culminated with the enshrinement of gender equality and the empowerment of women and girls as the 5th Sustainable Development Goal for the twenty-first century. Although women represent half of the world`s population, gender equality measures have resulted from the globalisation of the feminist movement's claims and a broad understanding of gender equality as a fundamental human right rather than from electoral choice worldwide. The second striking example is related to the right to a balanced environment. Beginning with the establishment of the United Nations Environmental Programme (UNEP) in 1972, passing through the many declarations, conventions and summits for climate action, all the way to the Paris Agreement (adopted in 2015) to strengthen the global response to the threat of climate change, the international environmental movement is probably behind the most powerful and endurable transnational agenda ever developed. In that scenario, the pressure on nations to reduce CO2 emissions comes much more strongly from NGOs, think tanks and multinational agreements than from local pieces of legislation or popular mobilisation.

The widening of the democracy analysis to encompass factors such as the existence and efficiency of institutional checks-and-balances mechanisms, gender equality, and the reduction of CO2 emissions challenges Brazilian mainstream constitutionalism's attachment to idealisations of 'popular will' or 'people's sovereign self-ruling'. Moreover, this move points to the take-over of the concept of democracy, once dominated by the political vocabulary of elections, vote competitiveness and the expansion of suffrage, by the semantics of rights – human rights.

To make this point, it seems sufficient to underline that the Democracy Index, published by the Economist Intelligence Unit, in its methodological definition of how to measure democracy, maintains that human rights integrate the index because 'the principle of the protection of basic human rights is widely accepted. It is embodied in constitutions throughout the world as well as in the UN Charter and international agreements such as the Helsinki Final Act.'[43] Campbell defines democracy as 'a system of self-ruling, self-government or self-governance by the people and of the people that is based on human rights'.[44] As we will see in more detail in the next section, the vocabulary through which the international consensus infiltrates, shapes and influences democracies all over the world is the vocabulary of rights. It manifests itself in the form of legal reform packages that sometimes meet popular expectations and claims at the national level, and then are enacted, while on other occasions they face resistance and reluctance, and are incorporated into local democracies incompletely. Since its very foundational

[43] The Economist, 'The Economist Intelligence Unit's Index of Democracy 2008' (2008) The Economist Intelligence Unit 2008 <https://graphics.eiu.com/pdf/democracy%20index%202008.pdf> accessed 13 March 2022 16.

[44] Campbell (n 30) 12.

moment, contemporary democracy bears this openness to the constant influx of content generated and spread internationally. Modern democracy has always been a system impregnated with the capacity of producing rights. Even if seen as a simple procedure of 'popular or general will' consultation, this procedure – *democracy* – has been invariably and forever open to the insemination of content generated internationally.

Not without reason, some authors argue that even if the international push for democracy and international human rights is not the same movement, their overlaps and intersections blur the boundaries between law and politics.[45]

By amalgamating democracy with human rights, those concepts make the democracy assessment more complex. It shows that democracy has an undeniable participatory core, in which elections and basic political rights are exercised in an environment of civil rights fruition. But it also demonstrates that other dimensions, institutional settings and rights have been aggregated to the participatory core over time, through processes of decision-making that rarely lie in the hands of the people or are produced by a manifestation of the 'general will' or 'popular sovereignty'. Largely, the adoption of 'electoral democracy' as the prevailing procedure to determine who rules is a decision that has been made for nations more frequently than by them. The international agenda on democracy that arose from the necessity to spread the 'electoral democracy' template around the globe has presented itself in various forms, from the imposition of conditionality to financial aid and trade to programmes of democratic assistance and electoral monitoring and, ultimately, even armed invasion.[46] Suffice it to say that the major military incursions of NATO superpowers into Arab States in recent times were underwritten by the necessity to 'free nations from tyranny' and lead them to *democracy*. The propaganda for the adoption of the Western electoral political model is so resounding that the very idea of democracy is now surrounded by an undisputed favourable aura, leading to the appropriation of the term even by its enemies. As Shapiro posits, 'authoritarian rulers seldom reject democracy outright', claiming to establish temporary transition regimes towards democracy, or even that their governments are, somehow, more democratic than the opposition would be if in power.[47] Once democracy was elevated to such canonical status, no regime, nation or country would happily accept the label of undemocratic or authoritarian. Democracy became a desired commodity in international relations, in which some countries are regarded as owners of institutional expertise and donors of reform packages, while others are considered needy and defective, and thus borrowers of such expertise and consumers of those packages. In other words, *electoral*, *minimalist* or *low-intensity democracy* imposes itself worldwide as a

[45] Thomas Carothers, 'Democracy and Human Rights: Policy Allies or Rivals?' (1994) 17(3) *The Washington Quarterly* 13.

[46] David Beetham, *Democracy: A Beginner's Guide* (Oneworld, 2012) 103–09.

[47] Ian Shapiro, *The State of Democracy Theory* (Princeton University Press, 2003) i.

political mode irrespective of manifestations of the 'people', the 'general will' or 'popular sovereignty'.

Likewise, the adoption of rule of law mechanisms and institutions, the adherence to human rights, the compliance with accountability packages, and so forth, witnessed from the last quarter of the twentieth century onwards, are decisions more pushed by multinational organisations, international agencies, transnational discourses and actors than longed for by the populace.

It is worth noticing that the presence of dimensions of democracy that are not produced through the quintessential democratic procedure face resistance by some or are ignored by others. Some understand rights derived from international sources as a challenge to the prevalence of the 'popular will' and a threat to 'self-government'.[48] Munck affirms that 'when everything is a right, there is no politics; and when there is no politics, there is no democracy'.[49] Their understanding of democracy is still anchored exclusively in the national-political component. They recognise no source of legitimacy other than 'self-rule', 'popular sovereignty', 'constituent power', and other descriptions conducive to the idea of an original manifestation of the *volonté general*. Their approach to the striking evidence of the ongoing role played by the cosmopolitan/universalist trait in founding, shaping and influencing democracy is blatant denial. On the other hand, other authors welcome rights and even absorb them as part of their democracy analysis,[50] but the fact that most such rights originated in the post-national realm, by initiatives of international organisations and courts, by efforts of multinational financial aid agencies, or as a consequence of transnational NGO campaigns is, yet, left unattended.

That is a stance prevalent in Brazilian constitutionalism. Given its adherents' need to reject the sceptical, elitist discourse that depicts the 1988 Constitution as an unfolding of the military regime, they engaged in the development of a constitutional theory of democracy that relies heavily on 'popular sovereignty', 'general will' and 'rule by the people'. The most influential constitutionalists in Brazil tend to understand international commitments to human rights as limitations or constraints on the manifestation of the 'constituent power'.[51] Their idea that the 'constituent power' cannot deny human rights, offend other nations' independence or self-determination, or harm supra-positive principles of justice, is an attempt to create a zone of prohibition, matters that a constitution cannot touch without denying its own legitimacy, something like a domestic version of *jus cogens*. The incapacity to see human rights basic guarantees as conditions of possibility for the

[48] Daniel H Levine and Jose Enrique Molina, *The Quality of Democracy in Latin America* (Lynne Rienner, 2011) 12; Brigitte Geissel, Marianne Kneuer and Hans-Joachim Lauth, 'Measuring the quality of democracy: Introduction' (2016) 37(5) *International Political Science Review*.

[49] Gerardo L Munck, 'What is democracy? A reconceptualization of the quality of democracy' (2016) 23(1) *Democratization* 18.

[50] Beetham, *Democracy and Human Rights* (n 40); O'Donnell et al (n 38); *The Economist* (n 43); Buhlmann et al (n 30); Campbell (n 30).

[51] Canotilho (n 20) 81; Neto and Sarmento (n 18) 224–25.

democratic order, rather than exogenous limitations on the 'constituent power', makes Brazilian mainstream constitutionalism fall prey to the same source of legitimacy that serves the scepticism they fight so hard against. The legitimation circular scheme, according to which the 1988 Constitution is democratic because the Constitutional Assembly was freely elected and its works were participatory, while Brazilian democracy stands on the provisions regarding universal suffrage in the very same 1988 Constitution, founds 'democracy's' merits on electoral participation, which is, with minor variations, trusting of the same source of legitimacy explored by 'elitist electoralism'. The 'continuity constitutional theory' sees the 1988 Constitution as one more episode of the Brazilian elite's manoeuvring, with just a stamp of legitimacy from elections and participation. The last-minute agreements and the behind-doors settlements between interest groups would make the 1988 Constitution a reflection of that view of Brazil's most historical events as signs of the society's lenience, lack of moral sense, intrinsic hypocrisy and corrupt nature. Meanwhile, Brazilian mainstream constitutional theory believes the constitutional moment was authentic but fails to understand it not only as a popular outburst for participation and the vote but also, and mainly, as a sign of a thirst for rights, generated by the secular drought described in sociological and anthropological accounts such as Ribeiro's and Fernandes'.

Moreover, they fail to note how contemporary democratic constitutions have been historically built upon the inextricable idea of a political regime based on the protection of and access to human rights. This entanglement between local political enfranchisement and the universalist assumption to protect the rights of men is foundational to French and German constitutionalism and became part of older constitutional traditions such as the British and American. Likewise, the Brazilian 1988 Constitution and the democratic cycle it flags did not happen by the sudden irruption of a 'constituent power', but by the incremental coupling of historical facts, social mobilisation, popular pressure, international geopolitics, and the appropriation by Brazilian society of its entitlement to universal human rights that go way beyond the right to vote.

As we have seen, for both historical sociological trends, the 1988 Constitution represented only a starting point in the direction of rupture they have long craved. While 'anti-corrruptioners' tend to cope well with a thin electoral version of democracy as long as the control and horizontal accountability are strengthened enough, those who have historically claimed inclusion long for a more substantial form of democracy, surrounded by robust levels of access to human rights. These different paths, though, cannot be achieved by popular will alone, as good governance, accountability, transparency and human rights are all agendas that have been posed, developed and pushed forward mainly in international forums.

The idea that there is a universalist element to popular participation that is foundational and constitutive of contemporary democracy has the inconvenience of inseminating the concept of democracy with characteristics that are not conducive to the manifestation of 'popular sovereignty' or the 'general will'. The consolidation of governance standards at the global level, or the development of legal orders beyond and throughout nation-states, presents a challenge that orthodox democracy theory fails to overcome.

1.4. Global Governance and the Necessity to Break with the Traditional Constitutional-Normative Paradigm to Understand Elements of Contemporary Democracy

The main claim of this chapter is that contemporary democracy is founded on and constituted by the constant interplay of two factors. One factor is substantiated by the participation of the *demos* in political decision-making and the necessary conditions to make that participation decisive and qualified. This factor is dominated by idealisations of 'self-rule', 'popular sovereignty' and 'constituent power' that are dear to Brazilian constitutionalism as sources of legitimacy for the democratic order and reasons to resist 'elitist scepticism' trends that undermine the transformative role of the 1988 Constitution. If the clamour found in Brazilian society for administrative efficiency, accountability and the fight against corruption, and moreover for the inclusion of historically disenfranchised minorities, is to be met, a mode of democracy must be found that is not only underpinned by institutional designs and rights that find support in local majoritarian consultation procedures, but that also comes from a universalist perspective. So, this other factor consists of the global flux of content, values and goals, normally originating in the international realm, that complete the regime with traits going beyond the work of the electorate or their representatives. This complementary element is related to the triumph of discourses, agendas and legal regimes produced by international bodies, multinational organisations and transnational agencies, and their incorporation into polities all over the world. The former is dominated by the national tide of political forces, interest groups, social movements, and so forth. The latter is achieved through the vocabulary of reform packages and rights, spreading like waves from the epicentre to the periphery and reverberating back from the edges to the centre of the 'civilised world'.

As noted, these qualified forms of democracy are hardly reconcilable with classical ideas of popular legitimacy. There is a lingering understanding that legal regimes produced by international forums must overcome an inescapable 'legitimisation gap', as the creation of norms, procedures and institutions above the State can hardly be traced back to a manifestation of 'popular will', 'rule of the people', 'self-government' or 'constituent power'. This concern makes Rosenfeld deem international law 'inherently unsuited to purposes of fulfilling the minimum requirements regarding democracy', although he acknowledges global constitutionalism as a two-way road.[52] He sees global constitutionalism as a dual

[52] Michel Rosenfeld, 'Is global constitutionalism meaningful or desirable?' (2014) 25(1) *European Journal of International Law* 191.

movement that encompasses the projection of constitutional standards onto international law, as much as it explains the infiltration of international law in shaping constitutionalism worldwide from the mid-twentieth century onwards. However, Rosenfeld is still in pursuit of a participatory element capable of legitimising power and law. Similarly, Besson sees that human rights regimes are consolidated by the dialectic relationship between international norms and domestic legal orders, but insists that they need to be legitimised by a system of mutual validation very much conditioned by domestic participatory practices.[53] The attempt to fill the so-called 'legitimisation gap' is what drives Walker to compose his version of post-constituent constitutionalism. For him, the constituent power of the supranational constitution manifests itself *ex post facto* by a dual factor: the consent of states, and the mechanisms that grant participation to 'peoples' in decision-making panels, constituting a democracy of many peoples, a *demoi*-cracy.[54]

A significant number of authors approach the emergence of international legal regimes 'by transferring key domestic concepts and institutions to regional and global levels'.[55] Although displaying remarkable differences between themselves, two prototypical proposals of the 'transfer' trend are the ones proposed by Held and Fassbender.[56] Held proposes a 'cosmopolitan democracy' as a solution to the legitimisation riddle. It would demand the creation of new participative institutions at the global level that would coexist with the traditional political systems of the States, but with the power to override the State's autonomy in clearly defined spheres of activities in which it is possible to demonstrate transnational/international consequences.[57] Fassbender identifies in the United Nations Charter the consolidation of a universal agreement around a set of rules, such as the prohibition of genocide, armed aggression, use of force, slavery, trafficking of human beings, and respect for self-determination.[58] He also outlines the provision for institutional guarantees of their enforcement, such as the Security Council (Chapter VII) and the International Court of Justice (Chapter XIV), and the existence of clauses of normative hierarchy, such as *jus cogens* and some obligations *erga omnes* as reflections of an expansion of constitutionalism beyond the sovereign State. While the former stands for the creation of effective and accountable political, administrative and regulative agencies in the international realm, the latter asserts that the UN Charter features 'all the homogeneity

[53] Samantha Besson, 'Human Rights as Transnational Constitutional Law' in AF Lang and A Wiener (eds), *Handbook on Global Constitutionalism* (Edward Elgar Publishing, 2017) 238.

[54] Neil Walker, 'Post-Constituent Constitutionalism? The Case of the European Union' in M Loughlin and N Walker (eds), *The Paradox of Constitutionalism: Constituent Power and Constitutional Form* (Oxford University Press, 2008).

[55] Nico Krisch, *Beyond Constitutionalism: The Pluralist Structure of Postnational Law* (Oxford University Press, 2010) 13–17.

[56] David Held, *Models of Democracy*, 3rd edn (Polity, 2006); Bardo Fassbender, *The United Nations Charter as the Constitution of the International Community* (Martinus Nijhoff Publishers, 2009).

[57] Held (n 56) 298–305.

[58] Fassbender (n 56) 73, 123.

which is needed'. Held sees the need to narrow the gap between the people and the decision-making processes carried on in the national, regional and global spheres. Fassbender believes that the original State consent to the UN Charter supplies the international community constitutional order with the legitimacy it needed to be founded, and thereafter it gains autonomy and independence from that initial building moment.[59] Despite their differences, both proposals are attempts to juxtapose constitutional concepts or make them suitable for the international legal order. That type of theoretical undertaking is similar to the way Lang and Wiener aim to adapt concepts like the rule of law, separation of powers and '*pouvoir constituant*' to the legal orders found in the post-national scenario.[60] Following those accounts, *global constitutionalism* would be

> a strand of thought (outlook of perspective) and a political agenda which advocates the application of constitutional principles, such as the Rule of Law, checks and balances, human rights protection, and democracy, in the international sphere to improve the effectivity and fairness of the international legal order.[61]

Brown maintains that this projection of constitutional traits onto the international legal order by global constitutionalist academics appears too apologetic, as if there were an intentionality behind it, trying to legitimise it at any cost. A different way to look at it would be Dunoff's 'functionalism', based on the idea that 'although no formal international constitution exists, certain international norms fulfil constitutional functions'.[62] One way or the other, to criticise it or to explain it objectively, both Brown and Dunoff only see the phenomenon of the rise of international legal regimes through 'transfer' lenses, projecting concepts, institutions and principles that pertain to traditional constitutionalism theory onto the praxis of international or supranational institutions. Although Dunoff and Trachtman mention 'supplemental constitutionalisation' as one of the forms of constitutionalisation produced by international legal orders, as the term suggests, it would consist of a complementary role played by international norms in filling gaps in domestic constitutional settings to integrate them in a context of legal globalisation.[63]

Our claim is bolder in the sense that international regimes have been part of the constitutional foundation and the adoption of democracy, shaping, influencing and driving constitutionalism paths in different nations all over the world

[59] ibid 54.

[60] Anthony F Lang and Antje Wiener, 'A constitutionalising global order: an introduction' in A Lang and A Wiener (eds), *Handbook on Global Constitutionalism* (Edward Elgar Publishing, 2017) 3.

[61] Garrett Wallace Brown, 'Cosmopolitanism and global constitutionalism' in A Lang and A Wiener (eds), *Handbook on Global Constitutionalism* (Edward Elgar Publishing, 2017) 100.

[62] Jeffrey L Dunoff, 'The multifaceted relationship between functionalism and global constitutionalism' in A Lang and A Wiener A (eds), *Handbook on Global Constitutionalism* (Edward Elgar Publishing, 2017) 188.

[63] Jeffrey L Dunoff and Joel P Trachtman, 'A Functional Approach to International Constitutionalization' in JL Dunoff and J Trachtman (eds), *Ruling the World?: Constitutionalism, International Law, and Global Governance* (Cambridge University Press, 2009).

in contemporary times. This is the point missed by the 'transfer' international constitutionalists. Such authors focus on the export of constitutional formulas of legitimation from the nation-state to the supranational or international landscapes and devote little or no attention to the flux that comes from the other side of this two-way road. In other words, they competently explain the emergence of international norms, the hypertrophy of international courts' competencies, the work of international organisations, transnational agencies' appellate bodies and arbitral mechanisms through the language of national constitutionalism in a bottom-up copy-and-paste theoretical exercise. Nevertheless, their vision is often blurred when they try to show how this very same machinery determines for whom, when and how democracy, human rights, developmental agendas, constitutional courts, environmental policies and anti-corruption toolkits are adopted in a top-down stream of legal and constitutional reforms. This blind eye to the phenomenon of the worldwide spread of certain legal/political features, such as electoral democracy, human rights, developmental agenda, environmental standards and anti-corruption mechanisms, seems to be accompanied by the requirement to find justification for the legal order in the 'consent', 'will', 'decision' or 'rule' of the 'people'.

This blind spot can only be illuminated by theoretical accounts that 'break' with the temptation to associate legal order legitimacy with popular participation. Krisch proposes this kind of rupture through an idea of legal pluralism that comprehends that monists and dualists have been superseded by the reality of multiple layers of law, from equally plural sources in the international, regional and national levels that have decoupled political processes from the nation-state, and detached legitimacy from traditional descriptions of democracy.[64]

Even Brunkhorst, who strongly believes that social evolutionary bursts and legal revolutions derive from class struggle and social mobilisation, concedes that in the aftermath of World War II 'mass democracy became an evolutionary universal'.[65] As he explains, 'democratic constitutionalisation' was a phenomenon that happened simultaneously at the national and cosmopolitan levels, so 'the idea of a universal democracy is co-original with human rights'.[66] As we have been stressing throughout this chapter, the coexistence between the participatory/national and the cosmopolitan/universal elements of democracy is not only constitutive; it is foundational to contemporary democracy. As Thornhill puts it, 'contemporary democracy has the paradoxical feature that it is not created democratically'.[67]

His historical recollections of democratic and constitutional advancements are very appealing in this sense. American and British systems are both presented as historically 'less democratic' than what is commonly agreed on. In the case of the

[64] Krisch (n 55).

[65] Hauke Brunkhorst, *Critical Theory, Legal Theory, and the Evolution of Contemporary Society* (Continuum, 2012) 391.

[66] ibid.

[67] Chris Thornhill, *The Sociology of Law and the Global Transformation of Democracy* (Cambridge University Press, 2018) 166.

United States, the exclusion of non-white voters from the political system until 1965 is the basis for the conclusion of the existence of a quasi-democratic system.[68] Similarly, the British mode of government is qualified as 'at least intermittently – less democratic than most other European polities' because of property qualification barriers to the universalisation of the right to vote.[69] It is only after a movement of adherence to ethnic minorities' civil rights, especially after the Warren Court period, that American democracy experienced a much more inclusive political system.[70] In the same way, the rise of British judicial human rights adjudication, with decisions very much aligned with supranational courts' paradigms, resulted in democratic advances in the United Kingdom.[71] The cosmopolitan/universalist component came in those cases to generate/improve political participation. Likewise, in contemporary democracies, the manifestations of 'popular will' do not happen randomly, but are accepted inasmuch as they are aligned to an elevated rationale; it must be 'a will that wills rights'.[72] As Tully shows, it is simply historically inaccurate to idealise a linear historical process by which autonomous, sovereign peoples found their way to build strong and well-established domestic constitutions and democracies, engaging, in a later evolutionary phase, in the construction of supranational institutions that mirror those same ideals. On the contrary, 'European states, as state empires, developed within global systems of imperial and colonial law from the beginning'.[73]

The idea that democracy and human rights were co-developed in the contemporary world, with reciprocal foundational influences between the international and the domestic/nation-state levels, does seem counter-intuitive, especially for the developed world and considering how self-conscious Western super-power nations are of their democracy. American democracy is based on a strong belief in the 'We the People' preamble to the Constitution. It has been praised as a bastion of freedom since the nineteenth century, and is considered the cradle of democratisation projects around the world (USAID, Freedom House, etc).[74] It is daring to affirm it as a 'faulty democracy' once the racial segregation regime had to cede to the embarrassment it caused the US before the international community.[75] Britain is proud of its unwritten constitutional tradition of more than 800 years of bills of rights, charters, and agreements based on 'self-government', and *rule by consent* of the ruled. The need to adopt a Human Rights Act and to empower a Supreme Court as late as the 2000s, in order to comply with the international consensus

[68] ibid 287.
[69] ibid 328.
[70] ibid 304.
[71] ibid 348.
[72] Chris Thornhill, 'The Enlightenment and global constitutionalism' in A Lang and A Wiener (eds), *Handbook on Global Constitutionalism* (Edward Elgar Publishing, 2017) 72.
[73] James Tully, 'The Imperialism of Modern Constitutional Democracy' in M Loughlin and N Walker (eds), *The Paradox of Constitutionalism: Constituent Power and Constitutional Form* (Oxford University Press, 2008) 319.
[74] Alexis de Tocqueville and Henry Reeve, *Democracy in America* (Saunders & Otley, 1835).
[75] Brunkhorst (n 65) 390.

on what democracy and the rule of law ought to be, also represents a challenge to that tradition. Similarly, Germany holds a constitutional tradition that dates back to treaties such as the ones that installed the kingdoms of Wurttemberg and Saxony and goes on to the Weimar Constitution and derivative influential constitutional theories. The fact that, after World War II, the commitment to international legal orders and human rights was imposed on German constitutionalism by the victorious Allied forces undermines assumptions about the strength of its *Rechtsstaat*. Germany as it is today, politically and socially, took shape in 1989/90, due to the inception of a geopolitical development foreign to it, leading to the end of the Soviet Union and the Cold War. As far as they deal with constitutionalism, the rule of law, democracy, human rights, and so forth, these societies often see themselves as 'expertise' donors, never borrowers. This is why there is a tendency to see constitutionalism and democracy as legal-political commodities that they created and developed as sovereign actors, rather than as components of a cosmopolitan community of reciprocal influences.

The obsession with the 'legitimisation gap' between the transnational legal orders and their addressees ignores the reality that 'there are no special legitimacy problems connected to international law that are not shared by constitutional law'.[76] In other words, there is a mythic aspect involving the idea of the 'legitimisation gap' that is very much based on an association between the concept of legitimacy and elections, voting and the factual participation of people in decision-making that is as unlikely in the international realm as it is in the national domestic one. Even enthusiasts of mechanisms of direct participation in modern democracies acknowledge that it has practical limitations and that factual mass deliberation on every issue simply lacks sense, is materially impossible, and is also inconvenient given the complexity of our industrial modern societies.[77] The 'legitimisation gap' solutions demand a capacity for the cognition of world issues, collective articulation, global or regional moral consensus, and consideration and regard for the mechanisms of participation that are beyond any known citizenship practice at the nation-state level.[78] In other words, if there is a 'legitimisation gap' affecting international legal regimes because the means of popular participation in their development are too slim or absent, the same can be said about many constitutions and legal statutes all over the world. The 'legitimisation gap' myth stems from a misconception of legitimacy itself that leads to disappointment and scepticism towards its functions.

Legitimacy is not a concept that has a substantial meaning of its own. It is, in this sense, a meta-concept that always refers to another semantic matter; it is

[76] Mathias Kumm, 'The Cosmopolitan Turn in Constitutionalism: On the Relationship between Constitutionalism in and beyond the State' in J Dunoff and J Trachtman (eds), *Ruling the World?: Constitutionalism, International Law, and Global Governance* (Cambridge University Press, 2009) 323.

[77] Norberto Bobbio, *The Future of Democracy: A Defence of the Rules of the Game* (University of Minnesota Press, 1987).

[78] Norbert Lechner, 'On the Imaginary of the Citizenry' in G O'Donnell, JV Cullell and OM Iazzetta (eds), *The Quality of Democracy* (University of Notre Dame Press, 2004) 208.

an effect, an outcome, or a symptom produced by something else. Some may ask if Carnival is a legitimate expression of Brazilian culture; others may question whether cryptoassets are a legitimate source of wealth, and so forth. In the logical regression one makes in seeking a justification for the legal order, legitimacy is produced by that ultimate persuasive argument or semantic category beyond which no more justification is required. It means that legitimacy is the bond that holds society together around a legal order even though, if confronted with the reality that such a legal order is the product of sheer power, will, and interest trade-offs, society would disintegrate into chaos, cataclysm or war. To avoid that unbearable degree of possibilities (complexity) and opportunities for disappointment (contingence), social systems develop concepts, ideas and abstractions that are capable of impeding access to the raw paradox or tautology that is at their core. The role in covering up such paradoxes must be performed 'latently' or 'without mentioning' by way of contingency formulas.[79] Contingency formulas operate like a veil, a barrier that contains the impetus to reveal systems' core paradoxes or tautologies. When Koskenniemi shows his scepticism towards the 'warm sense of contentment looking for no further justification' produced by rights regimes, he is misplaced in his disappointment.[80] He is not contesting the fragmentary rights regimes but legitimacy itself. The functional differentiation of law from politics provides rights with the ability to extract their legitimacy from the law itself. A constitution is amended, a statute is enacted, a constitutional court decision is laid down on the grounds of a rights requirement, a human rights exigency, and in the context of contemporary democracy, that is as much justification as you can get. The attempt to keep pushing the justification chain forward to its political roots is an evolutionary regression. If the legitimacy curtain is removed, as proposed by Koskenniemi, there is nothing else behind the screen except a naked king. The function of covering the backstage is performed by contingency formulas, and the contingency formula of the political system is legitimacy. As King and Thornhill present Luhmann's account, a legitimate political system is any political system that produces laws that are accepted as legitimate because the system itself sustains its legitimacy.[81] That sounds like a tautology, and it is indeed. We claim that the specific function to spare law from dealing with that tautology can be performed by multiple sources other than 'general will', 'constituent power', 'self-government', 'rule by the people' or 'popular will'. As King and Thornhill argue:

> The processes through which a political system creates legitimacy for itself are extremely complex and diverse. All endeavours to establish mono-causal models of legitimacy inevitably neglect the variable and endlessly evolving character of the political system.[82]

[79] Niklas Luhmann, *O direito da sociedade* (Martins Fontes Selo Martins, 2017).

[80] Martti Koskenniemi, 'Constitutionalism as Mindset: Reflections on Kantian Themes About International Law and Globalization' (2006) 8(1) *Theoretical Inquiries in Law* 14.

[81] Michael King and Chris Thornhill, *Niklas Luhmann's Theory of Politics and Law* (Palgrave Macmillan, 2003).

[82] ibid 72.

Thornhill's description of the 'global transformation of democracy' is, in one sense, a version of how the historical evolution of the idea of citizenship brought changes to political legitimisation. As he presents it, democracy as we know it has as one of its main features the transition from a collective political subject called 'people' or 'nation' as the legitimating source of law to a *fictionally universalised individual subject*, holder of human rights provisioned by international norms.[83] This new *citizen* is not an *a priori* author of the law but its centre of attribution, which decisively changes how we might think of democracy.[84] As Thornhill says:

> … the original chain of legitimization in more classical ideas of democracy is broken, and the presence of the people as a real aggregate of citizens is symbolically translated into an idea of the people as a holder of rights, internalized and cyclically reproduced within the law. The chain of legitimization becomes a chain that connects not real people to the organs of government, but different elements of the global legal system, each of which converges around human rights norms.[85]

The connection between democracy and human rights that derives from the understanding of the citizen as an agent and the consequent requirements for the exercise of that agency found in Thornhill's argument is common to O'Donnell et al.[86] It also points to democracy as more than just a system of participation, but primarily as a system of inclusion whereby elections and legislatures accomodate international norms. National and international courts are provoked by social movements and by transnational agencies, all to promote continuous and comprehensive inclusion through access to human rights.

The most important point we intend to make here is that democracy as we know it in the contemporary world, wherever we look at (or for) it, was founded and is constituted by the constant interaction between a participatory/local factor and a cosmopolitan/universalist element. This interaction is dialectical. Democracy is the synthesis of a relationship that can be of reinforcement or attrition, attraction or repulsion. The European Union's demands for austerity measures, cuts in wages and pension reforms faced a strong societal reaction in Greece during the 2010s. The supranational developmental agenda substantiated in legal reforms that aimed at reduction of the public revenue deficit were strongly repelled by a wave of protests, strikes and election results. The two constitutive elements of democracy clashed. In Portugal, the sequence of revisions to the Constitution made between 1992 and 2005 to adapt the Constitution to the provisions of the Treaties of Maastricht and Amsterdam, enacted to open Portuguese constitutionalism to the reception of rights such as non-discrimination on grounds of sexual orientation, found a much smoother environment. The reforms resulted in granting foreign citizens the right to vote, amplifying the means

[83] Thornhill (n 67) 216.
[84] ibid 276.
[85] ibid 216.
[86] O'Donnell et al (n 38).

for political participation with mechanisms of a popular legislative initiative. The cosmopolitan/universalist factors pushed for more participation and local constituencies' empowerment.

The reactions and resistances that one factor or element of democracy imposes on the other can be seen as manifestations of the expansionist and dominating tendency they both have. Koskenniemi affirms that the fragmented, technical, specific rights regimes in their expansion would bear a solipsistic and imperialist tendency to dominate issues and describe the world through their lenses.[87] His aversion to the 'extraordinary rhetorical power of rights' is a critique of the engulfment of politics by technocracy and 'managerialism'.[88] Indeed, the multiple partial legal regimes that are created and, then, spread to the four corners of the world tend to encapsulate that reality in their language. International human rights would describe the bad living/working conditions of cocoa producers through the idea of a human rights violation to be governed by ILO Conventions, while *lex mercatoria* would look at the same issue as a matter of inobservance of trade rules and WTO decisions and principles regarding the export/import of international goods. Social media juggernauts tend to set up their conflict resolution panels to discuss rules and procedures for the restriction/removal of abusive content, while democratic institutions would look at the same procedures through the prism of the necessary level of freedom of speech for free and fair elections.

The participatory/domestic element of democracy shares the dominant tendency shown by the cosmopolitan/universalist one. One might say that the prevalence of the national/majoritarian element over the cosmopolitan/universalist one is the basis for the most dangerous attacks on democracy today. Whether you consider the Brexit decision, the predominant discourses in Poland, Hungary, India, Italy,and Turkey, the far-right ascension in Brazil, or Venezuelan/Bolivian bolivarianism, the common appeal is for the renaissance of nationalist populism against the 'evil' forces of international organisations, multinational agencies and transnational legal bodies. As well identified by Kumm and others, aside from Islamic fundamentalist theocracies, and authoritarian technocracies, popular nationalist authoritarianism is the only alternative to liberal constitutional democracies in vogue. They all have in common the weakening of checks-and-balances institutions and their replacement by a sectarian view of 'the people' as a morally virtuous fragment of society.[89] Trumpism's strategy of bashing international institutions, withdrawing from treaties, questioning multinational organisations' intentions, and putting their rights proposals in conflict with the 'national', 'popular' or 'sovereign will', and its attacks on democracy are not

[87] Martti Koskenniemi, 'Hegemonic Regimes' in MA Young (ed), *Regime Interaction in International Law: Facing Fragmentation* (Cambridge University Press, 2012) 317.

[88] Martti Koskenniemi, *The Politics of International Law* (Hart, 2011) 136.

[89] Mattias Kumm, Jonathan Havercroft, Jeffrey Dunoff and Antje Wiener, 'Editorial: The end of "the West" and the future of global constitutionalism' (2017) 6(1) *Global Constitutionalism*.

two different positions.[90] Those arguments and their sub-products in Brazil, Hungary, Poland and Turkey represent an orchestrated attack on democracy as a whole in two steps. First, the participatory/national element of democracy negates any input from the cosmopolitan/universalist factor, and, then, the mechanisms of political/electoral participation are corrupted, co-opted and distorted. We see this incremental deterioration taking place mainly through attacks on, violations of and resistance to human rights, international scientific consensus, global environmental commitments, and so forth, in such a powerful and pervasive way that civil liberties constraints or political/electoral repercussions can happen after the point of no return has already been reached. To use an analogy that is dear to Koskenniemi and Brunkhorst, although Dr Jekyll and Mr Hyde both craved to be the dominating personality, they were both the same person and the prevalence of one would ultimately imply the doom of both.[91] The same is true for contemporary democracy. It is made up of both the participatory/local and cosmopolitan/universalist elements, with different reciprocal influences and forms to legitimise themselves.

We agree that international human rights became a source of democratic legitimacy itself. Yet, we have reason to believe that the cosmopolitan/universalist element of democracy relies upon other legitimising concepts. Indeed, democracy is a rights incubator; successful policies tend to be translated into rights and gain a life of their own, not depending on politics to reproduce themselves. Rights are the language through which contemporary democracy manifests itself, and they are often brought to the fore by international conventions, multinational organisations' reports and guidelines, transnational organisations' rankings, indexes and maps. But some rights and legal reform packages base their legitimacy on the 'developmental' agenda, or even on 'international scientific consensus', for instance. We have already mentioned how the international developmental agenda entered national democracies imposing constitutional revisions, institutional reforms and legal overhaul to decrease the size of the State under the discourse of rule of law improvement, collective rights to efficiency, and 'good governance' in public administration. Although articulated in the form of legal reforms necessary to give substance to diffuse rights in the better management of public resources, the accountability of public officials, the worldwide adoption of judicial independence monitoring agencies, public-private partnership legislation and administrative reforms found their legitimising basis in the idea of 'development'. Similarly, during the Covid-19 pandemic, we saw the adoption of unprecedented legal restrictions on freedom of circulation and businesses, based solely on what was regarded as the 'international scientific consensus' on the matter. Although all those international inputs were translated in the form

[90] Jonathan Havercroft, Antje Wiener, Mattias Kumm and Jeffrey Dunoff, 'Editorial: Donald Trump as global constitutional breaching experiment' (2018) 7(1) *Global Constitutionalism*.

[91] Koskenniemi, *The Politics of International Law* (n 88) 143; Brunkhorst (n 65) 48.

of law, speaking the 'rights vernacular', their source of legitimacy was economic developmental theory or scientific findings. That is to say that the cosmopolitan/universalist element of democracy can carry within itself inputs that present themselves in the form of legal reforms, principles and 'rights', but with different ultimate sources of legitimisation in the international forums. This assertion is decisive for the comprehension of the legitimising turn the international anti-corruption regime went through, as will be discussed in chapter 3, and its influences on democracies in Brazil, the subject of chapter 4.

Whatever their implications, these last remarks do not unsettle the fact that contemporary democracy hinges on the constant interaction between the inputs drawn from transnational legal regimes, whatever their source of legitimacy might be, and its national participatory element. That is how contemporary democracy came about and how it evolves wherever you look, including in Brazil, as we shall now see.

1.5. Democracy in Brazil: The Dual-Factor Democracy in Processes of Inclusion/Exclusion

It is fair to say that Brazil had not experienced any relevant democratic continuity until the Constituent Assembly was installed in the mid-1980s. After the general elections for the Constituent Assembly of 1933/34, Getúlio Vargas became constitutional President for another term, implanting the *Estado Novo* through an auto-*coup d'état* in 1937. It was a regime with no mechanisms of checks and balances between the branches of power. In fact, during the following nine years, both houses of the National Congress were closed, and elections were suspended. The absence of any political rights and the seizure of basic civil rights related to freedom of the press, for example, jeopardised an already stumbling template for citizenship. The 1946 Constitution initiated a period of democratic tendencies, with periodic elections disputed by a plurality of political parties, reasonable levels of access to civil rights, and independent judicial courts. The experience did not last long. In April of 1964, another *coup d'etat* occurred, this time by the military forces, which installed a regime of exception that endured until the 1986 Constituent Assembly.

During the military dictatorship, a hybrid political regime, with periodical elections to local assemblies and limited seats in the National Congress, was put in place back in 1974. The *anos de chumbo* (years of lead), during which press and artistic expression were subject to strong censorship and public gatherings were repressed by armed forces with arrests and violence, were left behind, and the opposition progressively gained political power and influence. In the 1978 and 1982 elections, with the support of civil organisations like the Brazilian Bar Association (OAB), the Brazilian Press Association, the National Conference of Brazilian Bishops (CNBB) and an already vigorous unionist movement present in the growing urban peripheries, the MDB (Brazilian Democratic Mobilization) party inflicted large and strategic defeats on the incumbent party. Battered by the worldwide petrol crises and the economic depression that came along with it, the backlash from the military rulers was incapable of preventing mass popular gatherings in favour of the '*Diretas-Já*' movement, which sought general direct elections for the presidency. The rising mobilised working and artistic classes, different social movements and interest groups, and broad media coverage realised the ideal of popular participation in the constituent assembly. As Barbosa reflects, 'even if it was not possible to identify some common claims, what brought together all the new actors was their effort to participate in the process, to influence the works, present their arguments …'. The 1988 Constitution was considered democratic because 'the civil society played a central role in the gestation of the new Brazilian constitutional order. An unprecedented role in our constitutional history'.[92]

As important as the national-political-participatory element was to the establishment of democracy in Brazil, it is undeniable that foreign aspects contributed to the transition from the military regime to the constitutional democracy. With the Cold War coming to an end, American foreign policy interest in spreading electoral democracy and 'freedom' to Latin America outweighed concerns of Brazil leaning towards the Soviet Union or Cuba. The shift in American foreign policy priorities removed the only international support the dictatorial regime had. International political isolation was accompanied by economic stagnation, price inflation out of control, and the absolute ineptitude of the military in dealing with a crisis that deemed the 1980s as 'the lost decade'. To that scenario of the absolute exhaustion of the pillars of the dictatorial regime, you can add a profound social discontentment expressed not only as a claim for more participation, but also for rights. Barbosa mentions two events that highlight the aspiration for a new Constitution that preceded and fuelled the constituent moment: the Vth National Conference of the Bar Association, which occurred in 1974, entitled 'The lawyer and the rights of men', and the National Conference of the Working Class, in 1981, which produced a report called 'Elaboration of a Constitution that guarantees the Fundamental Rights of the Working Class'.[93] In his assessment of the 1988 Constitution, Silva says that democracy 'is the regime of general guarantees for the realization of men's fundamental rights'.[94] Barroso concedes that 'the virtuous face of globalization' after World War II was the development of a 'universal ethic' around the idea of human rights, which is similar to what Neto and Sarmento call 'ethical cosmopolitism' regarding human rights.[95] Having regard to the historical response of Latin American constitutionalism to international human rights,

[92] Barbosa (n 22) 242–43.
[93] ibid 151, 169.
[94] Silva (n 16) 132.
[95] Barroso (n 19); Neto and Sarmento (n 18).

Gargarella affirms that, in the last decades, they came from a place of marginalisation to 'forge a new direction for public life in the region'.[96] The cosmopolitan/universalist push for the adoption of democracy and human rights, echoed in those local/political/participatory demands for change that Ulysses Guimarães insisted on his speech, meant a rupture, a new Constitution, more political participation, the enjoyment of civil liberties, and access to social, economic and cultural rights. The coupling of the two constitutive elements of contemporary democracy created a social boiling point, a build-up of pressure for citizenship, that was more than the armed forces, which did not have the economic resources to fuel tanks, could handle, and that is how Brazilian democracy came about and has since evolved.

As shown by Guilhot, the *promotion of electoral democracy* was part of an American propaganda strategy in which the periodicity of elections and the freedoms of expression, manifestation and the press were highlighted, while underachievement in healthcare and economic and ethnic inequality were relegated to discussions about governance performance.[97] O'Donnell et al say that democracy theory produced in the developed world tends to consider the universalisation of political rights as the last step of the journey towards democratisation because minimum standards of social rights and the homogeneous distribution of the State's authority over the territory are considered given facts or simply taken for granted.[98] Indeed, although European welfare provisions date from before the World Wars,[99] being a precondition for the flourishing of democracy throughout the continent, economic and social rights are often neglected or have a secondary role in some European initiatives to assess democracy, such as the Global State of Democracy, the Swedish V-Dem (Varieties of Democracy) or the Economist Intelligence Unit Democracy Index.

As for Latin America, the turn to constitutional democracy in the late twentieth century had to deal with a different quest. The difference is that, while in developed countries, democracy assessment implies electoral rights and basic civil liberties because minimum social living standards are considered given facts or simply taken out of the equation, in the reality of developing countries, democracy must be perceived differently.

[96] Roberto Gargarella, *Latin American Constitutionalism, 1810–2010: the Engine Room of the Constitution* (Oxford University Press, 2013) 169.

[97] Nicolas Guilhot, *The Democracy Makers: Human Rights and the Politics of Global Order* (Columbia University Press, 2005).

[98] O'Donnell et al (n 38) 47.

[99] In Germany, pension systems and other specific social security schemes were in place since the Bismarckian Empire, influencing, among others, the French welfare system. In Britain, beginning with the 1905 Unemployed Workmen Act and the 1911 National Insurance Act, the whole network of social rights was enacted by 1948, with two new National Insurance Acts and the creation of the National Health Service (NHS) in 1946. See Daniel J Whelan and Jack Donnelly, 'The West, Economic and Social Rights, and the Global Human Rights Regime: Setting the Record Straight' (2007) 28(4) *Human Rights Quarterly* 927.

As Karl presents it:

> … in countries where large parts of the population still are not ensured a minimal standard of living or where significant sectors are frustrated due to relative inequalities, democracy tends to be defined in socioeconomic terms (as gains in the standard of living or 'progress'), and a positive cycle is possible only to the extent that particular governments 'deliver'. When the attitudes and beliefs of ethnic minorities (or majorities in the case of some countries) are factored in, visions of democracy become even more complicated. For example, democracy can mean 'coming together', 'agreement', 'a spirit of solidarity', or 'doing what we need to survive', which is far cry from notions of electoral competition, alternation in power, or elections as conceived of by a political class or international organizations promoting democracy.[100]

Campbell's analysis of Brazilian democracy shows that Brazil has above-average levels of political freedom, considerably higher than China and Russia. It also demonstrates that GDP per capita is above Latin American and Asian averages, but the country underperforms strikingly on income equality, demonstrating that a wealth distribution system does not follow from an increase in wealth in Brazilian society.[101] Lauth would propose that the possible trade-offs between dimensions of equality and freedom in Brazil portray a democracy with a 'libertarian profile', while we would say it is evidence of the crossroads of Brazilian democracy. While the 'libertarian profile' of Brazilian democracy would provide the society with just enough participatory endowments to allow control over power, accountability and resistance against the political tendency to corruption, the lack of reach in terms of equality would be a sign of the constitutional failure to fulfil its vocation – generating inclusion. Here we align with democracy theories such as those proposed by O'Donnell, Huber et al, and Beetham in the sense that minimum standards of food security, access to drinkable water, and healthcare are constitutive elements of a democracy. Even if one considers that democracy is strictly about participation in elections and civil liberties, there must be a dignity baseline below which political and civil rights just do not make sense because people are not agents, they are sub-citizens, as highlighted by Prado, Ribeiro and Fernandes.

This whole book hinges on democracy's apparent contradictions and paradoxes. As we have seen, it presupposes broad popular participation, for in a democracy the people ought to own their destiny. A problem in that assertion is that democracy itself and, later on, human rights, 'good governance' mechanisms, gender and racial equality and environmental preservation are priorities rarely 'elected' by the 'common people', but result from foreign policies, multinational organisations' reports, financial aid programmes, transnational NGOs' activism, and so forth. Amid a clash of narratives or vocations, democracy in a country

[100] Terry Lynn Karl, 'Latin America Virtuous or Perverse Cycle' in G O'Donnell, JV Cullell and OM Iazzetta (eds), *The Quality of Democracy* (University of Notre Dame Press, 2004) 193.

[101] Campbell (n 30) 155–51.

like Brazil has different forms of responding to diverse historical claims. While a 'minimalist/low-intensity' version with episodic popular consultations under the tutelage of a technocrat intelligentsia would be fit for fighting corruption, only a comprehensive social democracy, with high levels of inclusion to the poor, the black, and the indigenous, would meet the constitutional objectives of a society based on 'freedom, justice and solidarity'.

The evaluation of the 'quality of democracy' in Brazil needs, necessarily, to address governance performance regarding the provision of social rights and its repercussions, not only in political or participatory aspects, but also for specific and crucial aspects of inclusion in the public sphere. In other words, Brazil's democracy was founded on and has been evolving since the mid-1980s through the coupling of international influences and its participatory procedures and institutions. That interaction is the subject of all the chapters to come, but its outcome for democracy cannot be limited to whether it increased political participation or generated electoral changes; the capacity of those cosmopolitan/universalist inputs to generate inclusion must be considered.

The need to balance all those tendencies leads us to affirm that if the two foundational and constitutive elements of democracy – the local/participatory and the universalist/cosmopolitan – are separated, or if one obliterates the other, the coupling ceases to exist, and democracy perishes. Democracy is not the sole dance of one partner, or the other, but the continuous dance of them together! The following chapters are an invitation to find out how that dance has evolved in Brazil over the last 35 years.

2

International Human Rights and Democracy in Brazil: Contributions to the Democratic Consolidation

2.1. Introduction

During the transition from the military regime to democracy that culminated with the promulgation of its new Constitution, Brazil ratified the Convention on the Elimination of All Forms of Discrimination against Women in 1984.

In the first four years that followed the enactment of the Constitution, Brazil ratified the Inter-American Convention to Prevent and Punish Torture, the UN Convention against Torture and Other Cruel, Inhuman and Degrading Treatment and Punishment, the UN Convention on the Rights of the Child, the International Covenant on Civil and Political Rights, the International Covenant on Economic, Social and Cultural Rights, and the American Convention on Human Rights.

Article 4 of the 1988 Constitution states that Brazil would follow the principle of human rights prevalence in its international relations. The Constitution also introduced an innovative clause concerning openness to human rights set forth in international treaties. Amendment 45 to the Constitution, passed in 2004, reinforced the constitutional commitment to international human rights law, granting human rights treaties supra-legal/constitutional *status*. This suggested that Brazil might adopt of a 'block of constitutionality': that is, a system of higher norms, incorporating both the original text of the Constitution and human rights provided by international law. According to the innovative constitutional mechanism (Article 5, para 3), once international human rights treaties pass through the same legislative procedure prescribed for the enactment of amendments to the Constitution – three-fifths of votes in two turnouts in each House of Parliament – they are incorporated as constitutional amendments themselves; they are integrated into the Brazilian constitutional *corpus*.

Considering that the 1988 Constitution was a democratic milestone in Brazilian history, Brazil's full integration into the international human rights movement can be considered contemporary to the process of democratisation. Moreover, human dignity is enshrined as a core principle for both the Brazilian Constitutional system inaugurated in 1988 and international human rights norms. As we have argued in chapter 1, this coordination suggests that Brazilian democracy was, decisively, longed for by the 'people', and pushed by societal mobilisation, but not only that. All the movements that espoused democracy during the constituent moment were wanting to participate, and to vote, but they were also craving rights: the right to education, the right to healthcare, the right to recognition, and the right to protection. Most of these rights claims were built through a dynamic in which societal needs meet international movements and are synthesised in the form of multinational organisations' declarations and agendas, legal norms and court decisions reverberating back into the local and national domains.

The Constitutional integration of international human rights set forth at the normative, formal level raises the question of how the interaction of international human rights and Brazilian democracy effectively worked out in the years that followed the 1988 Constitution. In other words, how have international human rights affected democracy in Brazil?

In the previous chapter, we explored how different accounts of Brazilian democracy and constitutional transition offer different responses to orthodox sociological claims for greater responsiveness of official representatives/human rights and inclusivity. We also highlighted that our analysis would focus on the specific challenges Brazilian society had ahead of the promulgation of the 1988 Constitution, which persist today. As set out there, our assessment covers the establishment of periodic elections with universal suffrage, and due process guarantees. However, it goes beyond those political and civil rights to address social, economic, environmental and intersubjective rights that provide the basic conditions of possibility for meaningful citizenship.

We proceed from the consideration that certain levels of exclusion and deprivation are conducive to generalised disenfranchisement, making approaches that equate democracy with electoral participation incomplete. We adopt a functionalist view according to which, in the context of the global society and the infinite links, relations and entanglements between national law, international treaties and covenants, multinational companies' pressures and transnational influences, the sources of law legitimisation are equally diverse. Sometimes, to be deemed as democratic, the law will rely on the political support of a 'people', 'nation', or correlated collective entities. On many other occasions, the law is considered legitimate as it endows people with human rights necessary to the exercise of citizenship, or, alternatively, it harbours its legitimacy on international managerial, economic or scientific consensus.

Democracy and citizenship certainly involve the capability to participate in elections consciously, and freely, but, especially in the Global South, that comes as a development of the free fruition of rights to food, healthcare, educational opportunities, and the right not to be extinguished. As stated in the introduction of this book, in order to identify the democratic consequences of international human rights in Brazil, we aim specifically to assess four of those basic rights: the right to food and the combating of extreme poverty; the right to health and the public healthcare system; the right to racial equality and the access of ethnic minorities to public universities; and the right of the indigenous population to recognition and protection.

As explained in the introductory chapter, the first two areas are related to social rights of which huge portions of Brazilian society have been historically deprived. The fight against poverty, the reduction of social inequalities and access to healthcare are issues that concern a considerable proportion of the population, affecting their capacity for effective participation in the public sphere and for promoting the consolidation of democracy in Brazil. Further, ethnic minority access to publicly funded universities and the recognition and protection of indigenous peoples are analysed to cover issues that often lack public attention, and which are of crucial importance for Brazilian society in overcoming historical inclusion deficits and democratic obstacles.

The democratic evaluation for each topic follows the same analytical framework. Domestic policies, legislative initiatives, the inputs of international legal regimes, transnational NGOs' reports, multinational organisations' rankings, and maps and their reciprocal relationships, are explored to highlight how the various regimes prompted the development of policies, statutory changes and judicial adjudication. Democracy is, then, assessed according to a twofold criteria: the outcomes of those regimes in terms of domestic participation, and in terms of inclusion and access to human rights.

As we shall see in the following sections, the influence of international human rights has been present in the process of constructing citizenship in Brazil from the mid-1980s constitutional movement onwards. The combination of constitutional rules and inputs from the international human rights regime resulted in both more opportunities for participation and rights attainment, and increased levels of inclusion that profoundly changed Brazilian society. In all the areas observed, Brazil has become considerably more receptive to the participation and engagement of people and ethnic minority groups who were deprived of full involvement in society before. Nevertheless, the processes by which this happened are very diverse and present different features according to the areas analysed.

Regarding the rights to food and social assistance, it is possible to identify a cycle of legitimisation between State action and international norms, targets, declarations or transnational institutions' indicators and assessments. The international human rights agenda infiltrated state policies in a more subtle and fluid manner. Its norms, protocols, goals and reports provide a source of rationales for the action of state officers, representatives and agencies. Although somewhat indirect, the linkage between the targets, goals and prescriptions found in international documents and the policies implemented is perceived in a common rhetoric of mutual reinforcement.

Conversely, if we consider the public healthcare system, it is possible to identify much stronger formal institutional connections between WHO initiatives and offices, and policies developed at the national level. The strength by which access to healthcare materialised as a right is shown by the fact that integration of international regimes overcame the mutual 'principle-guided' rhetoric to materialise into concrete joint projects and technical agreements, and by the increasing participation of healthcare system users in local councils and in judicial litigation on causes related to the right to health.

On the other hand, the rights of minority groups, such as the access of black students to publicly funded universities or the recognition and protection of indigenous people, followed a different path. The initial approach for international human rights support did not come from national political or representative bodies but from diverse initiatives from different stakeholders. The chain of cooperation between universities, social movements, international scientific community members, NGOs and international courts created the pressure needed to prompt State action. Judicial participation came late, in the case of affirmative action, and was somehow sceptical of and resistant to international human rights documents in the case of indigenous people's right to land.

The main conclusion of this chapter is that international human rights have, in general terms, contributed to increase levels of inclusion, the enhancement of citizenship and the consolidation of democracy in Brazil through different means and actors. While political and representative branches of power tend to continuously and circularly extract legitimacy for their actions from the international human rights apparatus, the participation of the judiciary in those processes vary and tend to absorb international norms and decisions normatively.

2.2. The Right to Food, the Fight against Poverty and Hunger, and Conditional Cash Transfer Programmes

The 1988 Constitution states as one of its fundamental objectives the *eradication of poverty and substandard living conditions.* It also establishes, in its Article 6, among other rights, the social rights to *health, food and housing* and, at item IV of Article 7, a minimum monthly wage capable of covering expenditure on 'housing, food, education, health' etc. Those constitutional provisions are very similar to those contained in Article 25 of the Universal Declaration of Human Rights (UDHR) regarding everyone's right to an 'adequate standard of living' that guarantees access to healthcare, food, clothing and housing, and so forth.

In 1993, the UN World Conference on Human Rights resulted in a Declaration that assured the human right to minimum standards of living conditions, including access to food. Although the UDHR dates from 1948 and Brazil assumed correspondent social responsibilities in its Constitution and before the international community in 1993, in 2005, the Brazilian Gini coefficient was 0.548, and 59.4% of the population had an income below the minimum legal wage, out of which 12% were in the poorest band, with monthly income per capita below one-quarter of the minimum wage, 20.4% receiving between one-quarter and one-half of the minimum wage, and 27% receiving between one-half and the level of the minimum wage.[1] In 1995, the UN promoted a World Summit for Social Development in Copenhagen. The Summit's final Declaration acknowledged the urgency to 'address profound social problems, especially poverty, unemployment and social exclusion' throughout the world. The States that attended the Summit also agreed on a commitment to 'eradicate poverty'.

Also in 1995, some regional initiatives on conditional cash transfer programmes started to take shape in the big cities of São Paulo state. In the Federal District, a programme called '*Bolsa Escola*' (School Allowance) set a conditionality related to primary school attendance by the children of families included.[2] At the national level, social protection initiatives were still very connected to the idea of 'safety nets', with State action towards the poorest section of the population being intermediated by NGOs and charities in general.[3]

The year 2000 was marked by the UN Millennium Declaration, which had very specific targets related to poverty eradication, like the one to halve, by 2015, 'the proportion of people who suffer from hunger'. It is symbolic that the first of the eight Millennium Development Goals (MDGs) was exactly to 'eradicate extreme poverty and hunger'.

In 2001, the World Bank put the fight against poverty on its developmental agenda, adopting a purposely holistic view on situations of social vulnerability that would guide States to develop their strategies and arrangements to fight poverty, a tool called 'social risk management'.

The Constitutional Amendment Proposal 21 was also presented to the Brazilian Senate in 2001. Its only intent was to add the word 'food' to the social rights listed in Article 6 of the Constitution, and its main reasoning was the Brazilian vote for the adoption of the 1993 Vienna Declaration and Programme of Action and the recognition of the right to food during that international conference. The proposal became Constitutional Amendment 64, from 2010.

Also in 2001, Brazil took some decisive steps to tackle poverty at a national level. The Federal Government created two different conditional cash transfer programmes, '*Bolsa Escola*' (School Allowance) and '*Bolsa Alimentação*' (Alimentary Allowance). The first mirrored the Federal District pioneer initiative, with similar values and conditionalities. The second was related to compliance with health assistance protocols regarding childhood vaccination and medical assistance in pregnancy.[4] Further, the Federal Government proposed a draft Bill to

[1] IBGE, *Síntese de indicadores sociais: uma análise das condições de vida da população brasileira* (Instituto Brasileiro de Geografia e Estatística IBGE 2016), https://biblioteca.ibge.gov.br/visualizacao/livros/liv98965.pdf, 91–93.

[2] Diego Sánchez-Ancochea and Lauro Mattei, 'Bolsa Família, poverty and inequality: Political and economic effects in the short and long run' (2011) 11(2)–(3) *Global Social Policy* 302.

[3] Romulo Paes-Sousa and Jeni Vaitsman, 'The Zero Hunger and Brazil without Extreme Poverty programs: a step forward in Brazilian social protection policy' (2014) 19(11) Ciência & Saude Coletiva 43–52.

[4] Romero Cavalcanti Barreto da Rocha, 'Programas condicionais de transferência de renda e fecundidade: Evidencias do bolsa família' (2018) 22(3) *Economia Aplicada* 6.

create the Poverty Fight and Eradication Fund, funded by both the public revenue and private donations, of which 85% should be applied to families and individuals living below relevant poverty standards.

It would be very simplistic to think that the sequence of international solemn declarations against poverty and hunger, the mobilisation of a transnational powerhouse like the World Bank towards this same subject and the institutional developments of the same nature in Brazil, briefly summarised here, are just a chronological coincidence. As Barrientos and Hulme affirm:

> The International Development Goals, Millennium Declaration in 2000 and subsequent agreement on the MDGs has focused the attention of international organizations, poor and rich governments and the citizens and celebrities of Europe and North America on poverty and vulnerability reduction more than any other global initiative in the past.[5]

Brazil's adherence to this global humanitarian agenda might have been strategic at its primary stages, and it might even have developed some original mechanisms. Yet, it certainly was not independent of international influences, as some studies would suggest.[6] The principles that informed international commitments aimed at attacking poverty and eradicating suffering were present in the policies and laws mentioned above. As noted above, the very proposal to amend the constitutional text to add the word 'food' to the list of social rights set out in Article 6 of the 1988 Constitution was expressly inspired by international commitments assumed by the Brazilian State before the international community, although it can be argued that the amendment, by itself, did not trigger substantial progress, but was more of a rhetorical manoeuvre to signify an undefined will to collaborate or comply with international standards on the matter. One way or the other, the discourse of international human rights activists and organisations was very concentrated on an agenda that was impossible to oppose. The fight against poverty invoked a sense of human solidarity; it appeared that a compelling international consensus gave propulsion to an increasing sum of efforts in the same direction: to reach out to the poorest human beings living below the most basic standards of dignity.

In 2003, the Brazilian government launched the '*Fome Zero*' (Zero Hunger) programme, aiming to boost State intervention against hunger and poverty. In another striking example of how national and international initiatives to fight poverty were discursively aligned, an official report on the programme asserted that 'the Fome Zero and the first Millennium Goal – Eradicate Hunger and Misery – symbolize and summarize one unique and comprehensive emancipation policy of inclusion and social justice'.[7]

[5] Armando Barrientos and David Hulme, 'Social Protection for the Poor and Poorest in Developing Countries: Reflections on a Quiet Revolution: Commentary' (2009) 37(4) *Oxford Development Studies* 443.

[6] Bernhard Leubolt, 'Institutions, discourse and welfare: Brazil as a distributional regime' (2013) 13(1) *Global Social Policy* 76.

[7] MDS, *Fome Zero: Uma História Brasileira*, Vol 3 (Ministério do Desenvolvimento Social e Combate à Fome, 2010), www.mds.gov.br/webarquivos/publicacao/Fome%20Zero%20Vol1.pdf, 169.

The most impressive achievements in attacking poverty and misery happened after all various policies were condensed into one major conditional cash transfer programme. Law 10.836, from January 2004, created the '*Bolsa Família*' (Family Allowance), rationalising institutional action under the management of one single Ministry of Social Development and Fight against Hunger.[8]

In 10 years, the number of households reached by the programme more than doubled, rising from 6,572,060 to 13,980,524 families from January 2005 to January 2015. In the same period, public expenditure on the programme increased even more sharply, from R$ 430,841,390 to R$ 2,342,594,866.[9] Studies register that *Bolsa Família* became an important source of income for one-quarter of the total Brazilian population, answering for a considerable share of improvement in inequality levels in Brazil in recent decades, amounting to a 44% reduction in the proportion of people in poverty between 1990 and 2009.[10]

In fact, although the conditional cash transfer (CCT) programme cannot be identified as its main cause, it is worth noting that the Gini coefficient dropped from 0.548 in 2005 to 0.491 points in 2015. After the *Bolsa Família* programme was initiated and structured nationwide, it was combined with a sustained and incremental increase in the real consumption capacity of the minimum legal wage, and the expansion of the *Benefício de Prestação Continuada* (Continuous Benefit), which is a lifetime non-contributory social insurance pension that covers the elderly and disabled. With all those policies put in place together, the proportion of the population with a monthly per capita income below the minimum legal wage fell from 59.4% to 57.3% in 10 years. The most significant changes happened, though, within the lowest group of earners. The poorest band of the population with a monthly income per capita below one-quarter of the minimum wage fell from 12% to 9.2%, the 20.4% that had a monthly income per capita between one-quarter and one-half of the minimum legal wage in 2005 fell to 17.8% in 2015, while the band between one-half and the level of the minimum wage increased from 27% in 2005 to 30.3% in 2015.[11] These data show a gradual, but progressive lifting of fringes of the population from a situation of extreme poverty and, especially, food insecurity. Official data show that, in 2004, 39.9% of the population were living in a situation of food insecurity, with 7.7% dealing with severe food insecurity, and 14.1% subject to moderate food insecurity. Those figures

[8] Jeni Vaitsman, Gabriela Rieveres Borges de Andrade and Luis Otavio Farias, 'Proteção social no Brasil: o que mudou na assistência social após a Constituição de 1988' (2009) 14(3) *Ciência & Saúde Coletiva* 736.

[9] Ministério da Cidadania, 'Programa Bolsa Família – quantidade de famílias e valores (até outubro/2021)' (Secretaria de Avaliação e Gestão da Informação), https://aplicacoes.cidadania.gov.br/vis/data3/data-explorer.php.

[10] Diego Sánchez-Ancochea and Lauro Mattei (n 2) 306; Sergei Soares, 'The efficiency and effectiveness of social protection against poverty and inequality in Brazil' in J Midgley and D Piachaud (eds), *Social Protection, Economic Growth and Social Change* (Edward Elgar Publishing, 2013); Flávio Eiró, 'The Vicious Cycle in the Bolsa Família Program's Implementation: Discretionality and the Challenge of Social Rights Consolidation in Brazil' (2019) 42(3) *Qualitative Sociology* 38.

[11] IBGE (n 1) 91–93.

plummeted until 2013, when 25.8% of the population were still in food insecurity, but the percentage of severe and moderate food insecurity more than halved to account for 3.6% and 5.1% of the population, respectively.[12]

This brief description of the *Bolsa Família* CCT programme's empirical outcomes helps to unveil another interesting interaction between national and international spheres of the fight against poverty and social inequality: the recurrence to international community approval as a source of legitimacy for State policies. The programme's official publicity mentions that *Bolsa Família* was one of the main factors for the achievement of the first Millennium Development Goal and contributed to Brazil's exclusion from the UN Food and Agriculture Organization's (FAO's)_ Hunger Map. An official report on the 10-year anniversary of *Bolsa Família* proudly presents the fact that Brazil received the 2013 Award for Outstanding Achievement in Social Security, an international prize awarded by the International Social Security Association (ISSA) for measures taken to tackle poverty and social inequality.[13] Another official source explores the benefits of mutual support between Brazilian governmental strategies to eradicate hunger and social mobilisation: ActionAid, an NGO that developed an index called the HungerFREE Scorecard, pointed to Brazil as the best performer in fighting hunger among 29 developing countries in 2009.[14] The 2015 UN Development Programme (UNDP) Human Development Report named *Bolsa Família* as one of the most successful programmes of social protection around the world.[15]

In consequence, the international agenda on human rights relating to dignity and the eradication of poverty and suffering and its institutional implementation in Brazil were intrinsically related in a circular, self-reinforcing dynamic. It takes effect, first, as an inspirational, principle-guided prompting force that advances State action, and second, as a legitimation source for its outcomes and achievements which, in turn, motivates more investment and institutional developments. In this legitimation cycle, international human rights operate predominately in a cognitive way. The constant interaction between international instruments, constitutional and legal changes, the conception of social policies and international community approval witnessed here can be described as a continuous process of institutional experimentation and learning. International declarations, targets and awards are often drawn upon by police makers and legislative authorities as political commitments that must orient expectations related to the fight against poverty and social inclusion within the society.

[12] ibid 38.

[13] Tereza Campello and Marcelo Côrtes Neri, *Bolsa Família Program: a decade of social inclusion in Brazil* (Ipea, 2014) 9.

[14] ActionAid, *HungerFREE Scorecard 2010: Who's Really Fighting Hunger* (2010).

[15] UNDP, *Human Development Report 2015* (United Nations Development Programme, 2015), http://report2015.archive.s3-website-us-east-1.amazonaws.com/, 170.

2.2.1. The Right to Food, the Fight against Poverty and Hunger, Conditional Cash Transfer Programmes, and Democracy

Even if it is difficult to identify an 'individual rights' discourse developed before or by the courts in this regard, an argument in favour of the improvement of Brazilian democracy through the conditional cash transfer programmes can be made: the international movement against poverty coupled with a cycle of inclusion that led to political mobilisation and the development of a new social right to a minimum income for the most vulnerable.

There are studies pointing out that the decentralised management of the *Bolsa Família* programme makes it susceptible to local government agents' bias and preferences in the selection of households, which impedes its concretisation as a right, leading to missed targets.[16] Conversely, another study shows that this very same mixed selection mechanism, with a federal spatial criterion that focuses on poor regions, complemented by local authority selection, means that '80% of Bolsa Familia funds currently reach families below the poverty line. 73% of Bolsa Familia benefits are distributed to the poorest quintile of the population, and 94% to the poorest two quintiles.'[17] Regardless of the index used to evaluate the effectiveness of coverage, the beneficiaries and the benefits of conditional cash transfer policies, the Brazilian *Bolsa Família* appears among the better-targeted programmes in Latin America, which is particularly remarkable considering its wide remit.[18]

The *Bolsa Família* programme also faced critiques that it would generate political clientelism.[19] The benefits would be granted in exchange for political support in a manoeuvre by incumbent politicians to capture society in a social assistance trap in order to stay in office. According to that claim, clientelism depends on a *quid pro quo* rationale. However, the recipients of social assistance can only be viewed as *clients* if the benefits are conditional on their vote. This trade-off logic erodes if there is no significant correlation between the concession of the benefit and electoral support or, in other words, if election results are not influenced in the targeting mechanism of the CCT programme at all.[20]

[16] Flávio Eiró (n 10) 388.

[17] Renee Gardner Sewall, 'Conditional Cash Transfer Programs in Latin America' (2008) 28(2) *The SAIS Review of International Affairs* 179.

[18] Gibrán Cruz-Martínez, 'Going beyond aggregated measures in the conditional cash transfer programs: The effective coverage of benefits and beneficiaries' (2015) 14(27) *Cadernos PROLAM/USP* 109.

[19] Felipe J Hevia, 'Society-State relationships, citizen participation and political clientelism inside programs that combat poverty. The case of Bolsa Familia in Brazil' (2011) 57 *América Latina Hoy*; Anthony Hall, 'The Last Shall be First: Political Dimensions of Conditional Cash Transfers in Brazil' (2012) 11 *Journal of Policy Practice*.

[20] Armando Barrientos and Juan Villa, 'Economic and Political Inclusion in Human Development Conditional Income Transfer Programmes in Latin America' (2016) 15 *Social Policy and Society*.

Further evidence against the 'clientelism theory' can be found where there is no indication that recipients' votes are fully determined by the concession of the benefit. Hunter and Sugiyama point out that the *Bolsa Família* design, with overlapping checkpoints either at local and national level, driven by technical and impersonal criteria, helps to create a sense of independence between the recipients of the benefit and specific political authorities.[21] As Bohn argues, *Bolsa Família* recipients tended to support the opposition candidate when the CCT programmes were first put in place and, even within this group, political support varies significantly by geographic region.[22] Similarly, Kerbauy concludes that CCT programmes cannot explain alone the results of the 2010 Brazilian election, as the decision to vote for a candidate (incumbent or opposition) was only slightly different if programme participants' and non-participants' voting intentions were compared.[23] The most recent general elections in Brazil provided striking evidence against the 'clientelism' theory, as the incumbent candidate lost to the opposition candidate for the Presidency in all 100 municipalities, with the greatest support coming from beneficiaries of the *Auxílio Brasil* (the name given to the benefit that succeeded the *Bolsa Família*, using as a data source the beneficiaries of emergency financial aid initiated to mitigate the economic effects of the Covid-19 pandemic in 2020).[24]

The clientelist critique is not only simplistic. It is also outdated, referring to jaundiced descriptions of the power relations found in orthodox Brazilian sociology, which has always seen policies related to social assistance as a crude reflection of the old authoritarian patrimonialism. Social protection policies seen through a patrimonialist lens would be nothing but a useful tool in the hands of an incumbent populist, be it Pedro II or Vargas, to prevent the beneficiaries from participating, rather than enhancing their capabilities.[25] Those descriptions of democratic deficits in Brazil that rely on traditional forms of domination exercised over the needy portion of the electorate by rural local authorities, known as *coronelism*, also often disregard empirical evidence that shows a profound change in the profile of the Brazilian electorate. A considerable proportion of the electorate is not chiefly isolated in rural communities in the deep countryside, as in the first half of the twentieth century, but is part of an urbanised working class living in the peripheric communities of the big cities.[26]

Nevertheless, it is possible to identify some connection between the programme beneficiaries' political preferences and the political actors often connected to those

[21] Wendy Hunter and Natasha Borges Sugiyama, 'Assessing the Bolsa Família Successes, Shortcomings, and Unknowns' in PR Kingstone and TJ Power (eds), *Democratic Brazil Divided* (University of Pittsburgh Press, 2017) 148.

[22] Simone R Bohn, 'Social policy and vote in Brazil: Bolsa Família and the Shifts in Lula's Electoral Base' (2011) 46(1) *Latin American Research Review*.

[23] Maria Tereza Miceli Kerbauy, 'Os programas de transferência de renda e o voto regional nas eleições presidenciais de 2010' (2011) 17(2) *Opinião Pública: Publicação do CESOP*.

[24] Beatriz Araújo et al, 'Lula liderou os votos em todas as 100 cidades que mais recebem Auxílio Brasil', *CNN Brasil* (São Paulo, 5 October 2022), www.cnnbrasil.com.br/politica/lula-liderou-os-votos-em-todas-as-100-cidades-que-mais-recebem-auxilio-brasil/.

[25] Raymundo Faoro, *Os Donos do Poder: Formação do Patronato Político Brasileiro* (Globo, 1975).

[26] Fernando Limongi F and Eoin Paul O'Neil, 'Democracy in Brazil: presidentialism, party coalitions and the decision-making process' (2007) 3 *Novos Estudos-Cebrap*.

social policies. Some studies show a link between aggregate electoral results and inequality maps. Kerbauy demonstrates that in the 2010 general election, the incumbent candidate's largest winning margin was in the region with the largest number of *Bolsa Família* beneficiaries.[27] Sewall, on the other hand, explores how the policy was part of the campaign discourse in the 2006 election.[28] A further study that used analytical data collected from surveys to assess beneficiaries' perception of political institutions and principles demonstrates that *Bolsa Família* recipients' and non-recipients' regard for abstract democratic values does not vary significantly. The first group tends to show more support for democratic institutions and actors immediately identified with the CCT programmes, which shows reciprocity trends in political support, but no variance in the perception of core democratic principles and institutional legitimacy.[29]

It is worth mentioning that there is literature identifying the positive effects of the Brazilian CCT programmes on primary school attendance, the consumption capacity of beneficiary families and well-being.[30] Thus, if the CCT programmes have a political impact – as some aggregate data might suggest – without any empirical evidence of a relevant correlation between individual programme participation and voting intention, it is possibly the result of a collective decision of the poorest part of the electorate to support policies that meet their interests and needs through voting.

If the first signs of a class balance brought by the consistent implementation of policies aimed to tackle extreme poverty have resulted in palpable electoral outcomes, it must be seen as a step forward in the transition from a formal democracy to a social one, as proposed by Huber et al, and not as a setback.[31] If the poorer part of the population, which is the vast majority, can articulate their voices in the direction of assuring their rights, this is not the characteristic behaviour of 'clients', but of rights holders well aware of their influence in the formation of the collective will, exercising it in the most classical democratic way. Beyond the electoral effect that the cash transfer programmes enacted to fight extreme poverty in Brazil might have brought to the citizenry, it is necessary to point to a sense of belonging to society for recipients endowed by it. From oblivion and invisibility, the poor gained the opportunity to consume, and to interact in different social environments. It is possible to suggest that millions of historically disenfranchised people could now articulate themselves to make their 'voices' heard.[32]

[27] Kerbauy (n 12) 478.

[28] Sewall (n 17) 183.

[29] Mathew L Layton, Maureen M Dounagly et al, 'Does Welfare Provision Promote Democratic State Legitimacy? Evidence from Brazil's Bolsa Família Program' (2017) 59(4) *Latin American Politics and Society*.

[30] Rocha (n 4) 12.

[31] Evelyne Huber, Dietrich Rueschemeyer and John D Stephens, 'The Paradoxes of Contemporary Democracy: Formal, Participatory, and Social Dimensions' (1997) 29(3) *Comparative Politics*.

[32] Dietrich Rueschemeyer, 'The Quality of Democracy: Addressing Inequality' (2004) 15(4) *Journal of Democracy* 83–84.

Here, we perceive the universal-cosmopolitan-rights-based element of democracy igniting the articulation of the local-popular-participatory one in a very cooperative manner. The incorporation of the international agenda on the fight against poverty and the eradication of hunger through policies and legislation brought about a cycle of inclusion that is a pre-condition for generalised citizenship. In fact, it is practically impossible to talk about citizenship when the main objective for a fifth of the population was not to die from starvation, as was the case in Brazil in 2005. If democracy is a system not only of increasing levels of participation, but also of broad inclusion that enables people to exercise a range of political rights, it is particularly problematic to have such a huge share of the population not even nurtured sufficiently to take part in a plural public sphere.

The elevation of more than 30,000,000 people from extreme poverty to minimum dignity standards is certainly one of the most remarkable social changes in the direction of the universalisation of citizenship based on human rights that the world may have witnessed at the beginning of the twenty-first century, and this phenomenon brought to the national political arena a part of society that could not previously articulate their political preferences.

The political ascension and strength of this new actor – the poor – can be felt through the almost 'untouchable' status of CCT programmes in the current political scenario, regardless of the ideological orientation of who governs. As said in the previous chapter, contemporary democracies are rights incubators; successful policies, developed from programmes and agendas created internationally, tend to be reproduced through the right lexicon and incorporated through participatory mechanisms, such as elections, legislative changes, or even constitutional amendments. Constitutional Amendment Draft Bill 29, from 2020, has been approved by the Senate and awaits voting by the Chamber of Deputies to enshrine the concession of a basic family income as a constitutional social right. CCT programmes that contributed to diminish food insecurity and poverty elevated deprived portions of the population that absorbed such policies as rights and not charity. This political empowerment means a significant improvement in the quality of democracy in a society in which the masses had been historically and systematically left out of the most important political decisions.

2.3. The Right to Health and the *Sistema Único de Saúde* (SUS): The Universal, Decentralised and Participative Healthcare System

The 1988 Constitution states in Article 196 that 'health is a right of all and a duty of the State'. In the following sections of its text, the 1988 Constitution establishes that the healthcare system should be decentralised, comprehensive and participative. Decentralisation means the effective participation of all federative spheres of government in its management, comprehensiveness indicates assistance that starts with preventive care and reaches complex treatments and interventions, and the participative character refers to the communitarian input in decision making.

Sarlet and Figueiredo consider, as a constitutional highlight in the dimension of health assistance, Brazil's adoption of an approach approximate to the healthcare definition adopted by the WHO following the Almaty Declaration guidelines.[33] Nevertheless, in the years that followed promulgation of the Constitution, Brazil faced a period of impacting economic measures adopted to contain hyperinflation and political turmoil that ultimately impeded Laws 8.080 and 8.142, from 1990, in substantially changing the healthcare system scenario.[34]

The formal creation of the *Sistema Único de Saúde* (SUS) (Unified Health System) was incapable of shifting an institutional culture still attached to the idea of a contribution-based social security system that offered health assistance only to formal workers. The real transformation came only after the closure of the National Institute of Medical Assistance and Social Security (INAMPS) by Law 8.689/1993 and the publication of the Basic Operational Rules No 01, in 1993 and 1996, by the Ministry of Health.[35]

Those norms brought concrete foundations to the principles of decentralisation, comprehensiveness and participation. Sarlet and Figueiredo point out that 'the budget handover from the Union to the Municipalities that reached 144 localities in 1996, came to encompass 5,539 cities in 2002'.[36] That is a major sign of practical management decentralisation by means of financial support from the national government to municipalities to enable them to better allocate resources.

The devolution of the administration of health assistance to the local sphere is demonstrable in the figures. According to Fleury and others, 96.4% of basic assistance and 43.4% of medium complexity procedures delivered by the SUS in 2009 happened in the municipalities' health care units, and 55.32% of hospital stays (more than 6 million) were under the municipalities' management.[37] If one thinks of comprehensiveness, it is worth mentioning that, according to Castro et al, primary assistance (PA) policies such as the '*Saúde da Família*' (Family Health) programme saw an expansion in family health teams (doctors, nurses and other health professionals) 'from about 2,000 in 1998 (the first available data) to 42,975 in 2018', and increased its coverage 'from 7 million (4% of the population)

[33] Ingo Wolfgang Sarlet and Mariana Filchtiner Figueiredo, 'Algumas considerações sobre o direito fundamental à proteção e promoção da saúde aos 20 anos da Constituição federal de 1988' (2008) 17 *Revista de Direito do Consumidor.*

[34] Tatiana Wargas de Faria Baptista, Cristiane Vieira Machado and Luciana Dias de Lima, 'State responsibility and right to health in Brazil: A balance of the Branches' actions' (2009) 14(3) *Ciência & Saude Coletiva* 831; Armando de Negri Filho, 'Brazil: a long journey towards a universal healthcare system' in JM Zuniga, SP Marks and LO Gostin (eds), *Advancing the Human Right to Health* (Oxford University Press, 2013) 3.

[35] Sarlet and Figueiredo (n 33); Filho (n 34).

[36] Sarlet and Figueiredo (n 33) 26.

[37] Sonia Fleury et al, 'Local governance in the decentralized health care system in Brazil' (2010) 28(6) *Revista Panamericana de Salud Pública* 447.

to 130 million (62% of the population) people, incorporating more than 264,000 health agents and 26,000 oral health teams'.[38]

In general terms, the combination of those attributes in SUS institutional dynamics was accompanied by a considerable improvement in many indices related to healthcare in recent decades. Preventive action increased the proportion of the population making at least one visit to a SUS doctor in the previous 12 months from 49.27% in 1998 to 69.32% in 2013. Between 1990 and 2015, life expectancy rose from 65.34 to 75.20 years, neonatal mortality decreased from 25.7 to 8.2 per 1,000 livebirths, infant mortality in children under one year old reduced from 53.4 to 14 per 1,000 livebirths. Mortality in children aged five years or younger also fell from 64.2 to 15.7 per 1,000 livebirths, and the maternal mortality ratio, which was 104 per 100,000 livebirths in 1990, decreased to 44 per 100,000 livebirths in 2015.[39]

In light of those results, Brazil's healthcare system has been cited by the WHO as a positive example of universal coverage.[40] Likewise, the Ministry of Health has referred to the authority of the WHO's assessments of healthcare systems and to its favourable appraisal of Brazilians policies such as the *Saúde da Família* strategy. The official report published in 2018 featuring a commemorative assessment of the SUS in its first 30 years of implementation was a co-production of the Brazilian Ministry of Health and the Pan American Health Organization, the regional office of the WHO.[41]

On this subject, once again, the cycle of legitimation is manifest. The Brazilian Constitution adopted a concept of health as a universal right very much aligned with WHO guidelines. This semantic convergence propelled a variety of laws and programmes, which were then validated according to the positive reaction to its achievements by the very same international organisations. If that aspect of the influence of the international human rights regime on the Brazilian healthcare system is somehow similar to the way in which social security, especially the CCT programmes, were generated from and integrated into the international humanitarian agenda, it is possible to identify that the liaison of the international human rights movement and Brazilian official agencies around the concretisation of a universal right to health assistance went a little further.

The discursive and rhetoric alignment was concretised in the form of institutional cooperation. International organisations and the Brazilian government have joined their efforts through around 70 technical cooperation agreements that reach all spheres of federal authority, for example the States of Espírito Santo,

[38] Marcia C Castro et al, 'Brazil's unified health system: the first 30 years and prospects for the future' (2019) 394 (10195) *The Lancet* (British edition) 348.

[39] ibid 394.

[40] WHO, 'The World Health Report: Health Systems Financing: The path to universal coverage' (World Health Organization, 2010), https://apps.who.int/iris/handle/10665/44371, 8.

[41] PAHO, 'Relatório 30 anos de SUS, que SUS para 2030?' (Pan American Health Organization, 2018), https://iris.paho.org/handle/10665.2/52517.

Pará and Tocantins, and the Municipalities of São Paulo and Florianópolis. Maybe one of the most emblematic examples of the intense cooperation between Brazil's healthcare agencies and the WHO was the implementation of '*Mais Médicos Para o Brasil*' (More Doctors for Brazil). The programme was focused on the nationwide spread of primary assistance through the allocation of doctors, including from overseas, in communities that are not particularly attractive in the usual working preferences of Brazilian doctors. Agreements between Brazil and other nations, especially Cuba, were intermediated by the WHO and the Pan American Health Organization. According to a WHO report on the subject, it mobilised more than 20,000 Cuban doctors, increasing the coverage of primary care assistance from 62.7% to 70.4% of the whole population, reducing avoidable hospitalisations from 45% to 41% in three years. The same report shows that 63% of that workforce went to the poorer municipalities in the northeast region of the country. The report also refers to the mobilisation, training and logistical preparations in the allocation of Cuban doctors in Brazil as 'an unprecedented challenge that was successfully conducted by PAHO/WHO'.[42]

It is fair to assert that while the influence of the international human rights agenda on *health* as a legally enforceable right is indirect, the mechanisms of international cooperation for the implementation of programmes and the production of technical reports of policy assessment are the result of a very much imbricated institutional dynamic between international and national agencies and offices.

2.3.1. The Health Care System and Democracy

It is hard to establish a connection between the right to health and electoral democratic outcomes. If a minimalist conception of democracy or 'low intensity democracy' is set as the standard, one would be tempted to say that healthcare and democracy are absolutely dissociated. As we have discussed, the national/popular/participatory element of democracy is not a seasonal device actioned from election to election. Social mobilisation around a right, manifested through litigation, can be considered a display of democratic enhancement and participation, even if it is mediated by courts. In other words, contemporary democracy in the globalised world is not fully perceived through a fixation on elections, but it is open to a broader sense of agency that acknowledges litigation over social rights as an important channel of democratic participation. In that regard, it is worth mentioning the considerable increase in the levels by which society has provoked the judicial machinery to rule on rights related to healthcare in Brazil.

The strong integration of international and national initiatives and stakeholders has created an amalgamated institutional culture towards a 'rights-based'

[42] WHO, 'Brazil: The mais médicos programme' (World Health Organization, 2018), https://apps.who.int/iris/bitstream/handle/10665/326084/WHO-HIS-SDS-2018.19-eng.pdf.

healthcare system in Brazil that was reflected in judicial intervention. According to research published by the Brazilian National Council of Justice, the number of new claims related to healthcare increased by 130% between 2008 and 2017, while the growth in the number of claims in general was around 50% in the same period.[43] The majority of those cases relate to two areas: (i) medicine provision, and (ii) hospital treatment. From 2014 to 2019, new claims logged as medicine provision and/or hospital treatment claims oscillated around 200,000 new cases per year.[44]

Despite the fact that participation of the judiciary has been predominantly concentrated in these two specific areas of the healthcare system, the Brazilian judiciary has made its contribution to the strengthening of the idea of health as a right. From 1997, the Brazilian Supreme Court started to produce a body of case law on the right to health. Even though the overall management of the public health service and the necessity of criteria for judicial intervention in healthcare were brought up in some cases, it is possible to affirm that the Supreme Court has granted the provision of medicine and treatment under the 'right to health' constitutional clause in almost all cases in which the claimant patient is successful in demonstrating the gravity of their situation.[45]

Discussions about the impact of judicial decisions on resources allocation were the subject of a public hearing held by the Supreme Court in 2009 and justified the creation, in 2010, of a permanent Health Forum in the National Council of Justice. Nevertheless, criteria such as the previous existence of a vindicated medicine/treatment in national policy, scientific or official recognition of its efficiency and safety, the inadequacy of other medicine/treatment provided by the system and a history of success in patients that can afford it, are either undefined in their internal rationing rules or simply ignored by the courts.[46] This radical interpretation of the *right to health* as an unconditional constitutional promise faces critiques in the sense that judicial intervention tends to increase inequality in the distribution of ambulatory and medical assistance, favouring those who can afford litigation, often represented by a limited and professionalised set of lawyers.[47] The percentage of healthcare cases issued by Public Attorneys' offices and other legal aid institutions is still below what would be expected in such an inequal society – 15%. Recent data also show that the share of claims related to private health insurance is disproportionately high in relation to cases related to the public healthcare system

[43] Insper, 'Judicialização da Saúde no Brasil: Perfil das demandas, causas e propostas de solução' (Conselho Nacional de Justiça, 2019).

[44] CNJ, 'Justice in Numbers' (2021), https://paineis.cnj.jus.br/QvAJAXZfc/opendoc.htm?document=qvw_l%2FPainelCNJ.qvw&host=QVS%40neodimio03&anonymous=true&sheet=shResumoDespFT.

[45] See STF [2010] SL 47 AgR/PE, j 17.03.2010; STF [2010] STA 175 AgR/CE, j 17/03/2010; STF [2018] STP 24/MG, j 02/08/2018; STF [2011] STA 558/PR, j 02/09/2011; STF [2010] SS 3962/SE, j 07/04/2010, etc.

[46] Daniel WL Wang, 'Courts and health care rationing: the case of the Brazilian Federal Supreme Court' (2013) 8(1) *Health Economics, Policy and Law*.

[47] Ana Luiza Chieffi, Rita de Cassia Barata Barradas and Moises Golbaum, 'Legal access to medications: a threat to Brazil's public health system?' (2017) 17 *BMC Health Services Research* https://link.gale.com/apps/doc/A511292175/AONE?u=jrycal5&sid=bookmarkAONE&xid=8254978e.

if considering the coverage of both, suggesting that litigation is a resource more accessed by the wealthier portion of the population.[48] Nevertheless, the openness of the judicial institutions, included Public Attorney and legal aid offices, to demands related to health assistance is a novelty brought about by the prominence of healthcare in the 1988 Constitution and the impact of the international human rights regime on State officials' perception of it.

Not without reason, observers show that through healthcare litigation, Brazilian citizens have been able to hold authorities from all federal spheres of the State accountable for the observation of principles underlying the healthcare system. Litigation has become a valuable tool for the inclusion of marginalised sections of the society, such as HIV patients, into the ambit of such policies.[49]

It is not possible to identify, in the Supreme Court case law on the right to health mentioned above, any direct reference to international norms related to healthcare. However, the judiciary has increased its influence as a forum for discussion of the healthcare system, adopting a view that connects the *right to health* to the *right to life* and *human dignity*. This sequential chain of rights has an unequivocal semantical resemblance to the way the WHO addresses the issue. Therefore, the usual judicial discourse is preferably underpinned by the Constitutional provisions on the *right to health*, which do not differ substantially to the UN organisations' consensus on the matter.

The SUS also features a remarkable participative character if one considers Law 8.142, from 1990, which created local Health Councils, permanent and deliberative bodies responsible for formulating strategies and the oversight of health policies in each federal sphere of government. Article 1, para 4, establishes that the Councils' composition should be evenly split between users and other segments of society, such as government representatives, health service providers and health professionals. Moreira and Escorel registered 5,463 local Health Councils functioning in Brazil in 2009, with 72,184 councillors, out of whom 36,638 were representatives of the health system users that came out of neighbourhood associations, religious groups, workers associations and other minorities' groups.[50]

Financial and structural deficiencies and councillors' lack of qualification were still felt in local Health Councils located in small towns, which contributes to knowledge asymmetries and political encroachments in some cases.[51] Nevertheless, in 2009, 82% of local Health Council meetings occurred monthly, with no cancellations due to a lack of quorum registered in the previous 12 months in 66% of cases. In more than 70% of local Health Councils, the president was

[48] Insper (n 43) 72–73.

[49] Baptista et al (n 34).

[50] Marcelo Rasga Moreira and Sarah Escorel, 'Municipal health councils of Brazil: A debate on the democratization of health in the twenty years of the UHS' (2009) 14(3) *Ciência & Saude Coletiva* 800–01.

[51] Andrea Cornwall and Alex Shankland, 'Engaging citizens: Lessons from building Brazil's national health system' (2008) 66(10) *Social Science & Medicine* 2173.

freely elected from the councillors, in 75% of Councils the right to a voice was granted to anyone who wished to participate, and 83% of meetings were open to the public.[52]

Another study, conducted through surveys applying to municipalities' heads of Health Offices in 1996 and again in 2006, shows that while, in 1996, only 15.3% of local Health Care managers considered the influence of Health Councils in budget allocation as important, in 2006, that percentage rose to 28.3%. No less than 92.7% of Health Offices were accountable to the Health Councils, including the duty to demonstrate and explain public expenditure to councillors on health-care assistance.[53]

One way or the other, when average common citizens, NGOs and health professionals have a say in budget placement, definition of priorities, management surveillance and control, the beneficiaries of the system are empowered as right holders and not only as clients. The achievements of the SUS can be considered the result of a complex engine by which users benefit from healthcare policies that they contribute to, elaborate and enforce, be through direct participation in local Councils, pushing Public Attorney and legal aid offices to pursue court action or litigating themselves.

The strong sense that access to healthcare belongs amongst their political and legal entitlements as citizens is a remarkable example of how, in democracies, successful policies tend to be converted into rights once their achievements are incorporated by their addressees as a component of citizenship. That is exactly the process of empowerment produced by the coordination and interaction between universalist/rights-based international law regimes and national legislators, policy-makers and the courts. It is a dialectic relationship between universal citizenship and democratic agency legitimised by human rights that characterises democracy in the context of world society.[54]

Despite the form in which the phenomena present themselves, it is possible to assert that international human rights principles, organisations and their overall influence are present in the way the SUS was conceived and consolidated, producing important levels of inclusion in the form of access to healthcare. The system informs nationwide primary assistance programmes such as *Saúde da Família* (Family Health) as well as the largest public organ transplant system in the world, responsible for financing 96% of this kind of complex procedure throughout the country. More than that, expanding access to healthcare and assistance may have contributed to a change in Brazilian society itself, reflected in the substantial improvement in life expectancy and child mortality rates. As Sen puts it, probably the most elementary of all freedoms is 'the ability to survive rather than succumb to premature mortality'.[55]

[52] Moreira and Escorel (n 50).

[53] Fleury et al (n 37).

[54] Chris Thornhill, *The Sociology of Law and the Global Transformation of Democracy* (Cambridge University Press, 2018) 422–23.

[55] Amartya Sen, *Development as Freedom* (Oxford University Press, 2001).

The decentralisation of healthcare management to the local arena has been coupled with the openness of the system to social oversight. Judicial intervention has held public officials accountable to policies and rights set forth by international forums, the Constitution, statute, or even technical cooperation agreements between national agencies and the WHO. The multivariate ways by which international human rights discourses on the right to health interacted with local and national initiatives and mobilisation most certainly contributed to the consolidation of Brazilian democracy in recent years.

2.4. The Right to Equality, Affirmative Action, and Ethnic Minority Access to Publicly Funded Universities

The 1988 Brazilian Constitution strongly condemns the practice of racism, considering it a non-bailable crime (Article 5, item XLII). The criminal approach seemed powerless to deal with situations of structural racism, often perpetrated by the State itself through its rules and institutional culture. The admission system to public funded universities is an example of such institutionalised racial inequality. Brazilian public universities have always faced a paradox. Due to their academic responsibilities, they have historically adopted a very strict admission process. The other side of that coin is that exam specifications privilege students from private schools, predominately attended by the white elite, to the detriment of poor and black students, coming out of precarious primary schools situated in the urban periphery.

The outcome is that public universities at the higher level are packed with white students who can afford a superior education, with less elite faculties attended by vulnerable members of the black community. Childs and Stromquist show that '66% of students enrolled in college in Brazil are from the highest income quintile, while only about 5% are from the lowest two'.[56]

The International Convention on the Elimination of All Forms of Racial Discrimination, adopted in 1965, provisioned the adoption of 'special measures' of positive discrimination to ensure the fruition of equal opportunities to historically discriminated against ethnic groups. However, discussions on strategies to overcome inequalities in admission to higher education in Brazil only gained traction through events organised in the mid-1990s by Brazilian publicly funded universities, in which theories and experiences on affirmative action measures were internalised.[57]

[56] P Childs and NP Stromquist, 'Academic and diversity consequences of affirmative action in Brazil' (2015) 45(5) *Compare* 792.

[57] Sales Augusto dos Santos, 'Affirmative Action and Political Dispute in Today's Brazilian Academe' (2014) 41(5) *Latin American Perspectives* 141.

The turning point was Brazil's participation in the Durban Conference against Racial Discrimination, in 2001. After the Declaration and Programme of Action urged the State Parties to adopt affirmative or positive action initiatives to overcome racial discrimination, the topic gained strength in different Brazilian forums with some institutional consequences, especially in the form of quotas schemes in admission processes carried out by important publicly funded Brazilian universities, starting in the State of Rio de Janeiro that same year.[58] The official recognition of racial fractures in Brazilian society and of the necessity to face them were intrinsically connected with the international discourse on the elimination of all forms of racial discrimination adopted by the UN Convention and, then, reinforced by the Durban World Conference discussions and report.

Official reports on racial and gender inequalities present some interesting data that could be related to the adoption of affirmative action in public universities' admission systems. In 2001, 67% of higher education students in publicly funded universities were white and 31.5% were black, while in 2015 the share of white students in publicly funded universities had declined to 53.5% with 45.1% black students, a figure closer to the non-white share of the whole population, which was 53.9% in 2015. The proportion of black graduates in the population rose from 26.6% in 2012 to 32% in 2017, and the share of the black population that had accomplished that level of education also increased by 8.8% in 2016 and by 10.1% in 2018.[59]

By the time the Supreme Court delivered a ruling on the adoption of affirmative action to grant access advantages to black students, 125 higher education public institutions already had 'quota' programmes in place, and the Congress had approved Law 12.228/2010, known as the Statute of Racial Equality.[60] The Statute of Racial Equality endorses the adoption of affirmative action to diminish racial disparities in the educational systems. During discussions in Parliament, the Brazilian State's contradictory approach to the subject was mentioned, especially considering the signing of the International Convention on the Elimination of All Forms of Racial Discrimination by a dictatorial government that, at the same time, repressed any attempt to freely discuss racial discrimination and injustice.

In the decision in ADPF 186, the Supreme Court also expressly brought up the sanctioning of positive discrimination policies in the International Convention on the Elimination of All Forms of Racial Discrimination and outlined its supra-legal normative status to uphold, once more, the constitutionality of affirmative action adopted to favour ethnic minority access to publicly funded universities in Brazil. Following directly after the decision, Law 12.711/2012 made the 'quotas' policy compulsory for all federal technical, secondary and higher education institutions.

[58] Stanley R Bailey, Fabricio Fialho and Michelle Peria, 'Support for race-targeted affirmative action in Brazil' (2018) 18(6) *Ethnicities* 768–69.

[59] IBGE, *Síntese de Indicadores Sociais* (Instituto Brasileiro de Geografia e Estatística (IBGE) 2012–2020), www.ibge.gov.br/estatisticas/multidominio/condicoes-de-vida-desigualdade-e-pobreza/9221-sintese-de-indicadores-sociais.html?=&t=resultados; Tatiana Dias Silva, 'Ação Afirmativa e População Negra na Educação Superior: Acesso e Perfil Discente' (Instituto de Pesquisa Econômica Aplicada (Ipea) 2020) 17–22.

[60] dos Santos (n 57) 142.

Despite coming late, the judicial intervention in this matter cannot be considered unimportant. If it is true that the Supreme Court played a mere supporting role in the adoption of affirmative action by public universities in Brazil, it is also certain that it conferred definitive legitimacy on such policies, avoiding the loss of their achievements to date and making possible their continuity.

Although it is a matter of citizenship, the factor that ignited state action towards the inclusion of black people in public higher education in Brazil did not come from elected representatives or the judiciary. On the contrary, different stakeholders diffusively and subtly incorporated it from the international agenda. Public universities adopted the 'quotas' system almost a decade before the Statute of Racial Equality and the Supreme Court decision in ADPF/DF 186. The policies derived from independent dialogue with international agencies. The data collected by the Brazilian scientific community, formed by sociologists, anthropologists and black people's rights movements were so compelling that Brazil had to recognise during the Durban Conference, before the international community, its racist vestiges, assuming a commitment to overcome them.

National and international movements dedicated to the racial equality cause created a decisive turning point for the Brazilian academic environment and society that, at later stages, were corroborated by the legislature and the judiciary. Nevertheless, the recognition of international conventions and declarations towards the necessity of positive discriminatory policies in favour of ethnic minorities consolidated the enrichment of citizenship in Brazil, making it much more difficult for subsequent governments to regress in the levels of inclusion achieved.

In consequence, even if one considers that the affirmative action in granting access to public higher education for the black community still falls short of its full potential in reducing racial inequalities in Brazil, it is possible to assert that it has started a broader movement to mitigate the intergenerational aspects of racial discrimination.

2.4.1. The Right to Equality, Affirmative Action, Ethnic Minority Access to Public Funded Universities, and Democracy

Structural and state discrimination against ethnic minorities in Brazil is not anecdotal. As discussed in a passage in the work of Holanda, slavery was mixed with policies 'to impede the excessive influence of the coloured man in the life of the colony', such as prohibitions on the occupation of public office, which were considered ineffective, accommodating too many exceptions like the case of a man appointed by the Crown to be a Public Attorney in the State of Pernambuco in 1731 'despite his problem of being brown'.[61]

[61] Sérgio Buarque de Holanda, *Raízes do Brasil*, 27th edn (Companhia das Letras, 2015) 55.

Possibly the crudest face of the regime in terms of access to public universities in Brazil was its capacity to perpetuate the racial inequality equation. The white elite formed by the renowned public universities would keep getting better jobs with higher pay grades, while black graduates would forever be deprived of opportunities to socially ascend, passing on the iniquity from generation to generation. A place in a public university in Brazil means more than just an opportunity to get a fancy diploma to hang on a wall; it means access and the possibility of contributing to the intellectual life of the country and to the democratic public sphere.

The necessity to extend affirmative action to the working market culminated in the enactment of Law 12.990, from 2014, that reserves 20% of vacancies in federal public offices filled through public selection procedures to black people. The Judiciary and the Federal Public Prosecutors office followed the measure in their mechanisms of appointment. A case study that took into consideration public selections of the Federal Police Department in 2006, 2007 and 2015 showed that the share of white candidates approved in 2006 was 71.69%, with non-white candidates at 23.07%. In the public selection of 2015, after the enactment of Law 12.990, of the newly appointed police force, 46.99% were white and 48.04% were non-white, which is a major shift in the racial composition of the main investigative agency of the Brazilian State.[62]

It might be still too early to identify major changes from a greater black presence in influential and strategic policy-making roles, but it seems feasible to believe that the normative framework needed to tackle the veiled form of racial apartheid that stained Brazilian society since slavery is now in effect, making citizenship reach black communities and enriching Brazilian democracy.

2.5. The Right to Recognition and Protection of Indigenous Peoples

The 1988 Brazilian Constitution dedicated a whole chapter of its text to enshrine the rights of the indigenous populations, stating that 'their social organization, customs, languages, creeds and traditions' should be recognised and the land traditionally occupied by them should be demarcated and protected by the Union.

This was an important innovation in the sense that, prior to the 1988 Constitution, all legislative acts related to indigenous people treated them with a discriminatory tone. The 1916 Civil Code considered the 'forestry' relatively incapable and subject to tutelage until their 'adaptation' (Civil Code, Article 6, IV and Paragraph), and Law 6.001/1973, known as the Indigenous Statute, established in

[62] Anderson Pereira dos Santos and Gilson Matilde Diana, 'O perfil racial nos quadros da administração pública no Brasil: um primeiro balanço dos efeitos da reserva de vagas para negros em uma organização de segurança pública' (2018) 69(4) *Revista do Serviço Público* 964.

its first article that one of its purposes was to, progressively and harmoniously, 'integrate' the indigenous communities to 'national communion'.

What is undisguised in those legal documents is the vision of the indigenous peoples as primitive and inferior beings that needed to be assimilated into the 'civilised' community in order to reach full citizenship. The 1988 Constitutional assertion of their rights to have their own way of life protected and preserved disrupted this 'assimilationist' approach.[63]

According to the constitutional view, indigenous people's diversity does not set them apart from Brazilian society, but, on the contrary, it is the very reason they must be recognised as part of it. This change of orientation did not occur suddenly. It was a result of an intense interaction between international anthropologists, local movements, catholic dissident missionaries (especially linked with liberation theology), journalists and international organisations that had been drawing attention to the situation of the indigenous people in Brazil since the 1960s.[64]

Transnational and international organisations offered support to social movements that were not strong enough to influence official representatives. Although none of the eight indigenous candidates for the Constitutional Assembly of 1986 was elected, the United Nations awarded Davi Yanomami for his environmental achievements, making it possible for the indigenist movement to have a voice in the constituent moment.[65] It is important to consider that, back in 1985, the Inter-American Commission of Human Rights recognised that the construction of a road and the concession of mining permits inside the Yanomami people's territory constituted violations of their rights to life, freedom and security, residence and locomotion, health and welfare. The Commission also recommended the demarcation of an indigenous reserve to protect Yanomami land and culture from invasion, increasing international community concerns and pressure on Brazil to take action on the issue. The Yanomami Park was only created after the enactment of the Constitution, in 1992, and was not very effective in abolishing mining activity in Yanomami territory after demarcation of the reserve into 'islands', showing that mining sector interests were still prevalent.

If compliance with international standards was an important reason for the adoption of concrete measures such as policies, programmes, statutes and Supreme Court decisions regarding the fight against poverty, the structure of the healthcare system and affirmative action towards ethnic minority inclusion in publicly funded universities, adherence to the main international landmarks relating to the protection of the indigenous population's rights came later. Among South American countries, Brazil was one of the last countries to ratify the Indigenous and Tribal Peoples Convention (ILO 169) in 2002. In 2004, the Inter-American

[63] Maria Guadalupe Moog Rodrigues, 'Indigenous Rights in Democratic Brazil' (2002) 24(2) *Human Rights Quarterly* 488.

[64] Ana Carolina Vieira and Sigrid Quack, 'Trajectories of transnational mobilization for indigenous rights in Brazil' 56(4) *RAE* 380, www.scielo.br/j/rae/a/FJdGRJhmQsHCjKJK9BHytCH/?lang=en#.

[65] Rodrigues (n 63) 500–01.

Commission on Human Rights adopted precautionary measures for the protection of the indigenous peoples of Ingarico, Macuxi, Wapichana, Patamona and Taurepang, all occupiers of the Raposa Serra do Sol region, in the northern state of Roraima, an indigenous reserve with a demarcation procedure that had been pending since 1977.

In the face of that embarrassment, the Supreme Court issued a controversial ruling on the case in 2009. The ruling itself can be considered a step forward in terms of protection of indigenous populations, determining the territorial continuity of the demarcated area, rejecting claims to the limitation of the reserved areas in 'islands' or 'clusters', and endorsing the immediate removal of non-indigenous occupiers of the area. Nevertheless, the indigenous people's right to recognition and land was subject to so many conditionalities that it is difficult to assert exactly the extent to which it was enhanced or hampered by the decision.[66]

Although the decision in Pet 3.388/RR has not become judicial precedent with binding judgments, it highlights opinions of the Justices that are very resistant to the recognition of the indigenous populations as 'peoples', reinforcing orthodox concepts of sovereignty and refusing to give effect to the UN Declaration on the Rights of Indigenous Peoples. Those opinions also ignored International Courts' case law on the matter.[67]

Brazil voted for the Declaration in 2007 in a demonstration of its increasing international commitment to the protection of indigenous cultural and land rights, which was acknowledged by another Justice's opinion in the Pet 3.388/RR decision. That Justice made clear that, although the UN Declaration on the Rights of Indigenous Peoples does not have the normative force of a treaty, it has an 'undeniable hermeneutic value, able to bound States' actions towards indigenous peoples'.

In fact, the pressures and constraints on Brazil brought by the scientific community, transnational and international organisations and national indigenist movements, setting the conditions for the 1988 Constitution's provisions regarding indigenous people's rights, were a reaction to a continuous process of atrocious genocide. According to the Brazilian Institute of Geography and Statistics (IBGE), the indigenous population in Brazil in the sixteenth century, estimated at 2,431,000 people, had reduced to 294,131 people by 1991. Entire populations were simply made extinct in that period, such as the Aimores, Caetes and Tamoios. By 2000, that population had recovered to 734,127 and totalled 817,963 people in the 2010 Demographic Census. Those figures mean that, in the first 20 years following the

[66] Christian Teófilo da Silva, 'A homologação da terra indígena Raposa/Serra do Sol e seus efeitos: Uma análise performativa das 19 condicionantes do STF' (2018) 33(98) *Revista Brasileira de Ciências Sociais*.

[67] Rafaela Teixeira Sena Neves and João Daniel Daibes Resque, 'Diálogo judicial transnacional: a Recepção dos Tratados Internacionais na Jurisprudência do Supremo Tribunal Federal sobre Territórios Indígenas' in AMDA Lopes and MM'AB Lima (eds), *A Internalizacao de Direitos Internacionais de Direitos Humanos na America do Sul* (Livraria do Advogado, 2017) 218–20.

1988 Constitution, the indigenous population in Brazil grew 64%, compared to 23% in the general population.[68]

Their struggle to become fully recognised as citizens is not over yet. The Yanomami people still suffer from the presence and activities of non-indigenous people in their living environment. Research conducted by the Oswaldo Cruz Foundation (Fiocruz) in 2014 shows that in the Yanomami communities in Aracaca, 66% of children and 100% of adults presented levels of mercury concentration above the limits accepted by the WHO.[69] The presence of mercury in their bloodstream was not a coincidence, but a direct result of its use in illegal mining activities inside the demarcated preservation areas which contaminated the indigenous people's main sources of water.

Even after the Pet 3.388/RR ruling by the Supreme Court, land conflicts in the Raposa Serra do Sol reserve continued, which motivated the Inter-American Court of Human Rights to admit the *Indigenous Council of Roraima (CIR) and Rainforest Foundation US v Brazil* case in 2010. Brazil also faced a conviction, imposed by the Inter-American Court of Human Rights in 2018, for violating the protection rights of the Xucuru people, not to mention the provisional measures adopted in the *Matter of Members of the Yanomami, Ye'kwana and Munduruku Indigenous People regarding Brazil*, laid by the Inter-American Court of Human Rights in July 2022, that will be discussed further in chapter 4.

2.5.1. Indigenous Rights Protection and Democracy

Due to the progressive embeddedness in Brazil of the international indigenous population's protection system, they certainly increased their visibility and capacity to participate in the Brazilian *demos*, asserting their rights in domestic and international courts.

Proof of their increased capacity to influence pivotal decisions related to their interests is found in Pet 3.368/RR, where the Supreme Court granted the right to participate as *amicus curiae* to seven indigenous communities. The indigenous communities of Soco, Barro, Maturuca, Jawari, Tamandua, Jacarezinho and Manalai could file petitions and present their briefings and oral arguments during sessions without any intermediaries. The opportunity for indigenous populations to be heard before the Brazilian Supreme Court, the protection of the reserves where they live and the preservation of their way of life corresponds to the basic right to not be extinguished as a people or a culture. All and all, it seems like a compelling example of integration between a universalist/rights-based element of

[68] IBGE, 'Indígenas: Gráficos e Tabelas' (Instituto Brasileiro de Geografia e Estatística), https://indigenas.ibge.gov.br/graficos-e-tabelas-2.html.

[69] Paulo Cesar Basta and Sandra de Souza Hacon, 'Avaliação da exposição ambiental ao mercúrio proveniente de atividade garimpeira de ouro na Terra Indígena Yanomami' (Fiocruz, PUC-RJ, Instituto Socioambiental Hutukara, Associação Yanomami, and Associação do Povo Ye'kwana do Brasil, 2016).

preservation of those indigenous rights and the internal, popular, participatory mobilisation to guarantee those rights in Parliament and the courts. We can speak of a process of increasing inclusion and recognition of indigenous rights by the whole country.

Nevertheless, as the indigenous population recovered in recent decades, some electoral repercussions might also be suggested as important changes in the participatory electoral element of democracy as well. No less than 38.22% of the indigenous population in Brazil dwell in the North Region of Brazil, which witnessed a 41.14% increase in the electorate between 2000 and 2010, the largest registered in the whole country. Roraima, the state in the North Region with the greatest proportional indigenous population in the country – 12.42% of the whole population – also experienced an increase of 45.89% in electoral registrations, almost two times the national average (23.41%) and more than the regional average.[70]

Not without reason, in the 2018 general elections, an Indigenous Parliamentary Front was created, with 130 candidates from 24 states spread across different parties. For the first time in Brazilian history, an indigenous person, Sonia Guajajara, was a candidate for the Deputy President of the Republic, and after 36 years, an indigenous person was elected to the Lower Chamber, Joenia Wapixana, the first indigenous woman ever to get a bachelor's degree in law. In the 2022 general elections, the number of indigenous representatives increased to five, in a sign of the capacity of political articulation and effective democratic participation.

[70] TSE, 'Estatísticas do eleitorado' (Tribunal Superior Eleitoral, 2020), www.tse.jus.br/eleitor/estatisticas-de-eleitorado/estatistica-do-eleitorado-por-sexo-e-grau-de-instrucao.

3

Human Rights, Corruption, and the International Regime Antidote

3.1. Introduction

Brazilians are known around the world for their devotion to samba and football. When it comes to football, one of the most iconic moments in the nation's long track-record of success was winning the 1970 World Cup title in a memorial performance against Italy in the final. The squad contained names such as Carlos Alberto, Tostão, Pelé, and Gérson, considered a manager on the pitch during the victorious campaign. In 1976, Gérson was invited to be the star of a Vila Rica cigarettes advertisement. In the footage, he talks about what he likes about the product, emphasising that since it was cheaper than the competition, why would he pay more for the same quality? He concludes the film with the slogan: 'I like to take advantage of everything, right? You too should take advantage …'[1] Gérson was known as a cerebral midfielder who could compensate for a certain lack of athleticism with smartness and improvisation. His words in that commercial became known in Brazil as the 'law of Gérson', meaning that the typical Brazilian is someone willing to do whatever it takes to exploit opportunities, circumstances and even people. It is an ode to the sociological representation of the Brazilian people as corrupt.

As we have seen in the previous chapter, throughout the 30 years that followed the democratic transition, international human rights covenants and treaties have inspired constitutional amendments and legislation. International agencies have engaged in implementing policies and programmes through technical cooperation; non-governmental organisations have appraised governmental initiatives with maps, rankings and ratings. Worldwide strategic goals have contributed, in different manners and degrees, to enhance citizenship and participation, as well as to promote inclusion and access to human rights. It is important to highlight that, as discussed in chapter 1, especially in developing countries of the Global South, where societies still struggle with high levels of inequality that deny the satisfaction of basic needs, democracy depends on the fulfilment of several underlying

[1] Propagandas Históricas, 'Cigarros Vila Rica (Lei de Gerson) – 1976' (YouTube, 17 March 2014), www.youtu.be/fh9u_amafFI?si=Z2XkMq99AKfmZAhx.

conditions. Therefore, citizenship requires the factual participation of individuals in political decisions that might affect their lives, as well as higher and higher levels of inclusion in human rights. Once contemporary democracy is established as a political mode by participation, that participation needs to be qualified by a diverse, plural and inclusionary environment. All the international regimes analysed so far were put to a double test, in which we assessed their capacity to generate participation and political enfranchisement, as well as inclusion and the fruition of rights. This chapter does not differ in terms of the analytical framework but focuses on a different topic: the international anti-corruption regime and its capacity to free Brazil, once and for all, from the 'law of Gérson'.

In the following section, we will explore how the protection of certain human rights was coupled with criminalisation mandates required of State Parties to international law instruments. That approach pushes for the expansion of the punitive arm of the State over areas of historical human rights violations, such as human trafficking or domestic violence against women. We will also address how the international anti-corruption movement attempted to legitimise itself by depicting corruption as a cause of human rights violations that demand international support for and cooperation with internal anti-corruption agents, despite concerns with the supposed causality implied by the official discourse and the legal implications of such correlation.

The second topic addresses how the fight against corruption came to be one of the beacons of the 'rule of law' developmental agenda. In fact, the international anti-corruption regime found its legitimising force as it departed from that criminalisation-command approach to a much broader movement going beyond prompt intervention by the criminal law. Although still present, the criminal approach is just a part of a combination of norms, reports, guidelines, toolkits and NGO activism that involve institutional overhaul and a surge of new modes and agencies of governance. The specific investigative mechanisms are less focused on traditional responses to crime than on its economic, managerial aspect.

The third section discusses how that international anti-corruption regime was incorporated in Brazil and how, from the OECD Convention on Combating Bribery of Foreign States to the UN Convention Against Corruption, passing through the OAS Convention Against Corruption, the Financial Action Task Force recommendations, and Transparency International interventions, many developments from those inputs took place in a multi-diversified way. As explained in the previous chapter, international regimes do not always interact and generate reflexes in the national arena through only one channel of influence. The integration happens simultaneously in many different fronts. It is a fluid and subtle flux of content that may occur via institutional adoption of international law provisions, such as the enactment of new national laws, institutional re-engineering, international mutual legal assistance, and the development of policies.

Lastly, the chapter is dedicated to presenting how the literature on democratic maturation by means of a more effective approach to corruption matches the current formal rhetoric of the international anti-corruption regime. Regarding this last aspect, it will be shown how a substantial part of the literature on democracy in Latin America and Brazil presents the 'modernisation' or the 'effectiveness' of the efforts to fight corruption as the 'missing part of the puzzle' for the definitive consolidation of democracy. Democracy is conditioned, according to those authors, by the adoption by Brazil of a specialised technocracy, or of a specific institutional machinery well equipped to monitor, detect, investigate and punish deviations related to public procurement, budget allocation, political campaigning, personnel recruitment, and so forth.

The main goal here is to outline that the impacts on democracy eventually caused by the way the international anti-corruption regime was incorporated in Brazil did not happen without an underlying social context. The triumphalist self-description of the international anti-corruption regime presents itself as a source of different tools and approaches to solve a problem portrayed as the root of all evil. The capacity of the international anti-corruption regime to fulfil its promise to bring Brazilian democracy through its full circle is the question that will inform our endeavour moving forward.

3.2. Human Rights, Transnational Criminal Law, and Corruption: An 'Empowerment' Strategy

The International Covenant on Civil and Political Rights (ICCPR) and the International Covenant on Economic, Social and Cultural Rights (ICESCR) are milestones of the international human rights movement. Articles 14 and 15 of the ICCPR provide universal rights to due process of law that shall be granted to any defendant under criminal prosecution, establishing boundaries, limitations and opposition to the States' punitive powers. Paradoxically, many issue-specific international human rights instruments opted for criminalisation as a means to protect the rights they provide for. As argued by Dissenha and Incott Jr, international human rights invoke a 'cosmopolitan conscience' not only relating to rights, but also to risks, insecurity and conflicts that, in some cases, make them a value to be protected by criminal law, working not at its limits but rather at its very basis.[2] This rationale underpins a transnational criminal law that consists of the incorporation in domestic legislation of criminal offences originating in international conventions.[3] Aside from international criminal law, as defined by the Rome Statute of the International Criminal Court, this other trend manifests

[2] Rui Carlo Dissenha and Paulo Roberto Incott Jr, 'A internacionalização do poder punitivo: riscos normativos e políticos da demanda por leis penais universais' (2018) 147 *Revista Brasileira de Ciências Criminais*.

[3] Nicolas Cordini, 'The internationalization of criminal law: Transnational criminal law, basis for a regional legal theory of criminal Law' (2018) 8(1) *Revista Brasileira de Políticas Públicas* 262.

itself by the transnational standardisation of the repression of certain human rights violations through criminalisation commands and innovative methods of prosecution. Provisions for the criminalisation of certain activities and behaviours, the deployment of new investigative devices, and international mutual legal assistance can be found in the 1979 Convention on the Physical Protection of Nuclear Material and Nuclear Facilities, the 1984 UN Convention against Torture and Other Cruel, Unhuman or Degrading Treatment or Punishment, the 1988 UN Convention against Illicit Traffic in Narcotic Drugs and Psychotropic Substances, the UN Convention against Transnational Organized Crime, and the Protocol to Prevent, Suppress and Punish Trafficking in Persons, especially Women and Children, as well as in the UN Convention against Corruption, to name just a few.

Brazil, for instance, has a long history of problems regarding misogyny. Although the country ratified the Convention on the Elimination of All Forms of Discrimination against Women back in 1984 and hosted the approval of the Inter-American Convention on the Prevention, Punishment and Eradication of Violence against Women in Belém in 1994, very little had been done to tackle the problem at that point. It was only after Brazil was censured by the Inter-American Commission on Human Rights in *Maria da Penha Maia Fernandes v Brazil*, in 2001, that the pressures for effective action arose. The applicant was shot by her husband while sleeping and was paralysed from the waist down. When she returned home from hospital, she suffered an attempt on her life by electrocution while she was in the shower by the same man, who ultimately remained free for 15 years until the case was finally taken to the international forum.[4] Law 11.340, of 2006, also known as the 'Maria da Penha Law', created new mechanisms to fight domestic violence against women, especially preventive protective measures such as restraint orders against the aggressor, preventing them from approaching the victim or the household, provisory alimonies in favour of the victim and children, and other restrictions. According to an Institute of Applied Economic Research report, in 2009, 1,447,694 women suffered physical assault, 43% of them were at home when it occurred, and almost 70% of those crimes were perpetrated by the partner, the ex-partner, someone known to the victim, or a relative.[5] In 2015, Law 13.104 established femicide as a homicide aggravated by gender reasons or as a consequence of domestic violence against women. The new offence has tougher penalties and is included in the heinous crimes list. The demand for an effective response to those iniquities against women was just, but it has undoubtedly added extra pressure on the criminal justice system. Another report, produced by the National Council of Justice, showed that 194,812 of the aforementioned protective

[4] Ludmila Aparecida Tavares and Carmen Hein de Campos, 'A Convenção Interamericana para prevenir, punir e erradicar a Violência contra a Mulher – Convenção de Belém do Pará – e a Lei Maria da Penha' (2018) 6(3) *Interfaces Científicas – Humanas e Sociais* 14.

[5] Cintia Liara Engel, 'A Violência Contra a Mulher' (Instituto de Pesquisa Economica Aplicada (IPEA), 2019), www.ipea.gov.br/retrato/pdf/190215_tema_d_a_violenca_contra_mulher.pdf.

measures were determined in 2016, while no less than 236,641 judicial restraints were imposed in 2017, an increase of 21% in the number of people under the surveillance of the criminal justice system in two years.[6] The same report registered 1,287 new formal charges of feminicide heard by the Brazilian judiciary in 2016, which more than doubled to 2,643 new prosecutions in 2017.[7] Legislative and judicial actors answered to pressure from international commissions, feminist NGOs' activism, and the general outcry against impunity in cases of violence against women, with an expansion of the criminal law to cover a wider group of offences and individuals. In this case, the human rights platform took the shape of criminalisation and statutory changes to increase penalties, which may pose a threat to other categories of human rights as these statistics point to an increase in sentencing and incarceration for years to come.

Similarly, the first Palermo Protocol, adopted to supplement the UN Convention against Transnational Organized Crime, highlights, in its Article 5, criminalisation as one of the preferred mechanisms to be used by State Parties to prevent, investigate and punish trafficking in persons. Since 2008, an inter-institutional task force led by the Ministry of Justice has put forward a National Plan to Counter Trafficking in Persons (*Plano Nacional de Enfrentamento ao Tráfico de Pessoas* (PNETP)) with strategic tools aimed at prevention, attention to victims, repression and prosecution, each with tasks, targets, stakeholders and timelines. The initiative is already in its third cycle and its work was decisive in structuring Draft Bill 479, in 2012, which resulted in the enactment of Law 13.344 in 2016. According to the opinion of the Rapporteur in the Chamber of Deputies, the Draft Bill's 'typification of the crime of trafficking in persons is in perfect consonance with the Palermo Protocol, comprehending all modalities of trafficking in persons, filling the existing gaps in the legislation'. An official report produced by the UN Office on Drugs and Crime and the Swedish and Brazilian Governments showed that since the adoption of Law 13.344, the number of investigations of trafficking in persons increased from 15 in 2017 to 218 in 2020, and the number of people convicted for those crimes also went up from 21 to 146 in the same period.[8] The human rights of the victims of trafficking in persons have become the prompting force for international criminalisation mandates, with several institutional and legislative repercussions in Brazil, such as the rise in investigations and criminal sanctions.

A similar attempt to link human rights and corruption has been made by the international anti-corruption movement. Transparency International has tried to establish that the 'promotion and protection of human rights and efforts to end

[6] CNJ, 'O Poder Judiciário na aplicação da Lei Maria da Penha' (Conselho Nacional de Justiça, 2018), www.cnj.jus.br/wpcontent/uploads/conteudo/arquivo/2018/06/2df3ba3e13e95bf17e33a9c10e60a5a1.pdf, 11.

[7] Ibid 19.

[8] UNODC and MJSP, 'Relatório Nacional sobre Tráfico de Pessoas: Dados 2017 a 2020' (Ministério da Justiça e Segurança Publica, 2021), www.unodc.org/documents/lpo-brazil/Topics_TIP/Publicacoes/relatorio-de-dados-2017-2020.pdf, 51–65.

corruption are mutually reinforcing'.[9] According to that view, in countries where there is a low adherence to human rights provisions, corruption tends to thrive, in the same way that where levels of corruption are high, human rights tend to fare not so well. To put it in Koechlin and Carmona's words, 'it is intuitively and empirically plausible that there is a significant correlation between low levels of development, human rights abuses, and the spread of corruption.'[10]

Most of the attempts to link anti-corruption measures to human rights protection rely on syllogisms that try to associate corruption with low economic growth and lack of foreign investment and the burden they represent to the poorest part of the population, or that simulated land sales and registration tend to harm indigenous people and minorities, or even that a bribe to a doctor or a teacher in exchange for treatment or a place in a school are violations of the right to non-discriminatory treatment and, consequently, of the rights to healthcare and access to education.[11] Intuitively sound as those hypotheses may seem, the causality between the adoption of anti-corruption packages and the improvement in human rights fruition is yet to be empirically demonstrated.[12] Many statistics used to highlight losses caused by corruption and show disinvestment in critical human rights issues are considered unfounded or, at least, imprecise.[13] As suggested by Khan, it is not accurate, either historically or empirically, to identify strong governance/anti-corruption capacity as a cause for higher per capita income in developed countries. This suggests the existence of a reverse causality that would advise caution in the adoption of anti-corruption reform packages in the developing world.[14] Even in legal terms, those who advocate the idea of corruption as a violation of international human rights concede that, under the UN Convention against Corruption (UNCAC), 'it is hardly possible to hold a State Party internationally responsible if it fails to fulfil its obligations or does so only poorly'.[15] The adoption of the so-called 'human rights approach' to corruption is more an attempt to bring the legitimising strength of human rights to the international anti-corruption regime. However still hypothetically linked, the international anti-corruption agenda would benefit greatly from borrowing the legitimation

[9] International Council on Human Rights Policy, 'Integrating Human Rights in the Anti-Corruption Agenda: Challenges, Possibilities and Opportunities' (2010), https://ssrn.com/abstract=1705396, vii.

[10] Lucy Koechlin and Magdalena S Carmona, 'Corruption and Human Rights: Exploring the Connection' in RI Rotberg (ed), *Corruption, Global Security, and World Order* (Brookings Institution Press, 2009) 310.

[11] International Council on Human Rights Policy, 'Corruption and Human Rights: Making the Connection' (ICHRP, 2009), https://ssrn.com/abstract=1551222; Anne Peters, 'Corruption as a violation of international human rights' (2018) 29(4) *European Journal of International Law*.

[12] Jomo Kwame Sundaram, 'Good Governance, Anti-Corruption, and Economic Development' in RI Rotberg (ed), *Corruption, Global Security, and World Order* (Brookings Institution Press, 2009) 458.

[13] Cecilie Wathne and Matthew C Stephenson, 'The Credibility of Corruption Statistics' (2021) Anti-Corruption Resource Centre (U4 Issue 2021:4).

[14] Mushtaq Khan, 'Governance and Anti-Corruption Reforms in Developing Countries: Policies, Evidence and Ways Forward' (2006) G-24 Discussion Papers 42, United Nations Conference on Trade and Development.

[15] Peters (n 11) 1276.

effect generated by human rights. According to Koechlin and Carmona, the linkage with human rights would 'persuade key actors to take a stronger stand against corruption' or, to rephrase it in Peters' terms, it would be a rhetorical strategy that would give the anti-corruption movement 'empowerment'.[16]

Aside from the previous examples related to violence against women and trafficking in persons, it cannot be clearly ascertained which human rights demand the expansion of the criminalisation of corruption or the adoption of new investigative methods to prevent and repress its transnational maleficent influence. So, if it is possible to assert that the cosmopolitan/universalist element of democracy can manifest itself in the form of criminalisation commands originating in international law, not all branches of this transnational criminal law can legitimise themselves as human rights exigencies. But human rights are not the only source of legitimacy that international legal regimes resort to in search of that ultimate semantic value capable of building broad consensus – or 'warm sense of contentment'[17] – that makes their exportation worldwide virtuous, advisable and desired. Created from demands for balancing business opportunities between multinationals from different countries, the international anti-corruption regime found legitimising strength when it tuned in the appropriate discourse to depart from its criminological origins to present itself as an inescapable trait of the transnational, complex and market-oriented new world order.

3.3. The International Anti-Corruption Regime: The 'Managerial' Turn from Crime to Business, Governance and Society

Corruption, just like democracy, is a term that can bear multiple meanings, and, in both cases, conceptual disputes do not take place in a vacuum of interests nor within an economically and politically void arena. As we have previously set out, in the case of democracy, scepticism led to a thin version of electoral competitiveness that fits well with the idea of the people as a supporting vertical accountability device working alongside well-oiled machines of corruption investigation, prosecution and punishment. Democracy, in that account, is presented as a compact mix of periodic, universal suffrage, surrounded by some handily picked civil liberties, such as freedom of speech, association and the press, for instance. Although neglected by contemporary theories of democracy and 'corruption-fighters', democracy as we know it was founded and is daily constituted by the local, popular, 'we-the-people' participatory element as much as by inputs of a

[16] ibid 1276.

[17] The expression is used by Koskenniemi in Martti Koskenniemi, 'Constitutionalism as Mindset: Reflections on Kantian Themes About International Law and Globalization' (2006) 8(1) *Theoretical Inquiries in Law*.

cosmopolitan/universalist component often developed internationally and, then, adopted domestically. Electoral democracy itself, constitutionalism and human rights have all been pushed forward by multinational organisations, international bodies, transnational NGOs and so forth, and it is not that which makes them democratic/undemocratic, but their capacity to promote/impede participation and inclusion.

In the case of corruption, as Hindess reminds us, the term carries a colloquial meaning related to any malfunction, impurity, or loss of essence. An electronic file damaged by a virus that prevents it from opening as it should is corrupted, an old syringe cannot be reused because it can corrupt its content, be it a medicine or a sample, and a wine that turns into vinegar is corrupted.[18] When it comes to the misapplication of public funds or property, or even if one thinks of the misuse of power to favour someone, the criminal law draws the conceptual boundaries between actions that amount to corruption and those that do not. Bribery, which happens when an undue advantage is given or received, offered, solicited or promised in exchange for an action or omission from an official, is a classic example of a corrupt act, often criminalised all over the world. Embezzlement and other modes of misappropriation of state property are also well-known forms of corruption proscribed by criminal law. Other behaviours that sit on the borderline of the public-private realm, such as trading in influence, illicit enrichment, or even situations in which there is favouritism towards the family (nepotism), friends (cronyism) or political allies and supporters (patronage), are increasingly not tolerated by some criminal justice systems, while still at the margins of legality in other cases.[19]

That was the way corruption was treated in the past: a criminal problem addressed by each nation-state according to its law.[20] Internationally, developed countries showed a relative complacency towards corruption in the developing world. Until the 1990s, German companies were entitled to tax deductions for expenditure on the bribery of foreign officials, and France showed a great reluctance to discuss the issue in global terms.[21] The inclusion of corruption-related issues in the international arena was an initiative of the United States. The US presented a 'Draft International Agreement on Illicit Payments' for discussion in the United Nations as early as 1976.[22] In 1977, the US passed a Foreign Corrupt Practices Act, criminalising the bribery of foreign officials, which created an

[18] Barry Hindess, 'Good government and corruption' in P Larmour and N Wolanin (eds), *Corruption and Anti-Corruption* (ANU Press, 2013) 5.

[19] Jean-Patrick Villeneuve, Giulia Mugellini and Marlen Heide, 'International Anti-Corruption Initiatives: A Classification of Policy Interventions' (2019) 26(4) *European Journal on Criminal Policy and Research* 440.

[20] Peter Larmour and Nick Wolanin, 'Introduction' in P Larmour and N Wolanin (eds), *Corruption and Anti-Corruption* (ANU Press, 2013) xi.

[21] Anja P Jakobi, 'Global Anti-Corruption Norms' in AP Jakobi (ed), *Common Good and Evils? The Formation of Global Crime Governance* (Oxford University Press, 2013) 244.

[22] ibid 252.

uncomfortable market disadvantage for American businesses abroad, increasing the pressure for an international covenant on the matter that could put companies from their OECD counterparts under similar constraints. The US emphatic effort to put the subject on the UN and OECD agenda did not bear fruit until the 1990s, when the first international norms against corruption were adopted.[23] The Organization of American States (OAS) summit in Miami, in 1994, resulted in the Inter-American Convention Against Corruption. In 1997, American diplomacy achieved its goal with the enactment of the OECD Convention on Combating Bribery of Foreign Officials in International Business Transactions.[24]

The Inter-American Convention Against Corruption came into force in 1996 and has been signed and ratified by 24 State Parties from all parts of the American continent. In its preamble, the Convention adopts premises that would become trademarks of the international anti-corruption movement: (i) it calls for a coordinated international response to the problem of corruption, seen as a transnational threat to markets linked to other criminal activities; (ii) it relates corruption to democratic deficits and administrative inefficiency, and (iii) it stresses the importance to involve civil society, through awareness campaigns, rallies and litigation, in the fight against corruption. Its Article VI sets out very detailed descriptions of the behaviours that consubstantiate acts of corruption, which could be seen as a reminiscent of Roman-Germanic principles of criminal law, such as strict legality and determinability. In Article VII, the Convention requires their specific criminalisation by the State Parties' domestic law. Another vestige is the centrality of transnational bribery of foreign officials. The Convention not only determines the enactment of laws that deny any favourable tax treatment for expenditures connected to bribery (Article III, item 7), but it also dedicates a specific Article just to reinforce the necessity of its criminalisation and consideration as an act of corruption (Article VIII). The condemnation of transnational bribery was to be expected as it was the driving force behind US efforts to take the subject to the international forum. The most interesting aspect of the Convention, though, is the transition from a purely criminal approach to corruption to a broader discourse that depicts it as more than a parochial criminal issue. Corruption is addressed as a transnational problem that requires international responses, something that can be repressed not only by criminal law, but prevented through governance improvement, and is a cause for civil society engagement. One of the tools of governance implemented by the Convention is the follow-up mechanism for its implementation (MESICIC), which involves periodic review of State Parties' legislation and institutions on the fight against corruption to assess levels of compliance with the Convention standards. The MESICIC consists of analysis carried out by Technical Secretariat experts who perform on-site visits, issue recommendations and reports

[23] Jo-Ann Gilbert and JC Sharman, 'Turning a Blind Eye to Bribery: Explaining Failures to Comply with the International Anti-corruption Regime' (2016) 64(1) *Political Studies* 77.

[24] Jakobi (n 21) 6.

on best practices, and provide guidelines and models to help areas in which the State Party under evaluation underperforms in combating corruption.

The description of corruption as a pervasive transnational phenomenon, found in the Inter-American Convention Against Corruption, has become one of the key features of the international anti-corruption rhetoric during the present century. According to that vision, corruption not only disregards nation-states' boundaries but is also a modality of crime that mobilises a worldwide industry of very sophisticated illicit networks, unbalancing international markets. Hypothetically, bribery is offered by a company from one country to an official from another, often paid in a third nation that features strict bank secrecy legislation and tax immunity, also known as 'tax havens', through multi-layered fake legal persons created to hide the proceeds of crime. It is commonly linked to public procurement frauds, favouritism in public funds allocation, and other forms of misuse of public funds that generate distortion in market opportunities for private entrepreneurs.

The twentieth century witnessed the development of organisations with multiple divisions specialised in mediating international connections between public and private actors, creating opportunities for corruption, and hiding the illicit financial outcomes of those transactions. Those organisations exploited a globalised environment of an ever-increasing flow of people, business and money to establish criminal networks powerful enough to defy State authorities' capacity to investigate or shut down their activities.[25] Wolf reports that multinationals, such as Siemens and Daimler, had already admitted, in prosecutions carried out in the United States, to have paid millions of dollars in bribes to Russian officials.[26] Meanwhile, massive data leaks have shown that some of those officials moved $2 billion through international bank accounts in singular transactions worth $200 million each, with a friend of President Putin holding an account with a £19 million balance in a Swiss bank. Estifania A Co mentions that Ferdinand Marcos' regime in the Philippines was characterised by the distribution of publicly owned companies, resources and concessions to cronies who would safeguard the proceedings of the illicit exploitation of public assets abroad. The scheme would be exemplified by the assets of the Lopez family, comprising the ownership of newspapers and television and radio stations in the Philippines, calculated at $400 million, headed by Eugenio Sr, who lived in the US during most of the 1970s and 1980s.[27] Okojie and Momoh argue that donors' incentives for internal solutions to combat corruption in developing countries, without coordinated efforts

[25] John McFarlane, 'Transnational crime: corruption, crony capitalism and nepotism in the twenty-first century' in P Larmour and N Wolanin (eds), *Corruption and Anti-Corruption* (ANU Press, 2013) 132.

[26] ML Wolf, 'The World Needs an International Anti-Corruption Court' (2018) 147(3) *Daedalus* 146–47.

[27] Edna Estefania A Co, 'Challenges to the Philippine Culture of Corruption' in S Bracking (ed), *Corruption and Development: The Anti-Corruption Campaigns* (Palgrave Macmillan, 2007) 125–26.

between international investigative agencies, are insufficient to solve the problem, as would be demonstrated by Transparency International data, according to which 140 million Nigerian nairas were diverted from the Nigerian National Petroleum Corporation, with stolen funds found in more than 130 different banks overseas.[28] Those cases are strikingly convincing in the sense that the indifference or even condescension of the international community towards corruption, which dominated the field for most of the twentieth century, would be at odds with complex criminal organisations that invade countries, pillage their resources and allocate funds into private hands through multi-level schemes of offshore fake companies, trusts and banks. More than that, they would evidence the incapacity of the traditional approach, rooted in each State criminal justice system, to adequately repress that new type of criminality. Souheil El Zein, Director for Legal Affairs at Interpol, stated that 'corruption has become an increasing international problem which needs to be addressed by the entire community … the need for international action against corruption may never have been more acute than today'.[29] Following the same thread, Chaikin says that:

> The tracing of assets is an extremely complex task, which has been made more difficult in a world where wealth is mobile and money laundering more sophisticated. … Few international investigations are supported by adequate intelligence and surveillance system. The traditional passive methods are often unsuitable in the context of detecting serious economic crime.[30]

Wolf describes the recovery of assets as 'legally complex, forensically difficult, and ponderously slow', citing the $30 million settlement between the US Department of Justice and Teodorin Obiang, son of the president and second vice president of Equatorial Guinea, as an example of how transnational corruption and money laundering can still pay off, in the long run, considering that his illicit profits would probably amount to $100 million laundered in mansions, sports cars and Michael Jackson memorabilia in the United States.[31] Prosecutors and investigative authorities needed a toolbox to overcome the limits of their respective national criminal justice systems, enabling them to engage in specialised and technically complex international operations that could match the level of expertise shown by the transnational criminal networks they are supposed to fight.

The move to treat corruption as a global threat was ignited by the US Government's attempts to internationalise concerns on the bribery of foreign officials, which influenced the adoption of the Inter-American Convention Against Corruption and the OECD Convention on Combating Bribery of

[28] P Okojie and A Momoh, 'Corruption and Reform in Nigeria' in S Bracking (ed), *Corruption and Development: The Anti-Corruption Campaigns* (Palgrave Macmillan, 2007) 104–06.

[29] McFarlane (n 25) 136.

[30] David A Chaikin, 'Controlling corruption by heads of government and political élites' in P Larmour and N Wolanin (eds), *Corruption and Anti-Corruption* (ANU Press, 2013) 100–01.

[31] Wolf (n 26) 148.

Foreign Public Officials in International Business Transactions. Corruption was categorically considered a transnational crime, though, in 2000, when the UN Convention against Transnational Organized Crime demanded, in its Article 8, the criminalisation of bribery and 'other forms of corruption' by the State Parties. To remediate those investigative bottlenecks and the incapacity of nation-states' prosecution authorities to cope with the intensification of transnational criminality, the UN Convention against Transnational Organized Crime provided a normative basis for international cooperation aimed at the seizure, freezing and confiscation of assets (Articles 12 and 13), mutual legal assistance between the State Parties (Article 18), the possibility of joint investigations (Article 19) and the adoption of special investigative techniques, such as controlled delivery, electronic surveillance and undercover operations (Article 20). The UN Convention against Transnational Organized Crime inaugurated a new moment in the international anti-corruption movement that advanced from the previous focus on the criminalisation of bribery to establish corruption, in a broader sense, as a transnational crime that demands internationally coordinated actions to be efficiently countered. By the time it was signed, negotiations for a specific international agreement on corruption were already in train, resulting in the 2003 UN Convention against Corruption (UNCAC). The UNCAC enshrines the connections between corruption, money laundering and transnational organised crime as premises for its enactment. In its Article 3, the prevention, investigation and prosecution of corruption are intertwined with the mechanisms of capture and return of misplaced resources. The UNCAC reproduces references to the freezing, seizure and confiscation of goods (Article 31), mutual legal assistance (Article 46), joint investigations (Article 49) and special investigative techniques (Article 50) already found in the UN Convention against Transnational Organized Crime, adding detailed procedural rules and best practice standards related to those topics. Further, it sets out provisions on mitigating the punishment for or granting immunity to accused persons giving evidence to law enforcement authorities (Article 37), on cooperation for the purposes of confiscation (Article 55), and even on training and technical assistance specifically designed for the recovery of the proceeds of corruption (Article 60). The UNCAC also adopts a peer review mechanism through which each State Party would eventually be evaluated in its level of compliance with the Convention by delegations of other State Parties.

As noted, once initial concerns with asymmetries in the way each country dealt with bribery in their respective legislation were resolved, the focus of the international anti-corruption agenda turned to the recovery of financial losses caused by corruption in all its forms. The 1997 OECD Convention on Combating Bribery of Foreign Public Officials in International Business Transactions, for instance, contained provisions relating to mutual legal assistance, but its main goal was to ban bribery and any favourable tax deduction schemes still present in some domains. The emphasis on international cooperation for the purposes of evidence exchange and the extradition, identification, freezing, seizure, confiscation and recovery of the proceeds of bribery came only after the Council for Further Combating Bribery of Foreign Public Officials in International Business Transactions added recommendations to the OECD Convention in 2009, when the UN Convention against Corruption was already in force and the anti-money laundering multilateral governance agency had considerable accumulated experience in tracing suspect financial behaviour worldwide.

The Financial Action Task Force (FATF), created in 1989 by the G7 as an initiative to establish standards for financial authorities in reducing money laundering worldwide, first added the financial encroachment of terrorist activities to its goals, and then measures to ensure transparency and the fight against corruption to its duties. The entity, which has 39 member States but no formal status in international public law, put forward 40 recommendations that form the international normative core of best practice and guidelines regarding the monitoring and investigation of suspicious financial transactions. Those recommendations were progressively revised and amplified over the following three decades to target terrorist financing, transparency, and the fight against corruption. The centrality of the FATF recommendations for anti-money laundering global governance was reached through mechanisms of coercion such as the Non-Cooperative Countries list, which was deactivated in 2007, when the last country was delisted, and the mutual evaluation system by which countries are assessed according to their technical compliance with and effectiveness of anti-money laundering standards.

The expansion of the focus of international anti-corruption efforts and their overlap with other global regimes, such as the FATF's anti-money laundering initiatives, did not signify that market competition had lost its importance. On the contrary, as a 2010 Anti-Corruption Action Plan approved by the G20 Anti-Corruption Working Group gathered in Toronto recalls, 'corruption threatens the integrity of markets, undermines fair competition, distorts resource allocation, destroys public trust, and undermines the rule of law'. For the international anti-corruption movement, as important as the conception of corruption as a transnational widespread evil is the representation of corruption as more than a criminal phenomenon. Corruption is depicted as a governance malfunction that can be explained from an economic point of view and, thus, more effectively tackled through institutional reform packages. The replacement of the traditional criminological roots of corruption by economic explanations for it through rent-seeking logic was very influential for the international anti-corruption regime. Klitgaard calls for the engagement of developmental policy studies to focus on the problem of corruption and presents a hypothetical scheme to understand its dynamics.[32] That scheme explores the possibilities for corruption that arise from an institutional set-up in which there is a continuous relationship between a principal, in the figure of the representative that conceives the

[32] Robert E Klitgaard, *Controlling Corruption* (University of California, 1988).

policies, an agent, represented by the state official bureaucrat responsible for the implementation of the policy, and the client or customer as the taxpayer, the private recipient of the policy. According to Klitgaard, corruption would result from agents empowered with the monopoly of a given service or activity, enjoying great discretion in public resources management and working in a scenario in which accountability mechanisms are weak. He even represents it by the formula, *Corruption = Monopoly + Discretion – Accountability*.[33] Similarly, Rose-Ackerman affirms that corruption has as a backdrop the organisation of the State and society, and that reforms should aim to reduce the incentives and increase the risks for State officials engaging in corruption behaviour.[34] Despite the limitations of those descriptions of corruption, in leaving out the possibility of non-financial (eg political, customary) purposes or even its occurrence within purely private organisations, they shaped the way the anti-corruption rhetoric evolved since the mid-1990s.[35] In 'Helping Countries Combat Corruption', a report published in 1997 by the World Bank, the idea that the causes of corruption are related to high incentives, represented by economic rent-seeking opportunities, and low accountability, identified with institutional weakness, was fully adopted.[36] Once the causes are known, the solutions involve measures that could diminish services offered by the State and the empowerment of accountability agencies. Corruption ceases to be a criminal problem to be solved *ex post facto* and becomes a preventable matter of good governance. That is the main subject of the 'Corruption and Good Governance' report, published by the UN Development Programme in 1997, which affirms that 'corruption is a symptom of something gone wrong in the management of the State', and adopts uncritically the principal-agent-client model of explaining how corruption takes place.[37] The UN Office for Drugs and Crime's 'Anti-Corruption Toolkit', from 2004, also shares the idea that corruption is the product of a considered analysis of the opportunities offered by the amount of discretion enjoyed by a public agent set against the risks of the illicit activity, and whether accountability mechanisms are efficient or not.[38] The World Bank developed a Governance and Anti-Corruption Strategy and presented a report, at the conclusion of the 2006 Singapore summit, linking the fight against corruption to governance

[33] ibid 75.

[34] Susan Rose-Ackerman and Bonnie J Palifka, 'Corruption, Organized Crime, and Money Laundering' in K Basu and T Cordella (eds), *Institutions, Governance and the Control of Corruption. International Economic Association Series* (Palgrave Macmillan, 2018).

[35] Ed Brown and Jonathan Cloke, 'Neoliberal Reform, Governance and Corruption in the South: Assessing the International Anti-Corruption Crusade' (2004) 36(2) *Antipode* 283.

[36] World Bank Group, 'Helping Countries Combat Corruption: The Role of the World Bank' (1997), http://documents.worldbank.org/curated/en/799831538245192753/Helping-countries-combat-corruption-the-role-of-the-World-Bank, 12.

[37] UNDP, 'Corruption and Good Governance' (United Nations Development Programme, 1997) https://digitallibrary.un.org/record/1491472, 7.

[38] UNODC, 'Anti-Corruption Toolkit' (United Nations Office on Drugs and Crime, 2004), www.unodc.org/documents/treaties/corruption/toolkit/toolkitv5_foreword.pdf.

improvement.[39] Transparency International highlights the shift in international anti-corruption efforts from their criminological origins to public management and good governance solutions as a turning point in the mid-1990s, calling it the 'birth of a diverse anti-corruption movement'.[40]

According to Brown and Cloke, the policies developed by organisations such as the UN Development Programme, the World Bank and the US Agency for International Development, under the connections established between the fight against corruption and good governance, were concentrated on the enactment of transparency legislation regarding public data, especially related to budget information, judicial reform, the creation and strengthening of agencies and institutions responsible for financial oversight and auditing, the professionalisation of recruitment and promotion criteria in the civil service, public procurement legislation and electoral reform.[41] To reach such a wide range of themes, the economic representation of the idea of corruption was more flexible than narrow definitions tied to criminal law principles that demand, *a priori*, complete, determined definitions of every aspect of the behaviour to be penalised by law. Based on economic theories of corruption, the World Bank defined corruption, in all its forms and manifestations, as 'the abuse of public office for private gain'.[42]

A conception of corruption that could be transformed into a catchy motto for the international anti-corruption movement was an important asset for the third aspect that characterises it: the involvement of civil society in the cause. The most prominent example of this particular trend is the role played by Transparency International in the conception, development and promotion of the international anti-corruption agenda worldwide. The NGO, founded in the early 1990s by former directors of the World Bank to champion the cause of the corruption fight worldwide, started publishing its Corruption Perceptions Index in 1995.[43] The Index has become an accepted reference for studies and corruption status diagnosis, exercising a huge influence in aid agencies' decision-making and in multinational investment strategies, despite the perception that indexes often reproduce stereotypes and biases. Further, Transparency International has intensively participated in the formulation of the main international anti-corruption norms, supplementary reports and detailed documents. Founders and directors of Transparency International, Peter Eigen and Jeremy Pope, contributed for the aforementioned 1997 World Bank Report, 'Helping Countries Combat

[39] World Bank Group, 'Strengthening World Bank Group engagement on governance and anticorruption: Main Report' (WBG, 2007), https://documents.worldbank.org/pt/publication/documentsreports/documentdetail/426381468340863478/main-report.

[40] International Council on Human Rights Policy, 'Integrating Human Rights in the Anti-Corruption Agenda: Challenges, Possibilities and Opportunities' (2010), https://ssrn.com/abstract=1705396.

[41] Brown and Cloke (n 35) 276–77.

[42] World Bank Group (n 36) 8.

[43] Kalin S Ivanov, 'The Limits of a Global Campaign against Corruption' in S Bracking (ed), *Corruption and Development: The Anti-Corruption Campaigns* (Palgrave Macmillan, 2007).

Corruption', which asserts that 'Civil society and the media are crucial to creating and maintaining an atmosphere in public life that discourages fraud and corruption … corruption is controlled only when citizens no longer tolerate it.'[44] The strong discourse on non-tolerance towards corruption is also found in the 2003 UN Convention against Corruption in Article 13(1)(c), which is entirely dedicated to the participation of society in combating corruption. The UN Office for Drugs and Crime's 2004 'Anti-Corruption Toolkit' says that 'policies and practical measures are most likely to succeed if they enjoy the full support, participation and ownership of civil society', and its 'Technical Guide to the UN Convention against Corruption', published in 2009, mentions public campaigns to raise awareness of corruption as a practical way to comply with Article 13 that should be a priority and a public commitment of governments around the globe.[45] In the Transparency International document, 'Together Against Corruption: Strategy 2020', the NGO presents itself as a spokesperson for civil society, highlighting how corruption revealed itself to be a rallying ground for citizen action in Brazil in recent years. Moreover, Transparency International defines corruption as 'the abuse of entrusted power for private gains', in a subtle manoeuvre to escape criticism of anti-Statism and to establish a partnership with people and institutions to build a strong movement able to prevent corruption and bring pressure for the enforcement of OECD and UN Conventions at country level.[46]

Starting in the last decades of the twentieth century, the international anti-corruption regime was incrementally built by the US Government interests, international covenants, additional protocols, revision mechanisms, reports from multinational organisations and NGOs that reciprocally reinforce each other, embodying a robust set of rules, initiatives, reform packages, indexes and discourses that influence the reality in many parts of the world. All this articulated effort made the anti-corruption agenda a 'mega hit'. The UN Convention against Corruption has 140 signatories and 187 State parties. The international anti-corruption regime is obviously centred in the criminalisation of corrupt behaviour, and the investigation, prosecution and punishment of those involved in it, but much more than that, it pushes for more comprehensive institutional reforms and deeper legislative changes. In portraying corruption as a global governance matter with economic causes and summoning society to take part in the process of preventing, detecting and whistleblowing corrupt practices, the international anti-corruption agenda becomes a concept with much greater pervasive penetration into local democracies. In that scenario, the jailing of the corrupt, as demanded by public outcry,

[44] World Bank Group (n 36) 44–46.

[45] UNODC (n 38) 21; UNODC, 'Technical Guide to the United Nations Convention Against Corruption' (United Nations Office on Drugs and Crime, 2009), www.unodc.org/documents/treaties/UNCAC/Publications/TechnicalGuide/0984395_Ebook.pdf, 62–63.

[46] Transparency International, 'Together Against Corruption: Transparency International Strategy 2020' (TI, 2015), TogetherAgainstCorruption_Strategy2020_EN.pdf (transparencycdn.org).

comes just as a side effect or a propaganda tool. In the next section of this chapter, we will attempt to describe the ways in which that international anti-corruption regime was incorporated in Brazil.

3.4. The Anti-Corruption Regime in Brazil: From State Efficiency to an Integrity System

Article 127 of the 1988 Constitution granted Public Prosecution offices functional independence and administrative autonomy. That means that criminal prosecution would be performed by a highly professionalised category of prosecutors with no hierarchical attachment to any representative of the three branches of power. According to the new constitutional order, the Public Prosecution offices would, beyond that, enjoy autonomy to prepare their budgetary proposals and to organise their internal bodies free from any interference from the legislature, executive or judiciary. Some argue that it could be considered a 'de facto fourth branch of power', authorised to independently investigate and prosecute even influential authorities and businesses.[47]

In the early 1990s, Brazil also engaged in constitutional and legal reforms intended to reorganise the state, make it lighter, more efficient, and more effectively managed by the implementation of new good governance principles and a comprehensive privatisation agenda.[48] Law 8.112, from 1990, established rules for federal public service recruitment through public selection exams, and laid out the career structure of federal public servants, including criteria for promotion and a detailed disciplinary regime to punish any kind of misbehaviour in public office. In 1992, Law 8.429 was enacted to regulate administrative improbity. It encompasses any type of illicit enrichment or undue advantage gained by public servants or representatives (Article 9), any act that could damage the public treasury (Article 10) and any position that contravenes the principles of public administration (Article 11) and provides administrative sanctions. Also, in 1992, Law 8.443 came into force to establish the Federal Account Court (TCU), responsible for the financial, operational, patrimonial and accounting supervision of any of the branches of power, including the assessment of the federal executive annual accounts. Law 8.666, of 1993, was enacted to regulate public procurement rules employing different modes of public bidding processes, criminalising many acts that would harm the regular flow of the procedures described in its rules.

[47] Lindsay Carson and Mariana Mota Prado, 'Mapping Corruption and its Institutional Determinants in Brazil' (2014) SSRN Electronic Journal, https://papers.ssrn.com/sol3/papers.cfm?abstract_id=2497935, 18.

[48] Luiz Carlos Bresser Pereira, *A reforma do estado dos anos 90: lógica e mecanismos de controle* (Ministério da Administração Federal e Reforma do Estado, 1997).

That first set of institutions and rules shaped the first cycle of efforts to build an accountability system, although, by that time, it was very much skewed to the professionalisation and control of public administration.

After some unpromising results from the first round of measures prescribed by the US Department of Treasury, the International Monetary Fund and the World Bank to tackle economic instability in the developing world, the so-called 'Washington Consensus' kept pushing for deeper institutional reforms that would attack elements of State inefficiency that were supposedly preventing public expenditure constraints and privatisation agendas to reach their full potential in triggering development.[49] The responses to that approach added to Brazil's institutional framework new auditing bodies, governance agencies and controlling bureaux aimed at increasing transparency, detecting suspicious financial transactions and coordinating efforts to bring Brazil into the international anti-money laundering and anti-corruption vanguard. In 1998, the first comprehensive legislation specifically dedicated to the criminalisation of money laundering and other crimes against the financial system created the Financial Activities Control Council (COAF) as an intelligence unit responsible for monitoring transactions and the flux of money, issuing reports about suspicious behaviour. In the motivation charter for Law 9.613, one of the rationales for its proposition was as follows:

> Such measures are found all over the compared legislation, which demonstrates the absolute necessity of its inclusion in Brazilian Law. See, for example, Belgium (Article 4 of the Law from January 11th, 1993), Spain (Article 3, number 1, Law 19/93, regulated by Article 3 of Royal Decree 925/95); Portugal (Article 3, number 1 of Law-Decree 3131, from September 15th, 1993), CICAD (Interamerican Drug Abuse Control Commission, Article 10 Model Regulations) and European Community (item 12 of 'The Forty Recommendations').

By some technical mistake, the Financial Action Task Force (FATF) recommendation was attributed to the European Union, which does not change the fact that it functioned as a driving force for the adoption of the new legislation. In 2002, Law 10.467 was approved to criminalise the bribery of foreign officials. Article 1 states that the Law's exclusive intent was to comply with the 1997 OECD Convention on Combating Bribery of Foreign Public Officials in International Business Transactions. In 2003, Law 10.683 created the Federal General Comptroller Office (CGU) with the missions to defend the public revenue, conduct internal audits and work as the federal administration ombudsman. One year later, the National Strategy to Combat Money Laundering (ENCLA) was inaugurated. It is a joint initiative by all spheres of

[49] Thomas Kelley, 'Beyond the Washington Consensus and new institutionalism: what is the future of law and development? (2010) 35(3) *North Carolina Journal of International Law and Commercial Regulation*.

government to engage multiple stakeholders in advancing the mechanisms of detection, monitoring and investigation of money laundering, and financing terrorism, which from 2006 onwards added the combating of corruption to its acronym, becoming ENCCLA (the National Strategy to Combat Corruption and Money Laundering).

ENCCLA brings together 88 participants from the three branches of power amongst federal and State bodies, and members of the Public Prosecution offices, and draws on contributions from NGOs such as the Ethos Institute and Transparency International. The initiative sets goals or actions to be achieved by participants in the intergovernmental web of institutions without any kind of sanctioning mechanisms. The failing agencies or branches of power are only accountable to public opinion as being non-cooperative with the anti-money laundering, anti-terrorism and anti-corruption agendas, a soft law approach that mirrors the naming and shaming strategy used by the FATF, for instance. ENCCLA is often cited in reports of international anti-corruption covenants' review mechanisms as a reference point for initiatives towards the fulfilment of their requirements. A 2011 MESICIC report mentions ENCCLA's articulation of policies to increase international legal cooperation and 'the formation of joint transnational investigative teams' and efforts behind the initiative to enact legislation to protect whistleblowers in corruption cases.[50] It is also referred to as a metric of success and good practice by the UN Convention against Corruption peer review mechanism report produced by Mexico and Haiti.[51] In fact, ENCCLA has championed the adoption, by Brazil, of many instruments imported from the FATF recommendations, guidelines and international law mechanisms. The insertion of ENCCLA as an interlocutor of the international anti-money laundering and anti-corruption regimes is explained by Barreto in the commemorative booklet of the Strategy's 10th anniversary:

> After the recognition of the transnational character of organized crime, Brazil has been negotiating a series of judicial and police international cooperation instruments, aiming at joint efforts to combat criminal activities that are executed, simultaneously, in many countries. In the UN, the Palermo Convention, from 2000, is a significative milestone in the transnational crime fight. The punishment of the guilty and the recovery of crime proceeds could not be threatened by the simple transpositions of one border. International cooperation mechanisms were established aiming at better criminal instruction, crime punishment, and the recovery of assets distorted abroad. The organization of a system to combat crime in the international instance, however,

[50] OAS, 'Mechanism for Follow-Up on the Implementation of the Inter-American Convention Against Corruption' (Organization of American States, 2011), www.oas.org/en/sla/dlc/mesicic/docs/mesicic3_bra_en.pdf.

[51] UNODC, 'Review by Haiti and Mexico of the Implementation by Brazil of articles 15–42 of Chapter III. 'Criminalization and law enforcement' and articles 44–50 of Chapter IV. 'International cooperation' of the United Nations Convention against Corruption for the review cycle 2010-2015' (United Nations Office on Drugs and Crime, 2016), www.unodc.org/documents/treaties/UNCAC/CountryVisitFinalReports/2017_01_19_Brazil_Final_Country_Report.pdf.

> needed to be accompanied by a solid national system, internal, based on cooperation, in which the joint efforts would promote work agility, avoiding the multiplication of initiatives.[52]

ENCCLA's targets have historically aimed at influencing the legislature not only to assure the approval of laws required by international law, but also to make international substantive consensus prevail in the internal discussions of Draft Bills. ENCCLA's Action 8, in 2010, for example, involved the follow-up and analysis of Draft Bill 5.228, from 2009, which later became Law 12.547, of 2011, known as the Access to Information Law, considered a landmark for Brazilian State transparency and corruption prevention and monitoring. Action 9, in 2011, focused on the push for Draft Bill 3.443, from 2008, which brought many modifications to the organised crime and money laundering legislation in Brazil. Action 9 is regarded as a development of the 2004 Target 20, which foresaw the proposition of alterations to the original proposal to amplify the premise of money laundering, to introduce the administrative seizure of assets and to provide a new definition of organised crime and terrorism. The Bill was enacted as Law 12.638, in 2012, and the ENCCLA influence was decisive in making Senator Pedro Simon's substitutive proposal successful, aligning Brazilian legislation on the matter to international provisions from the FATF and the UN Convention against Transnational Organized Crime in many aspects. The main change, from the Law 9.613 provisions and the original proposal, was the end of the list of precedent crimes, which made money laundering an autonomous offence to be prosecuted independently from the type of original crime or its investigative outcome. ENCCLA's Action 1, from 2018, was the elaboration of a National Plan to Fight Corruption, partly inspired by a joint project developed by the Getúlio Vargas Foundation and Transparency International that was endorsed by Transparency International itself as the 'greatest anti-corruption package ever produced in the world'.[53]

The ENCCLA initiative has played the role of an intergovernmental agency that works as a vector of influence from the international anti-money laundering and anti-corruption norms, guidelines and principles to Brazilian institutions. As Araújo points out, ENCCLA has no commitment to the use of incarceration as a response to transnational corruption; it is much more focused on the financial aspects of the phenomenon, such as the illicit flux of money and goods over borders, and with the dissemination of the anti-corruption movement, its mechanisms and tools to as many institutions as possible.[54] One of the main

[52] Luis Paulo Barreto, 'A Enccla e o Combate ao Crime no Âmbito Doméstico e Internacional' in *Enccla: Estratégia Nacional de Combate à Corrupção e à Lavagem de Dinheiro: 10 anos de Organização do Estado Brasileiro Contra o Crime Organizado* (Ministério da Justiça, 2012), http://enccla.camara.leg.br/quem-somos/enccla-10-anos, 56.

[53] Michael Freitas Mohallem et al, *Novas medidas contra a corrupção* (Fundação Getúlio Vargas-Rio, 2018), https://static.poder360.com.br/2019/05/Novas_Medidas_pacote_completo.pdf, 4.

[54] Felipe Dantas de Araújo, 'Uma análise da Estratégia Nacional contra a Corrupção e a Lavagem de Dinheiro (ENCCLA) por suas diretrizes' (2012) 2 *Revista Brasileira de Políticas Públicas* 53.

programmes developed by the initiative is the National Training Program to Combat Corruption and Money Laundering, a course offered to more than 19,000 public servants from the Federal and State administrations. ENCCLA's actions, thus, demonstrate a move away from the view of corruption as a criminal problem to present the international anti-corruption system as a more comprehensive response, which mandates criminalisation as just one element of the overall approach.

The criminal prosecution and punishment of acts of corruption are still a trademark of the international anti-corruption movement, but this has assumed a residual role in the context of managerial/good governance measures fostered by international anti-corruption agencies. The prevalence of modes of cooperation concentrated on asset recovery and the engagement of civil society in the anti-corruption debate is a consequence of the perception that criminal procedures run at their own pace, usually slow, and that a package of measures is needed to intervene in the problem of corruption at another, much faster gear.[55] Some would call this mode of broad governance of the anti-corruption efforts championed by ENCCLA as a 'whole of government approach' or 'joined-up government', by which administrative measures for monitoring and prevention prevail over criminal repression.[56] As Marona and Kerche point out, ENCCLA has been nothing less than 'a key factor to build the anti-corruption task forces'.[57]

The ENCCLA executive secretariat operates under the responsibility of the Department of Assets Recovery and International Mutual Legal Assistance of the Ministry of Justice (DRCI). The Department was also structured in the early 1990s and has the institutional role of overseeing mutual legal assistance requests that Brazilian authorities issue (active) and receive (passive), be they related to criminal prosecution, investigative measures, freezing of bank accounts and assets confiscation and recovery, or to civil matters such as international child adoption. The number of criminal mutual legal assistance requests, both active and passive, shows a progressive integration of Brazil into the international arena of information and investigative sharing. Between 2005 and 2011, criminal mutual legal assistance requests oscillated between 1,000 and 1,250. After that, they experienced a steep rise from 1,301 requests in 2013 to 2,329 in 2017, with ever-increasing figures in all the years in that period. In 2018 and 2019, there was a decline, but the numbers never fell below 2,000 requests. The monetary value of goods and assets frozen overseas shows a similar pattern. Except for a peak of

[55] Felipe Dantas de Araújo, 'Corrupção e Novas Concepções de Direito Punitivo: Rumo a um Direito de Intervenção Anticorrupção?' (2011) 8(2) *Brazilian Journal of International Law* 224.

[56] Michael Freitas Mohallem and Carlos Emmanuel J Ragazzo, 'Diagnóstico institucional: primeiros passos para um plano nacional anticorrupção' (Fundação Getúlio Vargas-Rio, 2017), https://biblioteca-digital.fgv.br/dspace/handle/10438/18167, 49–52.

[57] Marjorie Marona and Fábio Kerche, 'From the Banestado Case to Operation Car Wash: Building an Anti-Corruption Institutional Framework in Brazil' (2021) 64(3) *Dados, Rio de Janeiro* 8.

$195 million seized in 2004 and another high of $83 million in 2008, Brazil had never frozen more than $50 million of assets abroad until it documented a record $499 million in 2015, the same year that saw a record $145,218,000 repatriated. The impact of the '*Car Wash*' operation on those figures is undeniable. Between 2014 and 2020, that operation that was heavily underpinned by UNCATOC (UN Convention against Transnational Organized Crime) and UNCAC (UN Convention against Corruption) investigative methods, such as the cooperation of participants in criminal activity with law enforcement authorities (UNCATOC, Article 26; UNCAC, Article 37), corresponding alone to $728,960,600.64 in goods and assets frozen abroad and to the definitive recovery of $175,670,683.07.

Figure 3.1 Assets Recovered via International Legal Mutual Assistance/Operations (in USD Thousands)

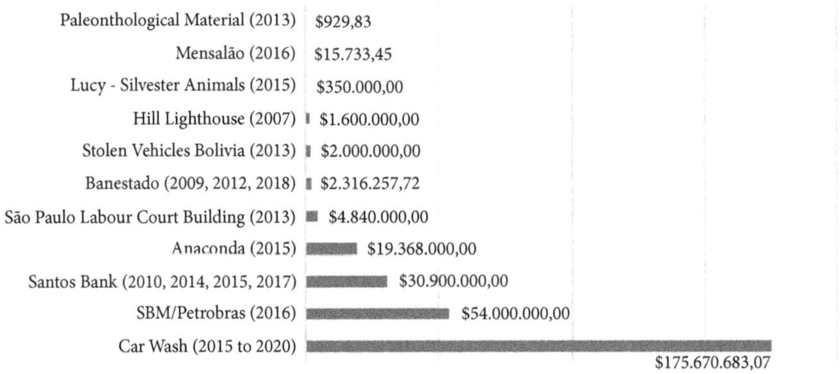

Source: DRCI – Department of Assets Recovery and International Mutual Legal Assistance of the Ministry of Justice.

The efficiency of the mutual legal assistance requests made by Brazil also increased considerably due to the enabling of direct cooperation between investigative authorities on the routine exchange of information that facilitates the tracking of offshore companies and accounts in tax havens. The debate over the necessity of judicial authorisation for that kind of cooperation between investigative authorities for preparatory measures to the request of mutual legal assistance was settled by a decision of the Superior Court of Justice in Reclamation 2.645, from 2009.

The judicial decision draws normative force from the UN Conventions to reinforce the relationship between investigative bodies of different countries, exempting the need for judicial authorisation for all those day-to-day investigative information exchanges for which the Constitution does not expressively require such authorisation. That decision opened the channels of communication between prosecution authorities and made the mutual legal assistance requests managed by DRCI more precise and effective.

Carson and Prado trace a very interesting history of how, despite its deficiencies, the arsenal of accountability institutions mentioned above contributed to uncovering a series of corruption scandals, beginning with the impeachment of former President Fernando Collor in 1992. A few years later, a Parliamentary Inquiry Committee investigation revealed the misuse of budget allocations by a group of congressmen known as the 'budget dwarves', in reference to their overall low stature. Those members of the Brazilian Congress used pork barrel prerogatives to deviate budget resources to fake social organisations and contractors in a kickback corruption system. The study also describes how a bribery scheme by Congress members in exchange for support for the approval of the 'Reelection Amendment' during President Fernando Henrique Cardoso's tenure became public, and the sequence of arrests and criminal convictions related to money distortion in the construction of the new São Paulo Labour Court building. The randomised audits carried out by the Federal General Comptroller (CGU) were responsible for the discovery of overpricing and corruption in the procurement of ambulances by local health authorities with decentralised federal money, called the 'Bloodsuckers Operation', and the Federal Police Department gained public credibility for the success of other nationwide operations related to corruption in regional aid programmes (Sudene/Sudam). The Federal Police also discovered a system of bribery in judicial decision-making, known as 'Operation Anaconda'. Last, but definitely not least, the Brazilian institutional fight against corruption unveiled the *Mensalão* case, a major scandal involving the use of overpriced contracts in State-owned companies to provide the continuous payment of a secret monthly wage to Congress members to assure their votes in Draft Bills of strategic interest to the government.[58] The case brought down the directive board of the Workers' Party, resulting in the criminal conviction for corruption, money laundering and criminal organisation of 26 people, including the General Treasurer and the former President of the Party, the former President of the Deputy Chamber, and the former Secretary of State.

By the time of those investigations, though, the main instruments of international anti-corruption were in their early stages of implementation and legislative reform to comply with the international standards in Brazil was not complete. A third round of Draft Bills and laws were enacted at the beginning of the 2010s. In 2011, Law 12.527 came into force to regulate the right to information provisioned by Article 5, item XXXIII of the 1988 Constitution. The Access to Information Law is considered a milestone in Brazil's integrity system in establishing the publication of information as the guiding principle of public administration, with confidentiality as an exception, setting forth the obligation to provide public information regardless of requests made to public offices, preferably through technological resources, and fostering the social control of public administration.

[58] Lindsay Carson and Mariana Mota Prado, 'Mapping Corruption and its Institutional Determinants in Brazil' (2014) SSRN Electronic Journal, https://papers.ssrn.com/sol3/papers.cfm?abstract_id=2497935, 18–22.

The motivation charter attached to Draft Bill 5.228, from 2009, a substitutive proposal presented by the Executive Branch to the original Draft Bill 219, from 2003, refers to the importance of the measure for democracy, citizenship, the fight against corruption, and transparency, as follows:

> In 2008, the United Nations Educational, Scientific and Cultural Organization – UNESCO released a report that shows that in 1990, only thirteen countries had regulated the right of access to information. Currently, more than 70 countries have already adopted this legislation, while dozens of others are in an advanced process for its elaboration. Another advance pointed out by UNESCO, lies in the recognition by many countries of the right to information as a fundamental right. The guarantee of the right of access to public information as a general rule is one of the great mechanisms for the consolidation of democratic regimes. Access to public information, in addition to being indispensable to the exercise of citizenship, is one of the strongest instruments for combating corruption. The preliminary project in question, therefore, appears as yet another measure adopted by the Federal Government to promote ethics and increasing transparency in the public sector.

In 2012, Brazil adopted a new anti-money laundering statute. As explained above, ENCCLA had a direct influence on legislative discussion of the matter. Senator Pedro Simon presented a substitutive proposal to Draft Bill 209, from 2003, before the Senate's Economic Affairs Committee in which he mentions the necessity of integrating Brazil into the 'third generation' of international anti-money laundering efforts:

> The most recent proposition, PLS no 225, of 2006, has the merit of inserting Brazil among countries that have the so-called 'third generation' of laws in the fight against money laundering, which consists in the elimination of the list of antecedent crimes. Thus, assets, rights and values arising from any criminal offense (crime or criminal misdemeanor) may characterize money laundering. For this reason, we believe that Amendment no 1, proposed by Senator Arthur Virgílio, which aims to recompose in PLS no 225, of 2006, the closed list of antecedent crimes, is against the most recent advances in the international landscape.

The legislative overhaul to expand anti-corruption measures way beyond criminal prosecution had another chapter in Law 12.813, from 2013, which regulates the conflict of interests in the Federal Public Administration. The communication attached to Draft Bill 7.528, from 2006, which generated Law 12.813, was produced by the Federal General Comptroller (CGU) and expressively clarified that the main goal of the proposition was to 'adapt domestic legislation to international conventions provisions, with emphasis on the United Nations Convention against Corruption, adopted by the United Nations General Assembly on October 31, 2003'.

In 2013, Law 12.846, also known as the Anti-Corruption Law, was approved to regulate responsibility for acts of corruption by legal entities, both domestic and foreign, against the Public Administration. The Anti-Corruption Law details the requisites and procedures for the attainment of cooperation agreements between companies involved in corruption and law enforcement authorities, a mechanism that has enabled the repatriation of goods and assets distorted abroad and has been widely used in recent investigations, such as the *Car Wash* operation, in which 22 cooperation agreements were concluded with many representatives of the private sector, including some of the country's biggest multinational contractors (Odebrecht, OAS, Andrade Gutierrez and Camargo Correa). According to Federal General Comptroller (CGU) information, those agreements were responsible for the return of R$3,840,367,468.77 to the public coffers, with more than R$10 billion to be repatriated thereafter. During the legislative procedure for Draft Bill 6.826, from 2010, the Special Committee for Acts Against the Administration of the Deputy Chamber issued the following opinion:

> The control of corruption has, therefore, become fundamentally important in strengthening democratic institutions and enabling countries to grow economically, which is why the United Nations Convention against Corruption, the Inter-American Convention to Combat Corruption and the Convention on Combating the Corruption of Foreign Public Officials in International Business Transactions were drafted, to all of which Brazil is a signatory. As a result, our country has forced itself to punish legal entities that commit acts of corruption, against the national public administration, and, in particular, those of transnational bribery, characterized by the active corruption of foreign public officials and international organizations' representatives. Hence, there arose the need to elaborate specific legislation that would reach, by means of administrative and civil accountability, the legal entities responsible for the acts of corruption described in international agreements.

Once more, not only was the necessity to comply with international laws brought up as a sufficient rationale for passing the new legislation, but it also incorporated international anti-corruption discourse on the causal relations between the effective fight against corruption, economic development and democratic consolidation. Likewise, Law 12.850, from 2013, which redefines criminal organisation and regulates new investigative methods is strongly backed up in international law provisions. The Deputy Chamber's Constitution and Justice Committee opinion on the Draft Bill 6.578, from 2009, highlights that:

> Indeed, this Bill, inspired by the aforementioned Palermo Convention, brings together the constituent elements of the criminal organization offense, allowing it to be distinguished, where appropriate, from the gang crime, now called 'criminal association', as provisioned in article 288 of the Penal Code. In addition, it brings specific rules on criminal procedure and regulates more robustly the means of obtaining evidence, such as rewarded cooperation, controlled action, and the infiltration of agents, currently provided for in Law 9.034/95 but seldomly applied due to the absence of necessary rules to ensure its effectiveness.

The investigative toolkit offered by the UN Convention against Transnational Organized Crime and the UN Convention against Corruption was fully adopted by Law 12.850. It introduced into Brazilian criminal procedural law mechanisms developed in a different legal system that reflects the American tradition of a negotiated criminal jurisdiction. In Brazil, criminal procedural law is affiliated with the Roman-Germanic legal framework, which imposes some difficulties in reconciling international norms with some constitutional principles and dogmas.[59] The possibility of rewarding someone under investigation for their collaboration, for instance, is not exactly a novelty in Brazilian criminal procedural law. The idea that the system should encourage participants in complex criminal offences to collaborate with the prosecution via a reduction in prison time is found in Article 25, para 2 of Law 7.429, from 1986 (Crimes Against the National Financial System Law), Article 8, para 1 of Law 8.072, from 1990 (Heinous Crimes Law) and Article 16, para 1 of Law 8.137, from 1990 (Crimes Against the National Tax System Law). Article 159, para 4 of the Penal Code, added by Law 9.249, from 1996, contains similar provisions related to kidnapping and the hostage's freedom. Nevertheless, in all those cases, the benefit is limited to a prescribed fraction of time in terms of sentence reduction, and its concession is subject to judicial discretion on the final verdict. The timing of the collaboration, the extent of its contribution to the investigation, and the participation of prosecution authorities in it have never been made clear in those statutes, and, probably due to their poor regulation, the mechanisms never achieved exposure.

Reward for collaboration is an autonomous procedural legal transaction between the police or the public prosecution authorities and the person under investigation, with the possibility of negotiating multiple levels of benefits, according to the significance of the collaboration. It only came into Brazilian law through the new Anti-Money Laundering Law (Law 12.638, from 2012) and then, more comprehensively, in the new Criminal Organizations Law (Law 12.850, from 2013). As explained above, both statutes were enacted with a significant influence from anti-corruption international law and guidelines produced by institutions committed to international anti-money laundering and anti-corruption, such as ENCCLA and DRCI.

The popularising of incentives for collaboration under the term '*delação*' (denouncement, accusation, incrimination) gained traction as the *Car Wash* operation made the headlines. Indeed, in that operation alone, 256 collaboration agreements were concluded, with 209 originating from the task force in Curitiba, State of Paraná. The terms of the collaboration agreements achieved by the Federal Public Prosecution office in Paraná, which headed the *Car Wash* operation task force, expressly mention as legal bases for their validity Article 26 of the Palermo Convention (UNTOC) and Article 37 of the Merida Convention (UNCAC). The collaboration agreements in the Paraná operation resulted in fines amounting to R$2.1 billion, with R$111.5 million recovered in voluntary payments from defendants.

The indiscriminate use of the mechanism is not free from critique, though. Some argue that the mob turmoil over the successes of '*delação*' led Brazilian

[59] Cordini (n 3) 271.

judicial institutions to elevate it to the status of a broad criminal policy, blocking any possibility of assessing its pros and cons and, ultimately, its fairness.[60] Rewarding collaboration is one procedural tool amongst many others that needs to be evaluated by those who formulate criminal policy with regard to its effectiveness in addressing the problem of corruption holistically, suppressing its economic and social causes and not only remediating its consequences.[61] Some specific cases show that the uncritical incorporation of incentives for collaboration into Brazilian criminal procedural law can lead to some distortions. One of the main collaborators in the *Car Wash* operation was Alberto Youssef, a key financial operator in the scheme of moving money from overpriced contracts between cartel companies and Petrobras to political parties and corrupt directors of the Brazilian State-owned oil company. The collaboration agreement between him and the *Car Wash* task force was not the first he secured with Curitiba's law enforcement authorities. A few years earlier, he had taken part in another collaboration agreement relating to his role as an illegal currency exchange agent in another major corruption scandal involving foreign currency evasion and the State of Paraná privatised bank, known as the *Banestado* case. That first agreement set out the collaborator's commitment not to engage in further criminal activity. In that sense, the collaboration agreement entered into by Alberto Youssef with the *Car Wash* task force was the recognition of the failure of the agreement signed during the *Banestado* case, which raised concerns over his loyalty to the prosecution institutions. Another case that illustrates problems with blind reliance on '*delação*' is that of Nestor Cerveró, a former director of Petrobras. He was preventively arrested at the beginning of 2015 and began to negotiate with the Federal Public Prosecution office in Curitiba the terms of an collaboration agreement. Fearing the results of his possible collaboration, Workers' Party and Government Leader in the Senate, Delcídio Amaral, contacted Cerveró's family to present a plan to bribe him and help him escape to Spain. It became public as Bernardo Cerveró, Nestor's son, secretly recorded his whole conversation with the Senator on tape, which he gave to the Federal Public Prosecution office and, ultimately, was used as evidence for the cautionary arrest of the Senator by the Supreme Court. The situation demonstrates that investigations based strongly on '*delação*' can make criminal prosecution susceptible to a 'marketisation', whereby the decision to collaborate with law enforcement authorities or protect peer criminals turns into a dangerous auction between judicial actors and criminal organisations to be won by those who offer the greater advantage.[62]

[60] Fernando Andrade Fernandes and Ana Cristina Gomes, 'Acerca da experiência brasileira com o Instituto da Delação Premiada, expectativas político-criminais transmudadas em Políticas Públicas Criminais' 83 *Revista Jurídica LEX* 369–70.

[61] ibid.

[62] Marcelo Rodrigues da Silva, 'A colaboração premiada como terceira via do direito penal no enfrentamento à corrupção administrativa organizada' (2017) 3 *Revista Brasileira de Direito Processual Penal* 305.

Those potential or theoretical concerns are not the only ones surrounding the obsession with incentives for collaboration that encapsulated criminal prosecution in Brazil, especially during the *Car Wash* operation. One of them relates to the legal requirements for a collaboration agreement, which is the voluntary decision to cooperate by the person under investigation (Article 4, para 7, item IV of Law 12.850, from 2013). It is debatable if people under custody for a prolonged amount of time can voluntarily decide to cooperate with the investigation, especially if, in addition to their cautionary arrest, the judiciary use coercion measures such as freezing accounts, arresting other participants in the criminal organisation, and compelling witnesses to attend interviews in the presence of police agents. Although it is impossible to tell what influence cautionary arrest may have on the will of the collaborator, the prospect of indefinite arrest under caution was specifically negotiated by some collaborators with the *Car Wash* task force. That is another curiosity of some collaboration agreements entered into by the *Car Wash* task force with many collaborators: the offer, by the prosecutors, of benefits that went beyond the parameters set out in Law 12.850 of 2013. Article 4 makes provision for the possibilities of a full pardon, a reduction in up to two-thirds of a prison sentence, or the substitution of imprisonment with other penalties such as fines, community service, and other constraints on rights. Nevertheless, one collaborator negotiated the exchange of cautionary arrest for provisory home detention, another negotiated the immediate release of his estate property for the benefit of his relatives, and many others that agreed to pay significant fines or to help with asset recovery were rewarded with a 'differentiated open regime', in which the collaborator had to serve time in an hybrid scheme with the ability to return home during the night and on weekends. Although such hybrid regimes do not find a parallel in Brazilian legislation, the negotiation of unprecedented 'prizes' with collaborators was not unexceptional during the *Car Wash* operation, as shown by the comprehensive analysis carried out by Schertel Mendes in which 106 agreements were examined.[63] The legality of such agreements is not the main focus of the discussion in this chapter. The striking aspect is the prevalence of a new approach of the criminal justice system, more focused on the economic aspects of corruption and the recovery of distorted money than on retribution by way of incarceration.[64] More than that, the canonical status attributed to rewarding collaboration represents the triumph of an alternative criminal law, less concentrated on retribution, and more inclined to a 'leniency revolution' based on a principal-agent structure that resembles how economic theory and managerial trends occupy the whole international anti-corruption movement.[65]

This relatively mild response to crimes that were confessed to and involved huge amounts of money is coherent with the international anti-corruption

[63] Francisco Schertel Mendes, *Leniency Policies in the Prosecution of Economic Crimes and Corruption* (Nomos Verlagsgesellschaft mbH & Co KG, 2021) 61.
[64] Silva (n 62) 293.
[65] Schertel Mendes (n 63) 148.

regime tendency to detach the phenomenon from its criminal roots, qualifying it in economic terms and as a broader governance disfunction. Transparency International considered the results of anti-corruption efforts in Brazil, such as those in the *Car Wash* operation, to be remarkable. The appreciation of the integration of international anti-corruption trends into the *Car Wash* operation is evidenced by the fact that the operation received the NGO's Anti-Corruption Award of 2016. The participation of Transparency International in Brazil's institutional efforts to fight corruption is extensive. As highlighted before, it has participated in joint projects, producing reports and technical proposals, attending ENCCLA meetings, and concluding agreements with Brazilian institutions, such as Cooperation Agreement 2, from 2017, reached with the National Council of Justice to promote studies and research on the best international practices on judicial management and the combat of corruption, with judges and clerks training in anti-corruption and anti-money laundering schemes, with international exchange, and with the development of publicity campaigns to sensitise public opinion towards transparency of data, corruption and social control. Here, the last trait of the anti-corruption regime reaches its full potential: the engagement of society with its causes. As this is probably the most impactful characteristic of the international anti-corruption agenda on Brazilian democracy, it will be addressed in more detail in the next chapter.

Although it has taken place through different actors and means, all the forms of interaction between the international anti-corruption movement and the Brazilian institutional framework analysed so far happened via formal mechanisms in the importation of legislation, targets, guidelines, agreements, covenant provisions, and discourses. So, be it through legal reforms carried on to increase State efficiency, as happened right after the enactment of the 1988 Constitution, through monitoring, audit and institutional reforms that brought COAF, CGU, ENCCLA and DRCI into existence in the early 2000s, or new legislation that incorporated FATF, MESICIC or UNODC standards with immediate outcomes in judicial adjudication, as happened in the 2010s, the penetration of international anti-corruption principles and methods in Brazil is undeniable. Some consider the changes in Brazilian legislation and institutional settings to battle corruption based on international guidance to be the 'main transformation in the Brazilian State and society' in recent decades, with the construction of a broad 'anti-corruption state of affairs'.[66] Indeed, Brazil's efforts to fully comply with international anti-corruption standards have generated favourable appraisal from important non-governmental anti-corruption organisations, with high scores and awards being granted by Amarribo Brasil, Global Integrity, and Transparency International. In the next

[66] Luciano Meneguetti Pereira, 'A Aplicação do Direito Internacional no Combate à Corrupção no Brasil: A Cooperação Jurídica Internacional e a Atuação do Ministério Público Federal na "Operação Lava Jato"' in W Menezes (ed), *Direito Internacional em Expansão*, vol VII (Arraes Editora, 2016) 87; Marcos Tourinho, 'Brazil in the global anticorruption regime' (2018) 61 *Revista Brasileira de Política Internacional* 15.

section, we will address the anticipated results of such a robust influence over Brazilian democracy.

3.5. The Struggle against Corruption: The Last Step Towards Democratic Consolidation?

Part of Brazilian mainstream sociological interpretation understands that the Brazilian democratic deficit is due to the inefficiency of the State agencies in fighting corruption. The compliance with international anti-corruption efforts is pointed out, by later literature, as a solution to that problem. Indicatively, Rose-Ackerman and Palifka have argued that international integration is of crucial importance if Brazil is holistically and efficiently to battle corruption.[67] Warf affirms that democratisation in Latin America 'left something to be desired', creating for itself new opportunities for corruption, as demonstrated in Brazil, where every government since the transition to democracy has had its own major corruption scandal to be remembered. His 2016 data, however, show that Brazil presents the second lowest – higher only than Trinidad and Tobago – percentage of people admitting to having been paid a bribe, and the second highest percentage of respondents declaring it socially acceptable to report bribes to the authorities (lower only than Costa Rica), among 20 countries in South America, Central America, the Caribbean and Mexico.[68] The assumption that corruption in Latin America, and by extension, in Brazil, is uncontrollable, impeding 'the further deepening and consolidation of democracy' or a 'prominent cause of low-quality democracy', is appealing for some reason, regardless of the achievements reached in those areas.[69] In that sense, Rehren points out that after the democratisation wave that swept Latin America in the last decades of the twentieth century, democratic legitimacy was subject to erosion in the region because of corruption.[70] Fighting corruption effectively is perceived as the 'unfinished' business in the transition from dictatorship to the definitive implementation of the 'rule of law'.[71] As seen in chapter 1, recent consensus in quality of democracy theories is that high quality democracies presuppose as one of their dimensions effective mechanisms of control capable of holding

[67] Rose-Ackerman and Palifka (n 34) 89.

[68] Barney Warf, *Global Corruption from a Geographic Perspective* (Springer, 2019) 25–26.

[69] John Bailey, 'Corruption and Democratic Governability' in CH Blake and SD Morris (eds), *Corruption and Democracy in Latin America* (University of Pittsburgh Press, 2009) 75; Stephen D Morris and Charles H Blake, 'Introduction: Political and Analytical Challenges of Corruption in Latin America' in SD Morris and CH Blake (eds), *Corruption and Democracy in Latin America* (University of Pittsburgh Press, 2009) 4.

[70] Alfredo Rehren, 'The Crisis of The Democratic State' in CH Blake and SD Morris (eds), *Corruption and Democracy in Latin America* (University of Pittsburgh Press, 2009) 46.

[71] JC Calleros-Alarcón, *The Unfinished Transition to Democracy in Latin America* (Routledge, 2007) 46–47.

representatives accountable to controlling agencies, bureaucracies and, ultimately, the electorate. Anti-corruption efficiency is one of the ways to show that the 'rule of law matters' to democracy assessment.[72]

The triumph over corruption, in all its manifestations, is considered by many as the last challenge to be overcome by Brazilian democracy for its definitive consolidation. As Power and Taylor state 'as Brazilian democracy evolves past some of the simpler institutional threats of its early transition, political corruption increasingly appears to be one of the main hurdles to achieving the promise of a consolidated and robust democratic polity'.[73] Although Brazil has engaged in a major institutional overhaul to enhance the capacity of its accountability agencies to identify, process and punish corruption, some argue that improvements perceived in the institutional arrangements employed in investigating corruption scandals were not followed by the judiciary in terms of sanctioning political agents severely enough.[74] Likewise, Taylor detects the lack of sanctions and effective punishment of influential political actors and businesspersons as a factor that inhibits Brazilian accountability mechanisms and organisations in providing their decisive contribution to the new democracy.[75] In other words, the missing piece of the democratic puzzle is the consolidation of an efficient multi-leveled accountability net, able to identify and punish corruption. Although recognising the institutional progress made by Brazil in identifying and investigating corruption scandals, the absence of effective punishment for corrupt actors is still pointed to as a major problem. Oliveira and Moisés say that 'the scale of corruption practices and their continuity over time are signs that the interinstitutional accountability system is malfunctioning'.[76] Efforts to adopt international anti-corruption packages just never seem to be enough.

The international anti-corruption regime found the force to fuel its worldwide spread when it detached itself from its criminal genesis to adopt a more comprehensive, interdisciplinary approach. The adoption of transparency, accountability and investigatory mechanisms became a jewel of the managerial, good governance and efficiency packages. As Trubek and Santos warn, these developmental projects and steps often misrepresent the realities in which they want to intervene.[77] Kennedy posits that the anti-corruption agenda was put forth along with human rights as 'a universal vocabulary of political legitimacy', presenting itself as a

[72] Guilhermo A O'Donnell, 'Why the rule of law matters' (2004) 15(4) *Journal of Democracy* 36.

[73] Timothy J Power and Mathew M Taylor, *Corruption and Democracy in Brazil. The Struggle for Accountability* (University of Notre Dame Press, 2011) 13.

[74] Carson and Prado (n 47) 32.

[75] Mathew M Taylor, 'Corruption, Accountability Reforms, and Democracy in Brazil' in CH Blake and SD Morris (eds), *Corruption and Democracy in Latin America* (University of Pittsburgh Press, 2009) 167.

[76] Emmanuel Nunes de Oliveira and José Álvaro Moisés, 'Corruption in the Perception of Brazilian Society: Persistence and Resilience' (2023) 29(2) *Revista do CESOP* 272.

[77] David M Trubek and Alvaro Santos, *The New Law and Economic Development: A Critical Appraisal* (Cambridge University Press, 2006) 17.

supposedly technical, apolitical and neutral intervention to take countries to the developmental and democratic promised land. Nevertheless, 'their criticism, strategies, and language all have consequences, allocate stakes, exercise power'.[78] In Brazil, the institutional machinery considered necessary for the enforcement of human rights, the eradication of corruption, and presumably the resultant democratic consolidation, involved the empowerment of lower-level judicial elites. How the discourse on those democratic deficiencies related to shortcomings in fighting corruption reached a pervasive semantic level that encapsulated the political mindset in Brazil, and its repercussions for democracy, will be discussed in the next chapter.

For now, it is important to stress that while street rallies and flag wavers engage in public campaigns against corruption and mobilise themselves to pressure democratic institutions thinking of themselves as holders of their own destiny, all they are doing is to mimic, as puppets in a ventriloquist's lap, discourses developed in summits, private meetings and conferences held oceans away from them, in which they cannot even dream of participating.

[78] D Kennedy, *The Dark Sides of Virtue: Reassessing International Humanitarianism* (Princeton University Press, 2004) 328–29.

4

The Fight against Corruption: From Societal Engagement to Social Poisoning

4.1. Introduction

At the end of 2020, one of the largest Brazilian retail companies launched a trainee programme exclusively for black applicants. They announced it as an initiative to open the doors of the company to a more diverse working environment, and also to offer better job opportunities for historically discriminated against people. In October 2020, a federal public attorney filed a class action against the trainee programme. In the petition, the attorney not only sought its cancellation, but also a R$10 million fine for collective damage.[1] Part of his reasoning was that the company had undisclosed marketing and political interests in promoting the trainee programme. According to the claim, behind the advertised concern with racial equality was the company's desire to assume a political cause and, thus, a marketing niche, which would only become clear if one could 'follow the money'. Again, the rhetoric on dissimulation, or the distortion of goals for private benefit, underpinned a class action filed by a State agent against a private company that had the initiative to offer inclusion opportunities for disadvantaged people.

The idea that behind every action and initiative, Brazilians have a second or third unconfessed intent links back to representations of society found in sociological works such as those of Freyre, Holanda or Faoro, which are imprinted in how Brazilians tend to see themselves. Once fed by a wave of facts, news and propaganda, that stigma can have a far longer reach. That is how campaigns and programmes aimed at human rights causes can be translated into the anti-corruption lexicon and dismantled under the need to prevent corruption.

In the previous chapters, we argued that democracy evolves as society mobilises itself to participate in elections, plebiscites and referendums, to exercise pressure and make representatives accountable or to litigate for their rights in courts. It also presupposes that more and more people ascend above sub-par living conditions, in which they are forced to deal with food insecurity, infant

[1] TRT 10 [2020] ACPCiv 0000790-37.2020.5.10.0015.

and childhood mortality, structural and institutionalised racial discrimination, or even the threat of extinction as a people. We also have seen how the integration of international anti-corruption initiatives and standards was highlighted as a necessary step toward Brazil's complete democratisation. However, the idea of an intrinsic correlation between the fight against corruption and democratic consolidation is not a peculiar trait of the Brazilian context. As Gutterman and Lohaus argue, one of the main premises on which the international anti-corruption movement is set forth is that corruption 'undermines democracy'.[2] Sousa and others also pinpoint that the international supporters of the good governance agenda assume that anti-corruption and democracy are indivisibly imbricated.[3] The fight against corruption became one of the main requirements for countries that were living through political transitions during the 1990s to be considered 'democratic' and, thus, to get a passport for 'modernity', represented here as membership of the EU or OECD.[4]

However, a constant problem with anti-corruption measures is that of assessing their effectiveness. As Sampson stresses, anti-corruption packages demand analysis of their impact as much as any other public policy, which generates the creation of perception indices and rankings that can be misleading.[5] Corruption is a difficult phenomenon to discern and identify and, thus, to measure. In some cases, when the effectiveness of anti-corruption provisions is at its peak, the perception of corruption also rises, while in others, complacent anti-corruption bodies can collaborate in a false perception of low corruption levels.

The challenge posed by the necessity to legitimise anti-corruption efforts with results, and the idea that the fight against corruption is a democratic cause, come together in the form of increasing public awareness of corruption. In chapter 3, we saw three main features that characterise the international anti-corruption regime. Firstly, corruption is depicted as a sophisticated and transnational phenomenon that cannot be fought without full compliance with international norms, agencies, and their investigation machinery. Secondly, corruption was progressively detached from its original definition as a criminological phenomenon, to be explained economically, through principal-agent/risk-reward syllogisms. Thus, investigation and punishment *ex post facto* were replaced by *a priori* adoption of good governance and transparency provisions and mechanisms to freeze, seize and recover financial proceeds of corruption.

[2] E Gutterman and M Lohaus, 'What is the "Anti-corruption" Norm in Global Politics?' in I Kubbe and A Engelbert (eds), *Corruption and Norms. Political Corruption and Governance* (Palgrave Macmillan, 2018) 246.

[3] Luis de Sousa, Peter Larmour and Barry Hindess, *Governments, NGOs and Anti-corruption: The New Integrity Warriors* (Routledge, 2009) 219.

[4] Matilda Dahl, 'How do International Organizations Scrutinize Transforming States? The Case of Transparency International and the Baltic States' in L de Sousa, PJ Larmour and B Hindess (eds), *Governments, NGOs and Anti-Corruption: The New Integrity Warriors* (Routledge, 2009).

[5] Steven Sampson, 'The anti-corruption industry: from movement to institution' (2010) 11(2) *Global Crime* 265.

Lastly, international norms, multinational organisations' reports and guidelines, and NGO activists invest in the idea of societal awareness as a crucial part of the anti-corruption movement.

Blake recognises that most Latin American countries engaged in institutional reforms aimed to reduce corruption during the 1990s and 2000s. But he emphasises that, although necessary, those initiatives were not sufficient to fight corruption: a further step forward in the direction of vertical societal accountability was needed to create social 'zero tolerance' towards corruption and a culture of 'probity, accountability and transparency'.[6]

In the first section of this chapter, we will see how this part of the international anti-corruption regime was incorporated in Brazil, and we will scrutinise its outcomes for democratic institutions and procedures. Review mechanism reports of the UN and Inter-American Conventions against Corruption are analysed to show this mix of favourable appraisal of legal and institutional reforms and demands for more effectiveness and data on the use of its instruments by Brazilian law enforcement institutions. We will also see how the international anti-corruption focus on public awareness explains the push by Brazilian lower-level judicial authorities for a transition from horizontal to vertical electoral accountability. In this first approach, our focus is on demonstrating how international pressure for practical outcomes and more societal mobilisation towards the problem of corruption affected traditional democratic institutions, such as the Presidency, and influenced the ultimate democratic procedure – elections. Studies on probative analysis and case law will be assessed to show that under the idea of increasing public awareness of corruption, lower-level law enforcement authorities implemented their political agenda, which culminated with the end of the elected President's mandate and decisive intervention in the 2018 general elections. We intend to show the strategic alliance between those authorities, their discourses, and campaigns in the media, and how this movement spread its influence to become a broad social and cultural obsession. Anti-corruption efforts did not only destabilise core political, participatory elements of Brazilian democracy but also colonised the public sphere, contributing not to 'enlighten the understanding of public affairs and control of the public agenda',[7] but to obscure and dominate them. Finally, we will address ways in which the loose definition of corruption adopted and advocated by Transparency International had a grip on the Brazilian political scene, not only generating an impoverishment of political debate but also extending its logic to different areas of public policies.

In the second section, this chapter goes back to the fight against poverty and hunger, and the conditional cash transfer programmes, to show how the 'clientelism' theory gained traction as a version of the anti-corruption discourse. It

[6] CH Blake, 'Public Attitudes toward Corruption' in CH Blake and SD Morris (eds), *Corruption and Democracy in Latin America* (University of Pittsburgh Press, 2009) 95–96.

[7] This is one of Dahl's polyarchal requirements. See Robert Alan Dahl and Ian Shapiro, *On Democracy* (Yale University Press, 1998).

prompted the idea of the existence of fraud in the cash transfer programmes and the necessity of audits as the main issues to be addressed to improve those policies. The section also analyses the impacts of those views on the social index observed in chapter 2 to evaluate if this approach brought inclusionary or exclusionary effects.

The third section is dedicated to the incursion of the anti-corruption logic into the right to health and the public healthcare system. We will address how it contributed to the end of a primary assistance programme and, ultimately, to the concentration of the main public efforts during the 2020 Covid-19 pandemic. Amid the most dramatic health emergency of the modern era, the Brazilian healthcare system was at the centre of investigations, arrests and inquiries to detect and punish the misallocation of public resources, healthcare equipment, materials and even vaccines.

The chapter goes on to examine if and how ideas of favouritism and manipulation of policies for political benefit were again brought to the fore to 'criminalise' ethnic minorities. It will be also explored how a new cycle of threats to indigenous populations was brought about, with unseen international repercussions related to the perpetration of genocide by the Brazilian State.

The chapter proposes that Brazil's full commitment to international anti-corruption initiatives and standards did not bring the democratic outcomes expected by the technical literature or experts. On the contrary, it seems like it played a considerable role in major political events related to the destabilisation of core democratic institutions – the Presidency – and procedures – general elections. Moreover, the penetration of anti-corruption discourses and practices into the Brazilian social fabric seems to have been deeper and more pervasive. It involves not only intervention in electoral democracy, but also the colonisation of the whole public sphere by its rhetoric, and agenda. The international anti-corruption vocabulary might be a major underlying influence on recent setbacks in human rights achievements, becoming the language of a new cycle of exclusion and democratic impoverishment.

4.2. From *Mensalão* to *Car Wash*: Societal Engagement to Take the Fight against Corruption to the Centre of Political Life

The idea of corruption is not only a defining concept for Brazilian sociology but also for Brazilian political history.[8] Daily accusations of public wealth deviation and mismanagement were haunting President Vargas when he 'left life to enter

[8] João Feres Júnior and Fábio Kerche, *Operação Lava Jato e a democracia brasileira* (Contracorrente, 2018) 254–56.

history' in August of 1954. The main discourse against Juscelino Kubitschek's developmental agenda was related to widespread corruption in infrastructure projects. In the 1960 general elections, conservative Jânio Quadros won the elections for President using a broom as his campaign symbol. According to his slogans and jingles, corruption and the corrupt needed to be swept out of Brazil. During his brief tenure as President, the Labour leader Joao Goulart, also known as Jango, also had to deal with accusations of corruption in his government, succumbing to a military coup in 1964. Months later, Juscelino Kubitschek, the heavy favourite in all polls for the elections set for 1965, lost his mandate as Senator owing to corruption charges, one of them being that he was bribed with an apartment in Ipanema beach, Rio de Janeiro. The general elections never took place and ultimately he had to go to exile. The first President elected directly by popular vote after the end of the military dictatorship won the elections calling himself the 'maharaja hunter', an allusion to his capacity to end favouritisms and privileges schemes. He ended up impeached by Congress after his brother disclosed his involvement in a corruption scandal. The case of buying votes in Parliament to pass the Constitutional re-election amendment was related to one of the most important rules of the Brazilian electoral system, but it was treated as a minor incident. It was only when the practice of granting deputies and senators a monthly payment for continuous support for executive proposals under the Workers' Party government became public that Brazilian society encountered 'the greatest corruption scandal of [its] history'.[9]

The *Mensalão* ('big monthly wage') case was discovered after an employee of the State-owned mail company was recorded seeking bribes in the name of one Congressman who was, up until that moment, a Workers' Party ally. In the face of the Government's refusal to protect him from the investigation, he decided to disclose a much bigger scheme that was run by almost all State-owned companies. The *Mensalão* case consisted of overpriced contracts in those State-owned companies and kickbacks to political party leaders in Congress in exchange for political support for the Government's legislative initiatives. Most of the money was destined for illegal electoral campaign financing in a sophisticated money laundering system that involved payments to political advertising companies in tax havens offshore. Discovered in 2005, the *Mensalão* scandal was the biggest criminal case ever heard by the Brazilian Supreme Court at the end of 2012. In total, 40 people were formally charged with corruption, money laundering, embezzlement, illegal money evasion, and criminal organisation. The group of defendants included 11 Congressmen, six from multiple political parties that were supporting the Government, and five from the Workers' Party itself, including the former President of the Deputies Chamber and the former Ministry Secretary of State and potential Presidential candidate for the Workers' Party. Three members of the Workers' Party directional board were also charged, including the National

[9] ibid 257–58.

Treasurer, the General Secretary, and the President. The lawsuit, registered as AP 470, contained around 50,000 pages, more than 600 witnesses were heard in 42 different cities, and the final trial in the Supreme Court lasted five months between the initial debates and the final ruling. In the end, 24 people were convicted. Some businesspersons directly involved in the overpriced contracts and bank directors that facilitated money laundering for the scheme were sentenced to more than 25 years' imprisonment. The main political figures involved in the scandal were also sentenced to tough penalties. The former President of the Workers' Party was convicted of corruption and criminal organisation and sentenced to six years and 11 months in prison and a fine. The former National Treasurer was convicted of the same crimes and sentenced to eight years and 11 months in jail and a fine. The former President of the Deputies Chamber was sentenced to nine years and four months' imprisonment and a fine, and the former Ministry Secretary of State, identified by the Public Prosecutors as the head of the criminal organisation, was convicted to 10 years and 10 months in prison and a fine.

When the case came to light, Brazil had recently ratified the Inter-American Convention Against Corruption in July 2002, and the UN Convention against Transnational Organized Crime in January 2004. The UN Convention against Corruption was only ratified by Brazil in June of 2005, one month after the scandal had already erupted. The legislative framework to enable the adoption of some new investigative weapons by the Brazilian authorities was not in place, and the institutional experience of mutual legal assistance between Brazilian law enforcement authorities and international investigative agencies was only starting to step up. In sum, the discourse on the importance of intensified efforts to fight corruption had the perfect scenario in which to flourish, but the machinery prescribed by the OECD, the Financial Action Task Force (FATF), the Organization of American States (OAS) and Transparency International had not been fully absorbed by judicial authorities and public prosecution agencies to allow for its deployment. The *Mensalão* case had great repercussions but were still insufficient to generate outcomes that could provide empirical evidence of Brazil's commitment to international standards in the fight against corruption. The third MESICIC (Mechanism for Follow-Up on the Implementation of the Inter-American Convention Against Corruption) Report, issued in September 2011, when the investigations were almost concluded, can be seen as an example of this ongoing pressure by the international community for results in the fight against corruption. Data provided by Brazilian authorities to show the adoption of measures to prevent favourable tax treatment for companies that violate anti-corruption laws, to prevent bribery of domestic and foreign officials, to tackle transnational bribery, or to criminalise illicit enrichment were considered either incomplete or non-existent. In the case of issues for which legislative measures were already in force, the absence of or the small number of cases brought by Brazilian authorities was considered a problem for implementation assessment. Regarding illicit enrichment, the absence of legislation was accompanied by a recommendation regarding the necessity to gauge the implementation of new legislation on the fight against corruption.

A constant in Recommendations 1.3 [35], 2.3 [121], 3.4.2 and 4.4.2 was the necessity to promote 'the selection and development of procedures and indicators' that could show results of the anti-corruption agenda.[10] The peer review report into the adoption of the UN Convention against Corruption by Brazil, produced by experts from Mexico and Haiti who visited Brazil in 2011, also reinforces the idea that the legislation enacted by Brazil to comply with international anti-corruption standards had to be followed by observable data on its implementation. The report acknowledges the existence of an 'advanced anti-corruption legal system' but states in item 2.3, related to provisions on the criminalisation of corruption, the necessity to develop 'its crime statistics system with a view to producing in a systematic manner consolidated statistical data in the whole anti-corruption criminal justice spectrum and for all stages of the relevant criminal proceedings'. Item 3.3, on international legal assistance, also stresses the importance 'to put in place – or improve – and render fully operational an information system, compiling in a systematic manner information on extradition and mutual legal assistance cases'.[11] The *Mensalão* case ruling seems to have produced an impact on the Transparency International (TI) Corruption Perceptions Index (CPI): between 2012 and 2014 Brazil reached its peak on the index, with a score oscillating between 43 and 42 in this period, which took Brazil to its historically highest ranking at position 69 among 180 countries. The TI analysis of corruption in the Americas in 2012 highlighted that 'the Mensalão case has shown that impunity does not prevail for cases of corruption. Sentences that added up to more than 250 years in prison were given to 25 out of the 37 individuals who were on trial, including prominent political figures'.[12] Yet the effects were quite temporary, and in 2015 Brazil's CPI score was back to the same level of 2011 (38 points) and the country was in position 76 of the ranking, three behind where it was in 2011. International anti-corruption bodies were asking Brazil to not only tell them what had been done to fight corruption, but they were also asking Brazil to show more tangible outcomes of the legislative packages introduced so far.

Some authors argue that there is a trend of continuity between the *Mensalão* ruling and the '*Car Wash*' operation. While some, like Prado and Machado, consider the efforts made in those cases as a 'turn toward the end of impunity',[13]

[10] OAS, *Mechanism for Follow-Up on the Implementation of the Inter-American Convention Against Corruption* (Organization of American States, 2011), www.oas.org/en/sla/dlc/mesicic/docs/mesicic3_bra_en.pdf.

[11] UNODC, *Review by Haiti and Mexico of the Implementation by Brazil of articles 15–42 of Chapter III. 'Criminalization and law enforcement' and articles 44–50 of Chapter IV. 'International cooperation' of the United Nations Convention against Corruption for the review cycle 2010-2015* (United Nations Office on Drugs and Crime, 2016), www.unodc.org/documents/treaties/UNCAC/CountryVisitFinalReports/2017_01_19_Brazil_Final_Country_Report.pdf.

[12] Transparency International, 'The Americas: Economies grow, democracies shrink. What does corruption have to do with it?' (Transparency International, 5 December 2012), https://blog.transparency.org/2012/12/05/the-americas-economies-grow-democracies-shrink-what-does-corruption-have-to-do-with-it/index.html.

[13] Mariana Mota Prado and Marta R de Assis Machado, 'Uso do Direito Penal para Combater a Corrupção: Potencial, Risos e Limitações da Operação Lava Jato' (2021) 17(2) *Revista Direito GV* 8.

others understand that the inquisitorial association between criminal prosecution authorities (police and public attorneys) and the judiciary that had traditionally labelled black people and the poor as 'bandits' was, in those cases, aimed at the criminalisation of politicians as the 'corrupt'.[14] Judicial authorities and elements of the press also appropriated the idea of continuity between one scandal and the other, justifying some different approaches that could take the results a little further. There was a sense, similar to the one found in the international anti-corruption movement, that, despite the long and deep investigations, and the harsh penalties imposed by the Supreme Court, the *Mensalão* case left something to be desired. As Fontainha and Lima outline, although the *Mensalão* case offered the political opposition the anti-corruption ethical banner, the discourse was not strong enough to impede the Workers' Party's wins in the 2006, 2010 or 2014 general elections.[15] In the authorised biography of the main lower-level judge from the Federal Regional Court Section in Curitiba in the *Car Wash* case, Hasselmann links the *Mensalão* and *Car Wash* cases.[16] The author presents them as variations of the way the Workers' Party governed, and that while their chief politician escaped prosecution in the first case, it was not going to happen in the second. As Barbabella stresses, when anti-corruption campaigns are able to 'fry big fish', they are more successful in motivating citizens.[17] The idea to use the social fatigue towards corruption created by the *Mensalão* case to fuel the *Car Wash* operation gained graphic representation in the press conference given by the *Car Wash* prosecution task force after filing the formal criminal charge against the Workers' Party leader and former President of the Republic.

The very idea of giving a press conference to present a criminal charge is, in itself, part of the strategy drawn from the international anti-corruption experience, movement and norms. A mundane task for the prosecution office, in filing an accusation that was still to be supported by proof and evidence under the rights to a full defence, the adversary system and the due process of law, received full media coverage. Public prosecutors and lower-level judicial authorities were determined to act on the mandate to 'raise public awareness' of corruption in Brazil – found in the UN Convention against Corruption (Article 13), and World Bank and Transparency International guidelines – to its extreme. According to that view, horizontal accountability, promoted by controlling agencies such as the

[14] Roberto Kant de Lima and Glaucia Maria Pontes Mouzinho, 'Produção e reprodução da tradição inquisitorial no Brasil: Entre delações e confissões premiadas' (2016) 9(3) *Dilemas – Revista de Estudos de Conflito e Controle Social*; L Pilau and R Azevedo, 'Os impactos da Operação Lava Jato na Polícia Federal brasileira' in JF Júnior and F Kerche (eds), *Operação Lava Jato e a democracia brasileira* (Contracorrente, 2018).

[15] Fernando Fontainha and Amanda Evelyn Cavalcanti de Lima, 'Judiciário e Crise Política no Brasil Hoje: Do Mensalão a Lava Jato' in JF Júnior and F Kerche (eds), *Operação Lava Jato e a democracia brasileira* (Contracorrente, 2018) 68.

[16] Joice Hasselmann, *Sérgio Moro – A história do homem por trás da operação que mudou o Brasil* (Universo dos Livros Editora, 2016) 20–1.

[17] Leticia Barbabella, 'Judicial Inconsistency and Citizen Anti-Corruption Demobilization: Evidence from Brazil' (2023) *Government & Opposition* 1–20.

Federal Public Prosecution Office and the judiciary, as seen in the *Mensalão* case, had to be deepened to the point where it would be translated into vertical electoral accountability. Audits, investigations, sanctions and fines imposed by controlling agencies had to be followed by a public desire to punish politicians and representatives labelled as corrupt with their vote. The idea of horizontal accountability being 'necessary but not sufficient' and the push for societal engagement in the fight against corruption had already been expressly advocated by Transparency International in a 2010 publication:

> While all forms of accountability are important to the integrity and quality of decision-making, this section examines particularly the role that 'bottom up' accountability (vertical accountability, broadly understood) can play in anti-corruption strategies. It argues that human rights perspective can deepen the understanding of 'vertical accountability' by emphasising the role that civil society and independent institutions can play in monitoring and influencing the behaviour of governments and government officials 'from below'.[18]

Here, we notice an entanglement between the two different elements of contemporary democracy, the universal and cosmopolitan element, represented by the idea of the fight against corruption as a proxy of democracy, and how it was brought to the scene to produce local, social mobilisation for the cause. There is nothing peculiar about this association. Democracy would, after all, be a result of this exact interaction. As seen in Chapter 2, the development of cash transfer programmes to address the problem raised by UN Millenium Development Goal No 1 sparked a very favourable social mobilisation for the entrenchment of those policies as rights. The adoption, by the 1988 Constitution, of the Alma Ata Convention lexicon on the right to health partially explains the appropriation of that right by the people and the high figures for litigation regarding State provision in that area. What is unprecedented in the case of anti-corruption international regimes is the intention to generate societal engagement as one of its mechanisms. This coupling between prosecution authorities and the media to generate social mobilisation was not 'circumstantial', as argued by Prado and Machado,[19] but a well-planned move, a pattern strategised by the international anti-corruption movement that would trigger in the Brazilian mind the deep-rooted corrupt essence of its society.

Intentions do not materialise themselves without agents. To embody the transit from a plethora of technocratic mechanisms to a social feeling, it was necessary to rely on a judicial actor who knew the *Mensalão* case and was well versed in the newest international trends on anti-corruption. In the huge *Mensalão* trial, some Supreme Court Justices had the assistance of lower-level judges, who specialised in criminal law, to prepare the case and their opinions.

[18] International Council on Human Rights Policy, 'Integrating Human Rights in the Anti-Corruption Agenda: Challenges, Possibilities and Opportunities' (2010), https://ssrn.com/abstract=1705396, 46.

[19] Prado and Machado (n 13) 9.

The judge that would later head the *Car Wash* lawsuits in Curitiba was one of them.[20] He had also taken part in the International Visitors Program of the US Department of State, promoted to provide training in the combating of money laundering, and was one of the main lecturers at the summit 'Illicit Financial Crimes', held in October 2009 in Rio de Janeiro.[21] The summit brought together judges, prosecutors and law enforcement authorities from Brazil and the United States, and it was lauded by the Brazilian participants as 'geared towards practical skills, not theory', which led them to request 'additional training on the collection of evidence, interrogation and interviewing courtroom skills, and the task force model'.[22] In an article published in 2004, entitled 'Considerations on the *Mani Pulite* Operation', the judge affirms that the conditions for the success of that operation in Italy were the progressive de-legitimisation of a corrupt political system and the legitimation of the '*Giudici raggazzini*', young lower-level judges recognised as strictly methodical and intolerant of corruption.[23] He also makes positive remarks on the use, by Italian authorities, of cautionary arrests, to show defendants the 'seriousness of the offences and the effectiveness of the prosecution', and on their alliance with the press.[24] In the conclusion, he points out that publicity and the support of public opinion are crucial for the fight against corruption and that Brazil had the 'institutional conditions needed for similar judicial action'.[25] That same judge had already headed up the *Banestado* case, in which fraudulent accounts in the Bank of the State of Parana were used for money laundering and currency evasion abroad by illegal currency exchange agents. When Alberto Youssef, one of the collaborators in the *Banestado* case, was caught for his involvement in illegal currency exchange and money laundering operations again in 2014, the opportunity presented itself. The difference between the two cases was that, while in the *Banestado* case the operations were very concentrated on bank accounts in the border city of Foz do Iguacu, in the State of Parana, in the second case, Alberto Youssef was working for political parties involved in overpriced contracts and corruption schemes in the massive State-owned Brazilian oil company, Petrobras.

To summarise, the investigations discovered a complex system of corruption that worked according to the following logic. Directors appointed by political parties headed three key departments of Petrobras. Those directors were responsible for granting overpriced contracts to a cartelised group of contractors and collecting kickbacks, which were then laundered by their financial operators and

[20] Vladimir Netto, *Lava Jato: O juiz Sergio Moro e os bastidores da operação que abalou o Brasil* (Primeira Pessoa, 2016) 44.

[21] Hasselmann (n 16) 28.

[22] Wikileaks, 'Brazil: Illicit Finance Conference Uses the T Word, Successfully' (30 October 2009), https://wikileaks.org/plusd/cables/09BRASILIA1282_a.html.

[23] Sergio Fernando Moro, 'Considerações sobre a operação mani pulite' (2004) 26 *Revista do Centro de Estudos Judiciários (CEJ)* 58.

[24] ibid 59.

[25] ibid 61.

redistributed to the directors themselves or the leaders of political parties. The *Car Wash* case was huge, and the infamous corruption scandal erupted from within Petrobras, the pride of the Workers' Party's developmental agenda. The company's capacity for oil prospecting in deep waters and the recently discovered oil base in the pre-salt layer of the Atlantic Ocean were an important part of the emancipatory propaganda of the Workers' Party government. Not without reason, the president of the Petrobras administrative board was ultimately elected twice to the Presidency of the Republic. The gravity and complexity of the criminal network demanded law enforcement authorities that specialised in those transnational criminal organisations. The political repercussions of the investigations provided a reason to make the anti-corruption movement bigger than the case itself. The main investigative efforts were undertaken by the *Car Wash* task force in Curitiba, and the figures are symptomatic of the size of the operation: there were 553 people charged with criminal offences, 295 cautionary arrests and 211 coercive questionings, 209 collaboration agreements reached between defendants and the prosecution authorities, 174 convictions, 723 international mutual legal assistance requests issued, and R$4.3 billion, destined for the public treasury or Petrobras itself, recovered.[26] The deployment of investigative methods promulgated by international anti-corruption agencies and norms, such as collaboration agreements and international mutual legal assistance to locate, freeze, seize and recover assets, was accompanied by intense publicity of all investigative initiatives and outcomes. All the warrants, arrests and diligent police work mentioned above were divided into 79 different operations spread over time, and the media covered every single action as if it belonged to an episode of a policing and political thriller. Fontainha and Lima refer to 'political-judicial incidents' whereby strict judicial/procedural acts were combined with publicity and advertising with clear political repercussions.[27] The authors cite as examples of that type of hybrid criminal litigation the securing of collaboration agreements and the leaking of their content to the press, the 'show business' media coverage of a simple coercive questioning order, and the aforementioned press conference after the filing of a criminal charge. The *Car Wash* case offered a platform from which judicial and prosecution authorities could build up the idea of societal awareness of corruption and gain the support of public opinion for the investigations.

In 2015, with the investigations already in course, the Federal Public Prosecution office decided to promote two broad campaigns on the fight against corruption. The *#CorrupcaoNao*, focused on the internet and social media, was a joint initiative with the Ibero-American Public Prosecution Association (AIAMP) and 20 National Public Prosecution offices, aimed at spreading the simple idea of the rejection of any kind of corruption, from day-to-day situations such as jumping a queue or bribing a traffic officer to major deviations of public funds. The second

[26] Ministério Público Federal (MPF), 'Caso Lava Jato', www.mpf.mp.br/grandes-casos/lava-jato.
[27] Fontainha and Lima (n 15) 69.

campaign, '*10 Medidas Contra a Corrupção*' ('10 Measures Against Corruption'), was much more audacious and targeted changes in Brazilian legislation. It sought the approval of a package of legislative reforms that would increase effectiveness in the investigation and punishment of corruption. The campaign was launched in March 2015 based on 'the experience of the Car Wash prosecution task force in Curitiba'. Measures 1 and 2, for instance, related to the protection of whistleblowers and the criminalisation of illicit enrichment of public agents, respectively, were aligned with recommendations from international anti-corruption agencies, specially the MESICIC reports. Measures 3, 4 and 9 encompassed the elevation of corruption to the status of a heinous crime, limitations on the constitutional right of *habeas corpus* and the utilisation of cautionary arrest as a coercive means for the recovery of distorted funds.

Despite their disputable constitutionality, the '10 Measures Against Corruption' received major investment, with the production of booklets, t-shirts, banners, billboards, a magazine, car stickers and celebrity support. As the Public Prosecution office does not have the standing to propose legislative bills to the National Congress, all that investment was necessary to raise public awareness and, especially, draw signatures. According to the constitutional rule in Article 61, para 2, a bill of popular initiative can only be accepted by the Chamber of Deputies if it is 'subscribed by at least one per cent of the national electorate, distributed throughout at least five states, with not less than three-tenths of one per cent of the voters in each of them'. In practical terms, the constitutional rule requires almost 1.5 million signatures to a bill. Considering the additional requirement of a minimum standard of regional distribution, it demands a level of national mass mobilisation quite difficult to achieve. After the enactment of the 1988 Constitution, only four bills proposed by popular initiative were approved by Congress. In March 2016, the Federal Public Prosecution Office had collected 2,028,263 signatures after one year of the campaign that involved 1,016 institutions such as churches, universities, associations, companies and NGOs mobilising volunteers across the country around the idea of the fight against corruption. The campaigns were fuelled by the constant participation of the Curitiba *Car Wash* prosecution task force in seminars, awards and think tanks, in which the proposals were legitimised by the results the operation was delivering in homeopathic doses. The discourses were always in the context that the *Car Wash* achievements were the result of this massive mobilisation of public opinion against corruption. In October 2015, the XXXII National Summit of Federal Prosecutors in Fortaleza had as its theme 'Societal Control in the Net of Corruption Fight'.[28] During the ceremony that celebrated the delivery of the '10 Measures Against Corruption' bills to Congress, the Chief Prosecutor of the *Car Wash* task force emphasised that 'today we say enough of corruption not

[28] Netto (n 20) 290.

only with words but with concrete action … the walk to the National Congress is a civic one and we want to make clear that the main role was played by society'.

Indeed, the campaigns to raise awareness of corruption marched in step with operations that enforced judicial decisions that were uncovering, layer by layer, a massive corruption network involving big companies, influential businesspersons and the core of the Workers' Party government. At that moment, a lower-level judge from a Section of the Regional Federal Court in Curitiba was bringing to their knees the owners of huge multinational contractors and political figures close to the centre of power in Brasilia. In November 2014, in an operation called '*Juízo Final*' ('Last Judgement or Doomsday'), executives of big contractors such as OAS, Engevix, UTC, Quiroz Galvao and Mendes Jr were provisorily arrested. In April 2015, operation '*A Origem*' ('The Origin') culminated in the arrests of former deputies, Pedro Correa, Luiz Argôlo and André Vargas, who had been an influential member of the Workers' Party and Vice-President of the Deputies Chamber. Five days after that, the National Treasurer of the Workers' Party, his wife and his daughter were also arrested, and he revealed that most of the misappropriated money was destined for the 2010 electoral campaign. In June of that year, operation '*Erga Omnes*' resulted in the imprisonment of the presidents of Odebrecht and Andrade Gutierrez, two multinational Brazilian contractors that combined had more than 300,000 employees around the world.[29] The indiscriminate use of temporary arrests and cautionary detention challenged the Supreme Court's established case law that limits those types of drastic measures, stressing principles of human dignity and the right to freedom. There are many decisions of the Brazilian Supreme Court establishing that generic claims for imprisonment for the convenience of a criminal investigation or reasons of public order are not sufficient reasons to arrest someone before their guilt is proven. In that set of rulings, the Brazilian Supreme Court rejects even assessments on the gravity of the crime supposedly committed by the defendant, or its social repercussions, as grounds for provisory or cautionary arrest, as provisioned by the American Convention on Human Rights.[30] The link between those provisory arrests, their length and the resultant reaching of collaboration agreements also drew the attention of the Supreme Court. In 2015, the *Supremo Tribuna Federal* (STF) acknowledged the importance of encouraging defendants to collaborate with criminal prosecution through penalty mitigation agreements, according to the Palermo (UN Convention against Transnational Organized Crime) and Merida Conventions (UN Convention against Corruption) provisions. But, in the same ruling, it stated that it is illegitimate, ie unconstitutional, to adopt personal cautionary measures, especially temporary or provisory arrests, as a means to

[29] Walfrido Warde, *O espetáculo da corrupção: Como um sistema corrupto e o modo de combatê-lo estão destruindo o país* (Leya, 2018) 45.

[30] eg STF [2004] HC 84.662, STF [2006] HC 86.915, STF [2006] HC 88.025, STF [2007] HC 90.074, STF [2008] HC 91.386, etc.

obtain the collaboration or the confession of the person under investigation.[31] The multitude of coercive questionings issued by *Car Wash* judicial authorities, used to take people into custody for a simple hearing or deposition, also led to a reaction from the Supreme Court. On 4 March 2016, 15 heavily armed men of the Federal Police elite troop in a tactical operations command van were responsible for the enforcement of the coercive questioning of the former President of the Republic and the main historical leader of the Workers' Party. The operation was broadcast from helicopters surrounding his apartment early that morning. He was ultimately taken for deposition in the Sao Paulo central airport and released hours after that, but the sense that evidence was mounting against him remained. Even enthusiasts of anti-corruption interventions acknowledged that the spectacle showcased by the task force on that specific occasion arguably traversed the borderline between aggressive prosecution and abusive judicial behaviour.[32] In 2018, the STF ultimately struck down the legislation that allowed coercive questioning to force defendants to make depositions, considering it incompatible with their fundamental rights.[33]

The succession of arrests, seizures of assets, coercive questionings and reward for collaboration agreements were interpreted by public opinion as a bold, technically sound, and heroic effort from a new generation of public prosecutors and judges willing to take the fight against corruption to the very end. In contrast, allegations of human rights violations and due process of law contraventions by the *Car Wash* task force were seen as a backlash from politically compromised organisations and institutions. That social consensus on the need to bring corrupt politicians to justice was fostered by the way the media covered the scandal. In a study that comprised 9,820 texts produced by the three main newspapers and the main TV news channel in Brazil between 2014 and 2017, including articles, editorials, headlines, columns and reports, Junior et al found that 20% of all media coverage in that period was dedicated to the *Car Wash* case.[34] Specifically focusing on editorials, as vehicles to express their institutional opinion to the public, the number of pieces that analysed the *Car Wash* case corresponded, on average, to one editorial every three days in each newspaper (*Estadão*, *Folha de São Paulo*, and *O Globo*) over the three years observed, or one editorial per day, every day, over the whole year, on the *Car Wash* probe alone. A similar figure was found when the analysis focused on headlines, which showed an informational storm around the subject. The authors set out the occurrence of a form of mutualism between the press and

[31] STF [2015] HC 127.186.

[32] Mariana Mota Prado and Marta R de Assis Machado, 'Turning Corruption Trials into Political Tools in the Name of Transparency: the Lava Jato Case' in S Botero, Daniel M Brinks and Ezequiel A Gonzalez-Ocantos (eds), *The Limits of Judicialization: From Progress to Backlash in Latin America* (Cambridge University Press, 2022) 269.

[33] STF [2018] ADPF 395; STF [2018] ADPF 444.

[34] João Feres Júnior, Eduardo Barbarela and Natasha Bachini, 'Lava Jato e a Mídia' in JF Júnior and F Kerche (eds), *Operação Lava Jato e a democracia brasileira* (Contracorrente, 2018).

the judicial authorities. The former can communicate to the public but lack the power to make their preferences prevail; the latter have the power to enforce decisions but lack channels to communicate their intentions.[35] The synergy between lower-level prosecutors, judicial authorities and the media around the *Car Wash* case found in the anti-corruption discourse a point of convergence. The main actors behind the case were valuable sources of information to journalists who would praise their achievements and fearless conduct of the case. The judge from the 13th Federal Criminal Court in the Regional Federal Section of Curitiba, Parana was elected 'Personality of the Year' in 2015 in the '*Faz Diferenca*' ('Makes a Difference') awards, sponsored by the *O Globo* newspaper, which is part of to the biggest communications network in Brazil.[36] He was also awarded the 'Brazilian of the Year' prize, offered in 2016 by the *Editora Tres*, the publisher of one of the main Brazilian weekly political magazines. The media anointment was not limited nationally; in the same year, he travelled to New York to receive the honour of being nominated as one of the 100 most influential people in the world, according to *Time Magazine*. Also in 2016, the *Car Wash* taskforce received the Anti-Corruption Award from Transparency International.

The most dramatic episode in the alliance between the *Car Wash* authorities and the media to mobilise public opinion also occurred in March 2016 and had major political repercussions. Tape recordings of intercepted phone calls captured a conversation between the President and the former President of the Republic about the possible appointment of the latter as Ministry Secretary of State. Assuming that it was a plot to grant the former President jurisdictional privilege and take the case out of the 13th Federal Criminal Court of Curitiba, the judge almost immediately released the content to the press, stating the primacy of publicity over the defendant's right to privacy or procedural secrecy, as it was more important for the people to know 'what politicians do in the shadows'.[37] As the media broadcast the audio file during the afternoon of 16 March 2016, thousands of millions took to the streets to protest against the government and ask for the President's impeachment. An impeachment procedure had been accepted by the President of the Deputies Chamber in December 2015 in a clear personal reprisal against the head of government for the fact the *Car Wash* investigations found connections between him and a department of Petrobras. The charge against the President was based on budgetary manoeuvres made by the government to delay payments to State-owned banks in order to improve fiscal balances and reduce public debt, in a sort of informal loan that would violate the Fiscal Responsibility Statute (Law 101). Identical actions had been carried out by all Presidents since 1994, and it had never been considered an offence before. The allegations were

[35] ibid.
[36] Netto (n 20) 177–79.
[37] Fontainha and Lima (n 15) 75.

very technical, and the procedure had been dormant for more than three months until 17 March 2016. One day after the leaking of the taped conversation between the two Workers' Party's leaders and the protests, the impeachment committee was finally installed in the Deputies Chamber. The influence of those events in the impeachment procedure was undeniable. The judge's biographer described his action as 'Moro's Check Mate', concluding that after that decision the impeachment of the President was unavoidable and that 'it created the collective feeling that would speed up the impeachment process'.[38] Regarding the March rallies, Netto remarks that

> the people on the streets were shouting against corruption, the President Dilma, the former President Lula and the Workers' Party. But it was not a manifestation in favour of any political party, since Senator Aécio Neves and São Paulo Governor Geraldo Alckmin, both from the Brazilian Social Democracy Party, were hostilely received in Paulista Avenue. The greatest honours of the day were to Sergio Moro, the Public Prosecution office, and the Federal Police.[39]

Later that month, the Supreme Court unanimously ruled the judge's decision to publicise the audio recordings unconstitutional on the grounds that he lacked jurisdiction to decide on investigations that involved the President of the Republic. The decision was also overruled as illegal as the judge disregarded legal provisions that forbid the publication of intercepted conversations, especially when they have no connection to the criminal investigation. In that ruling, the leading Supreme Court Justice affirmed 'at this point, we must acknowledge, the practical effects of the undue divulgation of the intercepted phone calls taped are irreversible'.[40]

Even considering that the government was struggling with an economic recession, the anti-corruption discourse was an element in the destabilisation and delegitimisation of the whole political spectrum, profoundly affecting governance and becoming an important, if not determinant, underlying cause of the 2016 Presidential impeachment. It is important to note that the formal charges against the President did not involve any accusation of corruption but a controversial budgetary allocation. In an analysis of the votes of the Deputies during the impeachment admissibility trial, Soares and Recuero found that the discussions were distanced from the President's responsibility for financial mismanagement.[41] In a list of the 12 prevailing concepts expressed by Congress representatives in that session, from those who voted in favour of and against impeachment, the most recurring words were 'vote', 'Brazil', 'president', 'people', 'Dilma', 'impeachment' and 'respect'. The most common word with the highest

[38] Hasselmann (n 16) 22–23, 55.
[39] Netto (n 20) 361.
[40] STF [2016] Rcl 23.457 MC.
[41] Felipe Soares and Raquel Recuero, 'A Argumentação dos Deputados na Votação do Processo de Impeachment de Dilma Rousseff' (2018) 1 *Estudos em Comunicação* 72.

semantic value used by those who endorsed the premature end of the President's mandate was 'corruption', repeated 43 times.

According to Teorell et al, the very first formative component of democracy is the 'decisiveness of elections', which is defined as the capacity of elected officials to effectively exercise power after elections.[42] Any disruption of tenure led by the defeated opposition represents an obvious threat to that first basic element of any democratic system. For all the facts summarised above, it is fair to assert that the Brazilian National Congress blatantly ignored the result of the 2014 general elections two years later. The Congressional impeachment of the President was strongly influenced by the successive operations, cautionary arrests, freezing of accounts abroad, collaboration agreements and media coverage of the *Car Wash* corruption scandal. The impeachment of President Dilma Roussef happened due to a multitude of different factors, one of which, maybe the most decisive, was the massive anti-corruption campaign put forward by the law enforcement authorities in the *Car Wash* case.

It is possible to affirm that the anti-corruption agenda propelled the *Car Wash* case, used it as a successful demonstration of its necessity and effectiveness, but was progressively gaining terrain to present itself as more than just a case. It was becoming an ideal, a whole new political vocabulary that entered the scene in deposing an elected President from her mandate but was going to stick to the public sphere for much longer. It would also have great electoral repercussions. The anti-corruption movement that played an important role in removing the Workers' Party from government was about to be decisive in the upcoming 2018 general elections.

The former President of the Republic, Luiz Inácio Lula da Silva (or Lula), was being investigated for supposedly receiving a beachfront apartment in Guarujá and a country house in Atibaia as bribes from contractors. Less than one year after the impeachment of President Dilma Roussef, the judge in the 13th Federal Criminal Court of Curitiba convicted him of corruption and money laundering and imposed a sentence of nine years and six months in prison. The conviction elicited one of the most enthusiastic endorsements from Transparency International (TI). The chair of the TI Board, José Ugaz, asserted at the time that the decision was 'a significative sign that the rule of law is working and that there is no impunity, even for the powerful'.[43] The arbitrary coercive questioning that made a special force of the Federal Police take the defendant into custody for questioning, broadcast live, was a distant incident to be forgotten. The leaking to the press of the defendant's private conversation for political purposes had been already censored by the Supreme Court. Doubts as to the reasons why a

[42] Jan Teorell et al, 'Measuring Polyarchy Across the Globe, 1900–2017' (2018) 54(1) Studies in Comparative International Development.

[43] Transparency International, 'The Conviction of Former Brazilian President Lula for Corruption Shows the Strength of the Judiciary' (TI, 13 July 2017), www.transparency.org/en/press/the-conviction-of-former-brazilian-president-lula-for-corruption-shows-the.

lower-level regional federal judge in the Southern State of Parana should have jurisdiction over a corruption case related to a public mandate exercised in Brasilia, by someone who had always lived in the State of São Paulo, where the contractors' headquarters and the real estates indicated as being the proceeds of a bribe were situated, seemed like just a minor technicality. Besides that, the links between those charges and Petrobras were not very clear, not to mention the fact that the State-owned company site is in Rio de Janeiro and most of the overpriced contracts were related to the construction of oil refineries and other works thousands of miles from Parana. The tactics in taking legal action against someone to the best battlefield, where the probability of a favourable decision is higher, is called 'forum shopping' and is considered one of the manifestations of what the literature identifies as 'lawfare'.[44]

Despite the existence of such an intention on the part of the public prosecutors, it is hard to think of a judge in Brazil who, by that point, had gathered so many attributes in pushing forward the anti-corruption banner and using the case for it. The judge of the 13th Federal Criminal Court of Curitiba, Parana, had ruled in the *Banestado* case and been the leading authority in the '*Farol da Colina*' ('Lighthouse on the Hill') operation, in which he had granted 215 search and seizure orders and 123 arrest warrants.[45] He was recognised as one of the most experienced and well-trained judicial authorities in Brazil in anti-transnational financial crimes norms and procedures, such as international corruption and money laundering regimes. He had personally participated in the *Mensalão* trial and shared the sense of disappointment in the face of the incapacity of the scandal to change the political scenario. He had accumulated institutional expertise second to none in the Brazil judicial system and, as an admirer of *Mani Pulite* and the Italian judge Giovanni Falcone, he was willing to use it in a massive anti-corruption crusade.

In 2018, the former President of the Republic was about to be imprisoned after an ordinary appeal court upheld the controversial verdict that sentenced him to more than nine years in prison. He appealed to the Supreme Court, invoking the presumption of innocence clause and the right to exhaust all appeals before starting his sentence. The court session was preceded by huge public demonstrations in at least 23 state capitals of Brazil, with millions of people taking to the streets to support the arrest. On the same day, a tweet from the National Army General Villas Boas said that the Army shared the 'nation's repudiation of impunity', being very aware of its 'institutional mission'. The Supreme Court decided by a very tight split decision – six Justices against five – that immediate imprisonment, even with appeals still being processed by the Superior Court of Justice and the Supreme Court itself, did not offend the Constitution.[46] The decision of

[44] Cristiano Zanin Martins, Valeska Teixeira Zanin Martins and Rafael Valim, *Lawfare: uma introdução* (Editora Contracorrente, 2019) 95–99.

[45] Marjorie Marona and Fábio Kerche, 'From the Banestado Case to Operation Car Wash: Building an Anti-Corruption Institutional Framework in Brazil' (2021) 64(3) *Dados, Rio de Janeiro* 8, 22.

[46] STF [2018] HC 152.752.

3 April 2018 ultimately resulted in the former President's arrest and ultimately blocked him from participating in person in the 2018 general elections, although he was considered frontrunner for the Presidency by polls even after his arrest. In August of the same year, ignoring an interim measure issued by the UN Office of the High Commissioner for Human Rights (OHCHR) to guarantee his participation in the general elections for which he was a heavy favourite, the Superior Electoral Court rejected the registration of the former President's candidacy. The Electoral Court decided to rule Lula out of the elections based on his conviction for crimes against the public administration, first imposed by the 13th Federal Criminal Court of Curitiba, Parana, and upheld by a collegiate panel of judges in the Federal Regional Court of Porto Alegre.

With its main historical leader out of contention, the Workers' Party appointed the former Ministry of Education and former mayor of São Paulo as its candidate. Under heavy accusations of being responsible for the *Mensalão* and *Car Wash* corruption scandals, the Workers' Party was striving to increase turnout for its candidate in the second vote. Six days before the elections, the 13th Federal Criminal Court of Curitiba released parts of Antônio Palocci's deposition to the press. Palocci was a former Workers' Party congressional representative, Economy Minister under Lula's government, and Ministry Secretary of State under Dilma Roussef's presidency, and in the footage broadcasted by all TV channels during the election week, he affirmed that both former Presidents knew about the Petrobras corruption scheme. He had been in 'provisory' imprisonment for more than one year and six months and had signed two different collaboration agreements with law enforcement authorities before he was sentenced to more than 12 years in prison by the judge of the 13th Federal Criminal Court in Curitiba. After his conviction, he decided to enter a third collaboration agreement and gave a deposition in which he confirmed all the investigatory threads followed by the public prosecutors. Parts of that statement were released and broadcast on television days before the general elections. The goal to translate horizontal into vertical accountability was about to be achieved. A far-right retired captain of the Brazilian army with a strong discourse on 'no tolerance' of corruption was elected President, his Party jumped from one to 52 representatives in the Deputies Chamber, and the Workers' Party lost two seats in the Senate and 13 seats in the Deputies Chamber. The judge of the 13th Federal Criminal Court of Curitiba resigned and was appointed the new President's Ministry of Justice with the mission to push forward the anti-corruption agenda.

Imported to produce democratic leverage, the international anti-corruption agenda, with its new investigative mechanisms and the ideal of social engagement in the fight against corruption, had a direct impact on Brazilian core democratic institutions and procedures. It was an important underlying cause for the premature end of a President's mandate, and a major factor in the outcome of the 2018 general elections. It could be argued that such events, yet traumatic, were steps towards more accountability, the consolidation of the rule of law and, thus, some sort of democratic growing pains. The fact that almost all the decisions that ultimately resulted in the exclusion of the former President from the general elections have been recently overturned shows that the anti-corruption discourse was probably just the means for an episodic anti-democratic intervention in Brazil. In November 2019, the Supreme Court overturned its understanding of the presumption of innocence clause once again. In the ruling of ADCs 43, 44 and 54, in a close decision – six Justices against five for the opposite thesis – the Court affirmed the constitutionality of the Criminal Procedural Code requirement for a specific reasoned decision for the imprisonment of a convicted person when any type of appeal is pending, which ultimately led to the former President's release. More recently, the Supreme Court declared that the 13th Federal Criminal Court of Curitiba, Parana had no jurisdiction to decide the criminal charges of corruption and money laundering against the former President, on the basis that the links between the facts imputed to him and the corruption schemes found in Petrobras were very blurry and uncertain.[47] The Supreme Court also decided that the 13th Federal Criminal Court's judge was biased and could not rule in the cases against the former President, as there was evidence that he worked in cooperation with the prosecution authorities, violating his impartiality and due process of law clauses.[48] The Supreme Court also decided to exclude the content of Antonio Palocci's collaboration agreements from all charges against the former President as it was included as evidence by the judge himself after the end of the probatory phase on the eve of the 2018 elections.[49]

Those decisions nullified all convictions that prevented the former President from exercising his political rights but were far from removing anti-corruption from Brazil's political centre stage. The way the international anti-corruption agenda was massively incorporated in Brazil gave it a grip over the whole public sphere that goes beyond a singular case. As Freixo and Machado argue, mass street protests and the occupation of public spaces that started in 2013 with a diffuse claim for lower public transport fares and more jobs were mixed with conservative agendas and religious groups that supported ideas such as nationalism, anti-politics, anti-democracy and anti-communism. However, they found a common ethos in the anti-corruption discourse, personified by the heroism shown by the *Car Wash* prosecution and judicial authorities.[50]

The fight against corruption penetrated the social fabric and set profound roots in the popular imagination. The societal engagement in the fight against corruption, championed by international anti-corruption norms, agencies and

[47] STF [2021] AgR HC 193.726.
[48] STF [2021] HC 164.493.
[49] STF [2020] HC 163.943.
[50] Adriano de Freixo and Rosana Pinheiro Machado, *Brasil em transe: Bolsonarismo, nova direita e desdemocratização* (Oficina Raquel, 2019).

guidelines, became a social poison. The fight against corruption became an obsession with its heroes and villains. The *Car Wash* public prosecutors were literally on the billboards, in the image of the judge of the 13th Federal, on protesters' t-shirts and banners, and even in the shape of a gigantic inflatable superhero set up in front of the National Congress. The history of the operation became a book and then a *Netflix* series, called '*O Mecanismo*' ('The Mechanism'), with two seasons of eight episodes each.[51] The fight against corruption was and has been everywhere, especially in the minds of Brazilians.

The National Confederation of Industry (CNI), the main syndicate of industrialists and company owners in Brazil, produces an annual public survey on the main problems the country faces at the year-end and the priorities for the year to come. In 2013, the main problems were healthcare, mentioned in 59% of responses, public security/violence, found in 39% of answers, followed by drugs and education, cited in 33% and 31% of the questionnaires, respectively. Corruption came in fifth, mentioned in 27% of the responses.[52] In 2014, the first year of the *Car Wash* operation, corruption was identified as the third gravest problem in Brazil, being referred to in 62% of the answers, behind only drugs and violence.[53] In 2015, the second year of *Car Wash*, when the cinematographic sequence of arrests, collaboration agreements, money freezing, seizure and recovery peaked, corruption reached the top of the ranking, named in 65% of answers as the most important problem in Brazil. It was followed by drugs, violence and the inefficiency/impunity of the justice system, all of which can be considered problems linked to corruption itself.[54] In 2016, the year of the impeachment and the conviction of the former President of the Republic, corruption was perceived as the joint second worst problem in Brazil, being pointed to in 32% of answers, along with healthcare. Both issues were behind unemployment, named as the most serious problem in 43% of the responses.[55] After that, corruption never left the top three public concerns in Brazil. In 2017, it again took second position as the worst problem to be faced, referred to in 55% of questionnaires, only 1% less than unemployment.[56] In 2018, it was identified as the third worst problem in Brazil, being present in 40% of questionnaires.[57] Oliveira and Moisés' study shows how intolerance towards corruption became an obsession for Brazilians. In the

[51] Netto (n 20).
[52] CNI, *Pesquisa CNI-Ibope: Problemas e Prioridades do Brasil para 2014* (Confederação Nacional da Indústria, 2014).
[53] CNI, *Retratos da Sociedade Brasileira: problemas e prioridades* (Confederação Nacional da Indústria, 2015).
[54] CNI, *Retratos da Sociedade Brasileira: problemas e prioridades para 2016* (Confederação Nacional da Indústria, 2016).
[55] CNI, *Retratos da Sociedade Brasileira: problemas e prioridades* (Confederação Nacional da Indústria, 2017).
[56] CNI, *Retratos da Sociedade Brasileira* (Confederação Nacional da Indústria, 2018).
[57] ibid.

Latinobarometro 2018, 58% of Brazilians said no level of corruption should be tolerated even if it was to solve a national problem. The second highest percentage in the region was in Colombia, where 27% of respondents demonstrated similar levels of intolerance.[58] As Netto reflects, the 'electrifying succession of events' during the *Car Wash* operation meant that 'from March 2014 to March 2016 it went from the prosecution of a renowned thief to the rules of the exercise of power in Brazil'.[59]

The fight against corruption absolutely dominated the political debate, emptying it of deeper discussion and transforming elections into a wide police inquiry in which every elector voted as if they were a law enforcement authority. Anderson and Heywood had already warned of a similar reduction of the political scene to a moral contest in East European countries such as Ukraine, Czechia, Bulgaria and Slovakia.[60] According to the authors, the persistent idea of corruption, and the fight against corruption, led to wide political distrust, which created a scenario of 'protest-vote' democracies, prone to the rise of 'anti-system' radicals and populists. Although that description resembles the events summarised above, the presence of corruption and the fight against corruption in the Brazilian public sphere seems to be even more profound. The same *Latinobarometro* survey explored by Oliveira and Moisés revealed that, while the average percentage of interviewees manifesting anti-democratic sentiment in the region was 35%, in Brazil that percentage was 44% in 2018.[61] The subtle change that Transparency International made to its definition of corruption helped in the overflow of anti-corruption language to other issues and policy evaluation. To curb critiques that its efforts were mainly concentrated on corruption in public administration while there was a certain complacency towards corruption in the private sector, Transparency International slightly changed its concept of corruption. What was once the 'the abuse of public office for private gain' became the 'misuse of entrusted power for private benefit', which loosens the definition to encompass any type of misallocation of resources or favouritism, not only for a bribe or financial profit, but also for familial or political reasons.[62] In the next three sections of this chapter, we will address how the obsession with audits, controls, and this open rhetoric on the necessity to prevent the concession of undue benefits and privileges to political allies or in exchange for political support, have colonised and dominated human rights policies addressed in chapter 2, bringing about a new cycle of exclusion and democratic decay.

[58] Emmanuel Nunes de Oliveira and José Álvaro Moisés, 'Corruption in the Perception of Brazilian Society: Persistence and Resilience' (2023) 29(2) *Revista do CESOP* 286.

[59] Netto (n 20) 15.

[60] S Anderson and PM Heywood, 'Anti-corruption as a risk to democracy: on the unintended consequences of international anti-corruption campaigns' in L de Sousa, PJ Larmour and B Hindess (eds), *Governments, NGOs and Anti-Corruption: The New Integrity Warriors* (Routledge, 2008) 41–42.

[61] Oliveira and Moisés (n 58) 292.

[62] Steven Sampson, 'Anti-corruption: Who Cares?' in S Arvidsson (ed), *Challenges in Managing Sustainable Business* (Palgrave Macmillan, 2018) 286.

4.3. The Fight against Poverty and Hunger and Conditional Cash Transfer Programmes: Fraud and the 'Nitcomb' Operation

The international anti-corruption regime was imported into Brazil to produce a definitive democratic consolidation. Nevertheless, the triumph of its mechanisms and logic drastically interfered in politics to the point that it interrupted a legitimate mandate and unbalanced general elections. As argued above, this intervention affected core democratic institutions and procedures. But, as also underlined earlier, democracy is about free, fair, periodic and competitive elections, but not just that. There is a myriad of social, cultural and economic rights that work as conditions for the possibility of democracy itself. Democracy, in that sense, presupposes the increasing capacity of the people to effectively participate in the life of the society. Citizenship involves being acknowledged, being heard, making behaviour and informed opinion accepted and meaningful for the collective destiny, and that can only be achieved through inclusion. In chapter 2, we analysed how conditional cash transfer programmes (CCTs), intended to aid people in situations of extreme poverty and hunger, contributed to the appraisal of Brazil's as one of the most successful international examples of the fight against hunger and misery. It does not mean that the CCT programmes were free from critique. The main argument against them relies on the idea of clientelism, a form of political corruption. This type of reasoning is found in studies, such as that of Manzetti and Wilson, in which they seek correlations between government effectiveness, corruption perception and government support, implying a tendency for the poor and uneducated to support corrupt governments since they are treated as clients of social benefits.[63]

In an ethnographic study carried out in a small town in the State of Ceará, Eiró explores the political use of CCT programmes in local elections. His intention is to identify how 'brokers persist in diverting public goods for private purposes' or the 'use of public resources for electoral purposes', which resembles Transparency International vocabulary on corruption.[64] Although his study shows compelling evidence of political packaging of the local social assistance service and pressure for electoral support by some of the social agents, the clientelism cycle was inhibited by political opposition monitoring, a Federal Police operation to guarantee the integrity of the programme registration system, and federal officers' supervision, especially from the Office of the Comptroller General (CGU). The attempt to divert the federal cash transfer programmes also faced resistance

[63] Luigi Manzetti and Carole J Wilson, 'Why Do Corrupt Governments Maintain Public Support?' (2007) 40(8) *Comparative Political Studies*.

[64] Flavio Eiró, 'Anti-poverty Programs and Vote-Buying Strategies: Lessons from Northeast Brazil' in I Kubbe and A Engelbert (eds), *Corruption and Norms: Why Informal Rules Matter* (Springer International Publishing, 2017) 136.

from some social agents and drew a social reaction that ultimately resulted in the electoral defeat of the incumbent mayoral candidate.[65] His study demonstrates that descriptions that devalue political participation from the poor are not quite accurate. In fact, the clientelism critique of CCT programmes is biased by *a priori* discrimination against the poor as corrupt or bandits. If the poor tend to support political parties that favour the improvement of CCT programmes, it means nothing more than political mobilisation around candidates that better represent their interests. That is exactly what the Federation of Industries of the State of Sao Paulo (FIESP) does before every Presidential election. The difference is that the former is labelled as 'clientelism' or 'political corruption', while the latter is simply advertised as 'political support'.

The idea that the '*Bolsa Família*' was plagued by distortions was present in the opposition discourse during the 2018 general elections campaign. The challenging candidate, Jair Bolsonaro, affirmed in an interview given between the first and second vote turnouts that 'the way to find resources to do many things is to combat fraud, fight corruption, even within the *Bolsa Família.* We believe that a third, approximately 30% are benefits granted without any criteria. People that don't need to receive this.'[66] In November 2018, speaking as President-elect, he affirmed that every social programme would be submitted to an audit from the first day of his administration.[67] The priority on audits aimed at identifying frauds in the programme was not a new idea. In November 2016, the government of President Michel Temer carried out the 'nitcomb' operation that blocked 654,000 benefits and cancelled 469,000 transfers.[68] The coverage of the programme shrank steadily from that moment until it reached its lowest figure in the decade in July 2017, with 12,640,740 families registered. After that, the number increased again, until the government elected in 2018 implemented another round of audits and cuts. In December 2018, 14,142,764 families were reached by *Bolsa Família*; in March 2020 that number was 13,058,228 households, the second lowest coverage figure since October 2011 when the programme surpassed 13,000,000 households for the first time in history. Total public expenditure on the programme also fell from R$2,641,616,078 in December 2018 to R$2,505,415,999 in March 2020. If we consider that the government decided to add an extra benefit, corresponding to another month's allowance, for each family, the reduction in total expenditure reveals a considerable diminution of the cash transfer programme.

[65] ibid 140.

[66] Talita Fernandes, 'Bolsonaro diz que há fraude em 30% do Bolsa Família', *Folha de São Paulo* (8 October 2018), www1.folha.uol.com.br/poder/2018/10/bolsonaro-diz-que-ha-fraude-em-30-do-bolsa-familia.shtml.

[67] Agência Brasil, 'Presidente eleito diz que programas sociais passarão por auditoria', *Agência Brasil* (24 November 2018), https://agenciabrasil.ebc.com.br/politica/noticia/2018-11/bolsonaro-diz-que-programas-sociais-passarao-por-auditoria.

[68] Ministério da Cidadania, 'Programa Bolsa Família – quantidade de famílias e valores (até outubro/2021)' (Secretaria de Avaliação e Gestão da Informação), https://aplicacoes.cidadania.gov.br/vis/data3/data-explorer.php.

From March 2020, the historical series was disrupted by the Covid-19 pandemic. Under pressure to aid families that were rapidly losing any income capacity, the number of beneficiaries rose sharply to reach 14,524,150 families in March 2021, when the amount transferred reached R$2,708,579,778.[69] Nevertheless, as pointed out in chapter 2, CCT programmes were never intended to replace families' income or were able to remedy poverty by themselves, but they were effective as complementary policies to wage enhancement and other social benefits. The unemployment rate that stood at 10.6% of the population in the first three months of 2016 reached 14.7% in the first trimester of 2021, the worst figure ever recorded. The minimum wage also reached its lowest value in dollar terms in a decade. Unemployment, wage stagnation and the constant rounds of audits that always resulted in the reduction in coverage of CCT programmes brought another cycle of general impoverishment. The percentage of people in extreme poverty grew from 4.7% of the population in 2014 to 5.7% in 2020, and those categorised as poor increased from 23.8% to 24.1% in the same period.[70] The number of families considered as having 'zero income' almost doubled in four years, jumping from 1,589,978 in May 2016 to 3,087,802 in January 2020.[71] According to a study produced by Fundação Getúlio Vargas (FGV), in 2021, Brazil recorded 62,930,194 people living below the US$5.50 per day poverty line, which corresponded to 29.62% of the population, the worst figure ever recorded.[72] With a great proportion of the population facing food insecurity, after years of favourable remarks on its efforts to eradicate hunger, Brazil was reinstated on the World Food Programme HungerMap.

Those figures were profoundly affected by the Covid-19 pandemic, but some of the setbacks discussed in this area are related to periods before March 2020, when the first cases of the disease were recorded in Brazil. They reflect a critical approach to CCT programmes, especially the *Bolsa Família*, often derided as a source of political clientelism, fraud, public resources misplacement, and corruption. Instead of a discourse around improving the targeting or coverage of the programme, the discourse and practice until the pandemic were dominated by an emphasis on audits, data analysis and 'nitcomb' operations that have always resulted in a reduction of recipient families. This move represents the colonisation of the fight against poverty and hunger by the vocabulary and semantics of the fight against corruption, with clear exclusionary outcomes. Exclusion in the form of food insecurity and poverty consists of the deprivation of a minimum level of individual capability, undermining citizenship and hindering democracy.

[69] ibid.

[70] IBGE, 'Síntese de Indicadores Sociais: uma análise das condições de vida da população brasileira' (Instituto Brasileiro de Geografia e Estatística IBGE, 2021), https://biblioteca.ibge.gov.br/visualizacao/livros/liv101760.pdf, 61.

[71] Ministério da Cidadania (n 68).

[72] Marcelo Neri, 'Mapa da Nova Pobreza' (Fundação Getúlio Vargas (FGV), 2022).

4.4. The Right to Healthcare: The End of '*Mais Médicos*', and the Police (and not Policy) Response to the Covid-19 Pandemic

In chapter 2, we associated the creation and consolidation of a public, comprehensive and decentralised healthcare system with the recognition, by the Brazilian constitutional and judicial system, of international organisations' claims for a right to health. The internationalisation of that perception of health as a right of the population and the elaboration of different procedures to litigate or participate in the healthcare system management were highlighted as citizenship-enhancing experiences, as evidence of inclusion, and therefore as democratic advances.

One of the most striking examples of how policies developed internationally affected the recognition of the right to health by the Brazilian population was the '*Mais Médicos Para o Brasil*' ('More Doctors to Brazil') programme. It was a joint initiative, coordinated by the Pan American Health Organization (PAHO), the regional chapter of the WHO, to fill vacancies, especially in primary care, in regions difficult to access in the countryside and poorer areas of Brazilian territory, where the ratio of doctors per 1,000 residents was far below the national average. The programme recruited 18.337 doctors out of whom, in December 2014, 11,185 were Cubans, spread throughout 73% of Brazilian cities.[73] During the 2018 general elections campaign, the far-right candidate who ultimately won the contest asserted that he would 'expel' the Cuban doctors from Brazil through the introduction of an examination to revalidate their diplomas in Brazil. In his own words, 'Together we can make Brazil better for all and not only to a small group that has seized power and has mugged us for more than 20 years taking us to a path we don't want. It is time to put an end to São Paulo Foro. We will kick Cubans out of Brazil with the *Revalida*.'[74] In a tweet from 27 November 2018, the President-elect announced that the continuity of the programme would be conditioned on the revalidation of foreign doctors' diplomas, and on a change in the way the programme was financed, because, in his words, 'the biggest part was destined to the dictatorship' in Cuba.[75] The financial agreement intermediated by the PAHO involved a bursary scheme offered to Cuban doctors that was already in place in more than 67 different countries. The bursary value corresponded to

[73] Governo Federal, 'Mais Médicos Resultado para o País', http://maismedicos.gov.br/resultados-para-o-pais.

[74] Gabriel Tibaldo and Wellington Roberto, 'Bolsonaro diz que vai usar Revalida para "expulsa" médicos cubanos do Brasil', *G1 News Web Site*, 22 August 2018, https://g1.globo.com/sp/presidente-prudente-regiao/noticia/2018/08/22/bolsonaro-diz-que-vai-usar-revalida-para-expulsar-medicos-cubanos-do-brasil.ghtml.

[75] JM Bolsonaro, 'Após Cuba irresponsavelmente retirar-se do Mais Médicos por não aceitar dar liberdade e salário integral aos seus cidadãos, quase 100% das vagas já foram preenchidas por brasileiros. Está claro que o acordo do PT era pretexto para financiar a ditadura membro do foro de São Paulo' (Twitter, 27 November 2018), https://twitter.com/jairbolsonaro/status/1067495309431980033.

25% paid by the Brazilian government, with 75% shared between the PAHO and the Cuban government. This was portrayed by the President-elect as a wicked agreement to distort Brazilian public funds to finance a dictatorship in Cuba and to privilege foreign doctors at the expense of Brazilian professionals. The capacity or incapacity of the programme to bring primary care to distant and economically underdeveloped cities in the North and Northeast regions was never on the horizon of the critique. It was always surrounded by the idea of a plot to misuse the public budget for international ideological alliances and political benefit. It was translated, once more, into the vocabulary of anti-corruption and ultimately led to Cuba withdrawing from the agreement. It immediately resulted in the resignation of Cuban doctors who were linked to the programme, generating 8,517 vacancies that were offered to Brazilian doctors in two consecutive public calls sponsored by the Brazilian government in 2018. According to preliminary data provided by the Ministry of Health, 29% of the Brazilian doctors selected to replace the Cubans did not attend the healthcare facility they were ascribed to. In addition to that, a decline in uptake encouraged the Brazilian government to launch another public call to fill approximately 2,500 vacancies in May 2019. In August 2019, the Brazilian government issued a Presidential Decree replacing the '*Mais Médicos para o Brasil*' with a different programme called '*Médicos pelo Brasil*' ('Doctors for Brazil'). On the day he signed the Decree, the President of the Republic affirmed that with the introduction of Cuban doctors into Brazil's poor and rural communities, the '*Mais Médicos para o Brasil*' had as a goal the formation of a 'guerrilla nucleus in Brazil'.[76] In 2020, the Federal Account Court (TCU) carried out an audit of the new programme and laid down a decision stating that it lacked a detailed diagnosis of the problem from the point of view of the policy recipient, did not consider any alternatives, unintended effects or disadvantages of the programme, adopted an insufficient indicator of the adequacy of the policy, and did not contemplate a plan for implementation of the programme with regard to the distribution of doctors, among other findings.[77] Although the number of doctors under the new '*Médicos pelo Brasil*' programme had reduced from 18,337 to 15,003 in October 2019, data on the impact of changes in primary care caused by the disruption of the programme are still nebulous, especially considering that the Covid-19 pandemic produced figures off the scale in many healthcare categories. The aspect that cannot escape our observation is the employment of the broad idea of the misplacement of public resources for political benefit, or the strong rhetoric on the presence of cronyism, the concession of privileged access to international allies, the use of a healthcare programme to conceal a political coup as the language behind the public policy shift. It means the contamination of an issue that should

[76] Julia Lindner and Daniel Weterman, 'Mais Médicos formava "núcleos de guerrilha", diz Bolsonaro', *Terra News Web Portal* (1 August 2019), www.terra.com.br/vida-e-estilo/saude/bolsonaro-diz-que-mais-medicos-tinha-objetivo-de-formar-nucleos-de-guerrilha,7ed4229d8ed1383a3fd685880d2b-0998mqcwe5cr.html.

[77] TCU [2020] Acórdão 994/2020.

be assessed through health indicators, such as vaccination rates, infant mortality, maternity mortality, or hospitalisations by allegations of different manifestations of corruption.

When it comes to healthcare or public health assistance, few events can have had such a huge impact as the Covid-19 pandemic. Suffice it to say that 2020 was the deadliest year in Brazil's history, with 1.4 million deaths registered, of which 194,976 were caused by SARS-CoV-2. This regrettable record was only surpassed in 2021, when a further 412,880 people died in Brazil due to complications related to the Covid-19 disease, not to mention the catastrophic number of hospitalisations and the skyrocketing figures related to expenditure on tests, sedatives, anaesthetics and other materials required in diagnosis and treatment.

Nevertheless, it is fair to say that none of those figures were able to mobilise the Brazilian institutions during the Covid-19 pandemic in the same way as the fight against corruption. Since the first case was registered on 26 February 2020, the Brazilian government tried to underplay the importance of the disease and refused to determine any national measure to mitigate contamination, such as the mandatory use of masks, social distancing or lockdowns. The Ministry of Health itself was changed twice during the pandemic, showing an erratic response to the health crisis that afflicted the country. The federal government has concentrated its efforts and discourses on the idea that resources decentralised to states' management had been either embezzled or misallocated. The Federal Police website states that there have been more than '100 operations to repress the misuse and deviation of federal funds destined to combat COVID-19', investigating contracts that amount to approximately R$3.2 billion. In less than two years, they executed 175 provisory arrest warrants and 1536 search and seizure orders in 205 municipalities in all 26 states.[78] One of the operations targeted the Governor of the State of Rio de Janeiro, identified by the prosecutorial authorities as the chief of a corruption scheme that involved the fraudulent appointment of a non-profit social organisation to manage campaign hospitals that would be built to receive Covid-19 patients. The Governor was preventively removed from office by a judicial decision in August 2018 that took in evidence the content of a collaboration agreement. In April 2021, he was impeached and lost his mandate based on accusations of mismanagement of resources during the Covid-19 pandemic. The opposition discourse was also encapsulated by the idea of the fight against corruption. The government's negligence in failing to adopt any national measure to effectively prevent the spread of the SARS-CoV-2 virus led Brazil to having amongst the worst outcomes of the pandemic in the world. It was the third-placed country in terms of total cases, with more than 34 million people diagnosed with Covid-19, second in the total of deaths, with approximately 700,000 lives

[78] Ministério da Justiça e Segurança Pública (MJSP), 'Polícia Federal completa mais de 100 operações contra fraudes relacionadas às ações de enfrentamento à pandemia' (*Polícia Federal*, 2021), www.gov.br/pf/pt-br/assuntos/noticias/2021/07/policia-federal-completa-mais-de-100-operacoes-contra-fraudes-relacionadas-as-acoes-de-enfrentamento-a-pandemia.

lost during the pandemic, and the 10th worst for deaths per 1 million people, behind countries with very small populations such as Gibraltar, San Marino and Montenegro. It figures in 120th place in the list of Covid-19 tests per 1 million residents.[79] All those data and evidence of government inefficiency were very poorly communicated to the public and did not shake public support for the President until a Parliamentary Investigatory Committee (CPI), installed by the Senate to investigate government action during the pandemic and a bribery scheme in the acquisition of vaccines, became public.

Discourses on management inefficiency, one of the world's worst death tolls, and anti-scientific and anti-vaccine campaigns from the government were not able to engage with public opinion with the same intensity as a corruption scandal. The incapacity to articulate a public, comprehensive and decentralised healthcare system to effectively fight the most devastating health crisis of the last 100 years was easily outshone by the idea of the detection, prosecution and punishment of corruption. The ways in which the population can participate in and reclaim the right to health have been absorbed by a never-ending debate on the fight against corruption in health policy management. Healthcare has ceased to be a matter of citizenship-enhancing policy, to be discussed instead in police inquiry terms by actors from both ends of the political spectrum. The results of this suppression of public debate on the right to health by anti-corruption rhetoric are difficult to evaluate by data, but it definitely did not help the development of a better response to the Covid-19 pandemic.

The broad idea of 'administrative rationalisation', the need to avoid the 'waste' of public resources with 'unfruitful' meetings and to stop the threat of 'political coordination' to impose a 'Bolivarian' agenda through communitarian councils, was contained in the message that followed Presidential Decree 9.759, enacted on 11 April 2019. The Decree brought a general ban on participative councils and a series of limitations for the operation and creation of new bodies of direct communitarian participation in the Federal Public Administration. The Decree put in jeopardy the functioning of important councils such as the National Council of Sustainable Rural Development, the National Education Council, the National Council for the Rights of Children, the National Council for the Rights of Women, and, ultimately, the National Health Council, and the local Health Councils, created by Law 8.080, through which healthcare management in Brazil became famously participative. The Supreme Court issued a cautionary measure to withdraw the effects of the provision in the Decree that allowed the closure of or interference in Councils previously created by law.[80] The decision safeguarded all the issue-specific bodies of popular participation in the public administration that had legal *status*, but the logic of equating participative councils with a waste of

[79] Ritchie H et al, 'Coronavirus Pandemic (COVID-19)' (OurWorldinData.org, 2020), https://ourworldindata.org/coronavirus.

[80] STF [2019] ADI 6121 MC.

public funds, or as a misuse of power for some sort of political manipulation, was the rationale of Presidential Decree 9.759. The effects of such official discourses on local health councils are still to be determined, but it seems obvious that they will not foster further political participation.

For all those reasons, there are signs that the overspread of the 'zero tolerance against corruption' obsession into the understanding and realisation of the right to health brought about discouragement in political mobilisation and social participation, the rejection of inclusionary programmes and policies, and an overall incapacity to properly respond to the Covid-19 pandemic.

4.5. Ethnic Minority Rights: Affirmative Action as Undue Privilege for Black Students and Workers, Mining Activity in Demarcated Areas, and Indigenous Genocide

In this last section, we will consider again how variations of the anti-corruption agenda impacted policies that were adopted in Brazil to reverse a scenario of structural racism that has prevented people from ethnic minorities from accessing public higher education institutions and market positions. We will also assess how it has come to play a role in threats to the demarcation of indigenous reserves, and to the preservation of the original communities that live within those areas.

As seen in chapter 2, after Brazil finally admitted its racism before the international community, Brazilian public higher education universities engaged in a broad movement to secure admission vacancies for ethnic minorities, especially black people. That initiative prompted a series of institutional developments, such as the Supreme Court decision to assure the constitutionality of those affirmative policies and the enactment of statutes that brought the 'quotas' in force, not only in the educational system, but also in personnel recruitment examinations for public offices. Although a radical change in social dynamics to grant better opportunities for poor black people takes time, it is already possible to witness signs of those transformations in the Brazilian academic environment.[81] It is also possible to identify the progressive appropriation of quota policies as rights and not privileges by their recipients.[82]

The chances of more inclusion for ethnic minorities also depend on the continuity of such programmes, which has been recently challenged in Brazil. When participating in one of the most traditional Brazilian political interview TV shows

[81] Adriano Souza Senkevics and Ursula Mattioli Mello, 'O perfil discente das universidades federais mudou pós-Lei de Cotas?' (2021) 49(172) *Cadernos de Pesquisa* 184.

[82] Camille Giraut, 'From privileges to rights: changing perceptions of racial quotas in Brazil' (2023) *Ethnic and Racial Studies* 1–24.

before the 2018 elections, the ultimately victorious far-right candidate declared that he owed no personal debt to the black community, as he 'had never enslaved anyone in his life', and that 'no black is better than me, and I am no better than any black'. He also asserted that access to publicly funded universities and public offices should be granted exclusively on merit and asked, 'why don't they study since elementary school to have a strong base and follow their careers in a situation of equality?' He also affirmed that he could not end the quota policies himself, as he would depend on Congress to change the laws to do that, but he would at least propose a reduction in the percentage of positions or vacancies reserved to ethnic minorities.[83] The measures adopted to include people from ethnic minorities in the educational system and job market were not discussed in their capacity to effectively produce the intended changes. No indicator, statistical figures, or any other kind of empirical evidence was brought to the debate to assess the efficiency or adequacy of the affirmative action measures adopted in Brazil. On the contrary, the very idea of imposing positive discrimination to overcome historic processes of racial inequality that deprive black people of opportunities for higher education and better jobs was translated as a form of deviation, undue privilege, and absence of merit. The discourse depicts the racial quotas policy as a way to misallocate places in publicly funded universities or vacancies for public office positions to favour ethnic minorities to the detriment of candidates from different ethnic backgrounds.

The fact that affirmative action in access to publicly funded universities and public office in Brazil is set in stone, not only by a Supreme Court decision, but mainly by Laws 12.711, of 2012, and 12.990, of 2014, has been a hurdle to the implementation of counter-policies. Nevertheless, some attempts at regression have been made. In June 2020, the Ministry of Education issued a normative order abrogating a previous norm that had extended the affirmative action rules to graduate programmes in all federal public universities. The decision generated a strong reaction in Parliament, with some Congress representatives discussing the possibility of passing a Bill to guarantee the 'quotas' for postgraduate degrees, and Parties filing a constitutional action to strike down the decision, which was ultimately overturned by the Government itself. The practical outcomes of such backlash measures have been limited, especially because, as said, affirmative action is well established in Brazilian legislation and case law. But the fact is that, even sporadically, the discourse on undue privilege given to black people and the existence of veiled political or economic interests behind quota policies has risen to influence State action. Suffice to say, we can consider the importance that 'so-called' hetero-identification committees or verification commissions have gained in the implementation of affirmative action in Brazil. To prevent fraud

[83] Roda Viva, 'O Roda Viva recebe o candidato à Presidência da República pelo Partido Social Liberal (PSL), Jair Bolsonaro, que fala sobre seus planos para a presidência, caso venha a ser eleito', *YouTube*, (31 July 2018), www.youtube.com/watch?v=lDL59dkeTi0&t=1s.

in self-declarations, universities and public institutions have adopted panels of specialists to check applicants who have registered themselves as brown or black. Resolution No 531, of the Brazilian National Council of Justice, for example, regulates the works of the hetero-identification commission in all public selection examinations promoted by the Brazilian judiciary, establishing a complex two-step process according to which self-declaration if followed by a photo check by the committee and, if necessary, a face-to-face verification that must adopt phenotypical criteria to determine who qualifies for a quota or not. It can be questioned how degrading such a verification process might be for someone who has dealt with structural racism throughout their life, especially considering that the experience would be necessary only for the sake of control, and fraud prevention. It can be argued whether, through the hetero-identification committees, the State is not in fact redefining races and aggravating racial inequality at the individual level.[84] The fact is that the works of such commissions have spread and dominated much of the debate around affirmative action in Brazil, generating increasing levels of judicial litigation around the subject. The number of cases related to vacancies reserved for ethnic minorities in public selection examinations in Brazil grew from 1,030 new lawsuits in 2020 to 2,729 new cases in 2023.[85] The growing concern with fraud prevention and detection is a variation of the broad anti-corruption agenda and correlated discourses on the need for 'objectiveness' and 'meritocracy' for every opportunity offered with public or private funds. Its capacity to penetrate State action towards affirmative action cannot be underestimated in its potential to generate exclusionary effects.

The situation is considerably different when we consider the protection of indigenous populations. As seen in chapter 2, pushed by various decisions from International Human Rights Courts and Commissions, Brazil accelerated the processes of indigenous land demarcation, which is a crucial step to guarantee that, inside those reserved areas, the indigenous populations can live in their environment with minimum intervention from others, particularly farmers and miners. After the rise in the number and areas designated as indigenous reserves, after 2016, not a single reserve was approved by the Brazilian government. If that alone would be reason for concern, it is important to outline that the executive handed a message to the Brazilian Congress with 34 priorities for 2021 that included Draft Bill 191, from 2020, an initiative proposed in March 2020 by the executive itself to regulate the economic exploitation of natural resources inside indigenous reservations. By economic exploitation, the Bill refers to mining activities and the use of water resources to produce energy. The government also pushed for the approval of Draft Bill 490, from 2007, which changes the procedure for the demarcation of indigenous reserves. The Draft Bill would diminish the

[84] Graziella Moraes Silva, Veronica Toste Daflon and Camille Giraut, 'Seeing race like a state: higher education affirmative action verification commissions in Brazil' (2024) 66(1) *Latin American Politics and Society*.

[85] CNJ, 'Justice in Figures' (2024), https://justica-em-numeros.cnj.jus.br/painel-estatisticas/.

authority of *FUNAI* (*Fundação Nacional do Índio*), the administrative agency that works for the protection of indigenous populations, limit exclusive possession and development rights over the lands demarcated to indigenous populations, affecting projects already in train, and nullify previous decisions that were not taken according to the new requirements. The approval of such measures would not only represent a major setback for populations awaiting decisions on the demarcation of their areas, but could jeopardise areas already reserved for indigenous populations, such as the *Raposa Serra do Sol*. The case ultimately decided by the Supreme Court was a milestone in terms of indigenous rights in Brazilian history, not only because the demarcation adopted a continuity approach, but because the Supreme Court affirmed the constitutionality of the whole procedure and its compliance with international human rights provisions. At the same time, it was the target of criticism from former Ministry-Chief of the Institutional Security Cabinet (GSI), General Augusto Heleno. Speaking as President-elect in November 2018, the far-right President of Brazil asserted that 'if it is up to me, there will be no more demarcation of indigenous land'. In the same interview, he suggested that the areas demarcated were 'superdimensioned'. His position became clearer in August 2019, when in a Facebook live address, accompanied by Heleno, he said:

> These demarcations, they all deserve to be reviewed, as there is evidence, within FUNAI, of allegations of fraudulent demarcations of indigenous lands. There are demarcations that were forged, very increased in their extension, by people interested in profit from it. This needs to be studied. The very *Raposa Serra do Sol* report has been under doubt and it is practically proven it is a fraudulent report. Thus, all these demarcations must be revised, to verify if they really correspond to the truth.[86]

The line of thinking that inspired the decision to stop all the demarcation procedures is very much influenced by the broad idea that there are undercover interests at play in the demarcation of indigenous lands. That is, it is believed that the bureaucracy responsible for identifying and certifying those areas is involved in fraud, forgery, and other types of misbehaviour to benefit those shady interests. In sum, the main ideas that entered the Brazilian government's indigenist policy were corruption and anti-corruption. And behind the vocabulary of checks, controls, audits and triumphs in fraud detection was a lenient approach towards farming and mining activities in indigenous reserves. The intense traffic of people in and out of indigenous reserves motivated the APIB (Articulation of Brazil's Indigenous Peoples) to file a constitutional lawsuit before the Supreme Court to compel the Brazilian government to adopt measures to avoid the spread of Covid-19 in indigenous populations. The Supreme Court Justice, ahead of the case, called a meeting with government and indigenous representatives to discuss the measures that needed to be taken to avoid the disastrous effects the disease

[86] Jair Messias Bolsonaro, 'Live de Quinta-feira – 19:00', *Facebook* (29 August 2019), https://pt-br.facebook.com/jairmessias.bolsonaro/videos/-live-de-quinta-feira-1900-29082019-fatos-da-semana-link-no-youtube-httpsyoutube/481394389360908/.

could cause to indigenous populations. The first meeting ended with the indigenous representative leaving the room, alleging that General Augusto Heleno had made threats and was verbally aggressive towards them.[87] The threat of extinction through territorial encroachment caused by alarming rates of forest destruction in the previous couple of years, and the death toll from Covid-19 among indigenous populations, motivated many organisations to file accusations of crimes against humanity by the Brazilian President before the International Criminal Court.

Moreover, in July 2022, installed to adopt provisional measures to protect the Yanomami, Ye'kwana, and Munduruku peoples by the Inter-American Commission of Human Rights, the Inter-American Court of Human Rights laid down a paradigmatic decision in which the provisional measures were granted, after the Court recognised:

> Regarding the requirement of extreme gravity, as is apparent from the information provided by the Commission, members of the Yanomami, Ye'kwana and Munduruku Indigenous Peoples are allegedly subject to significant advances in the exploitation of so-called illegal mining activities on their indigenous lands, among others, carried out by third parties not authorized to enter their territory, which is causing: (i) homicides of indigenous adults and children, as well as deaths resulting from mining operations; (ii) acts of sexual violence against indigenous women and children; (iii) threats to indigenous leaders, some of whom play a very important role within the community; (iv) involuntary displacement of some indigenous communities that are threatened by the increasingly close presence of prospectors and the products of their activities; (v) the spread of diseases, especially due to COVID-19 infection, in a population that has a particular immunological vulnerability, and (vi) contamination, especially with mercury – a product of gold mining – of rivers that serve the subsistence of indigenous peoples, and deforestation, seriously impacting the health and food security of the proposed beneficiaries.[88]

It is hard to think of one subject in which the broad idea of corruption and the fight against corruption had such dramatic impacts as in the case of the policies related to the preservation of indigenous populations' rights. The perception that the demarcation of indigenous lands has been tainted by fraudulent reports, unscrupulous interests and so forth motivated the adoption of an anti-indigenous governmental prejudice with serious repercussions for those people's lives, not to mention their inclusion in the Brazilian society.

4.6. Conclusion

It is fair to assert that the positive impact of full compliance with the international anti-corruption regime on democratic consolidation in Brazil has fallen

[87] STF [2020] ADPF 709 MC.

[88] *Matter of Members of the Yanomami, Ye'Kwana, and Munduruku Peoples Regarding Brazil – Provisional Measures* (IACtHR, 1 July 2022).

short of the expectations expressed in specialised literature. In fact, as seen in this chapter, the institutional machinery imported from international norms, protocols, guidelines and toolkits, epitomised in the *Car Wash* outcomes, had a decisive role in the destabilisation of core democratic institutions and procedures. It was an underlying cause for the controversial impeachment of an elected President and had direct consequences for the 2018 general elections. The push to translate horizontal accountability into vertical electoral accountability led to an unprecedented sequence of cautionary arrests, coercive questionings, and the release of investigatory material to the press with a considerable influence over the President's impeachment process. The leaking of an illegal recording of a President's private communications, the pressure of public opinion that made the Supreme Court vacillate in its interpretation of the presumption of innocence constitutional clause, and its repercussions for the 2018 general elections, are all signs of a 'state of exception' installed in Brazil during the 2010s.[89] This would in itself show enough evidence of serious democratic repercussions from the international anti-corruption arsenal in Brazil, once the domestic, participatory, electoral element of democracy was directly influenced and subverted.

However, as we have seen, more than that, basic conditions of democracy, such as freedom of the press, manifestation, and access to alternative sources of information that could give 'the people' an 'enlightened understanding of public affairs', were severely contaminated by the anti-corruption discourse. The broad and massive exploitation of investigative measures by the media contributed decisively to discrediting the whole political spectrum. A comprehensive investigation such as the *Car Wash* probe, which involved politicians from all parties and political orientations, and the sequence of arrests, convictions, and removals from office on the grounds of corruption, culminated not only in the ineligibility of the former President of the Republic but also combined to taint allies and traditional oppositions. Political scepticism and broad social discontentment fuelled by massive anti-corruption propaganda paved the way for the victory of a conservative, self-proclaimed outsider populist with support in Parliament to implement his agenda. The appropriation of the international anti-corruption discourse by Brazilian legal elites put forward a punitive approach that created an adversarial social environment that divides the 'we (the people)' from 'them (the corrupt politicians)'. In this chapter, we have tried to describe the actors, their motives and processes, as well as how the international consensus on the necessity to fight corruption infiltrated and met a very strong tradition in interpretations of Brazilian society. Following Vieira's warning, we do not put forward the triumph of the anti-corruption movement as the single cause of the political crisis witnessed in Brazil from 2013 onwards. However, we propose that through mechanisms and strategies propelled by the international anti-corruption

[89] Emilio Peluso Neder Meyer, 'Judges and Courts Destabilizing Constitutionalism: The Brazilian Judiciary Branch's Political and Authoritarian Character' (2018) 19(4) *German Law Journal* 728.

industry, law enforcement and judicial authorities promoted more than an institutional clash caused by defects in constitutional design that allowed a 'hardball' exchange between the branches of power.[90] As Vieira himself concedes, the fight against corruption was the banner under which diffuse social dissent and even anti-democratic tendencies found a dwelling.[91] This social mobilisation around the subject propitiated a favourable environment for an anti-corruption crusade by judicial and semi-judicial corporate associations, with the active engagement of public prosecutors in think tanks, and even evangelical churches, to preach the 'anti-corruption gospel'.[92]

Corruption and its combat became more than just a matter of 'judicial activism' or 'juristocracy', as proposed by Meyer.[93] Reciprocal corruption accusations, support for cinematographic investigations, and theatrical meetings held by Inquiry Committees in Parliament are not only symptoms of a flawed coalition presidentialism prescribed by the Constitution, as suggested by Vieira.[94] They became the only language through which Brazilian political institutions, parties, and the electorate communicated with each other. Schertel Mendes originally proposes that ideas such as intolerance towards 'systemic corruption', and the need to put an end to the impunity of economic and political elites involved in 'white collar' crimes, had a far reach into Brazilian governance institutions.[95] He draws similarities between how the ideas of crime and the war on crime became the way through which power was exercised in America, 'from the President of the United States to the classroom teacher',[96] and the way corruption and the fight against corruption became the dominant political-legal vocabulary in Brazil.

The push for societal awareness and engagement in the anti-corruption cause had deeper repercussions for Brazilian democracy. It not only generated an emptiness in political debate around issues unrelated to accusations of corruption, but it overflowed to become the language of State intervention in many other areas, producing setbacks in access to and inclusion in human rights. Here, we can witness an interesting dynamic that might not be peculiar to Brazil, nor to the way the international anti-corruption agenda was implemented. An international regime that draws its legitimacy from ideas such as 'good governance', 'development' and 'accountability' colonises and dominates the local, electoral, popular,

[90] Oscar Vilhena Vieira, 'Clash of powers: Did Operation Car Wash trigger a constitutional crisis in Brazil?' (2021) 71(1) *University of Toronto Law Journal.*

[91] ibid 174.

[92] Fabiano Engelmann, 'The "Fight against Corruption" in Brazil from the 2000s: A Political Crusade through Judicial Activism' (2020) 47 *Journal of Law and Society*.

[93] Meyer (n 89).

[94] Vieira (n 90).

[95] Francisco Schertel Mendes, *Leniency Policies in the Prosecution of Economic Crimes and Corruption* (Nomos Verlagsgesellschaft mbH & Co KG, 2021) 302–16.

[96] Jonathan Simon, *Governing Through Crime: How the War on Crime Transformed American Democracy and Created a Culture of Fear* (Oxford University Press, 2007).

participatory element of democracy to repel other international human rights regimes that integrate the cosmopolitan and universal element of democracy, bringing about exclusion. Policies adopted to fight poverty, such as the conditional cash transfer programmes, have come under severe scrutiny for being prone to deviations and corruption. As discussed in chapter 3, the shift in the international anti-corruption movement approach, dislocating it from its pure criminological roots to translate it into managerial terms, theories and concepts, has loosened the very idea of corruption to depict it as any form of 'abuse of power' for a 'benefit'. That comprehensive and elastic definition underpins critiques that describe conditional cash transfer programmes as sources of political clientelism. The 'clientelism' critique has been usually relied upon to justify cuts and adjustments. Since the Temer administration, many audits have been carried out to detect benefit fraud and mismanagement, accompanied by a decline in coverage and the rise of poverty, inequality and food insecurity, until the Covid-19 pandemic struck and data were distorted by the need to implement emergency financial aid for a great portion of the population.

The dominance of anti-corruption over other issues is also clear in the right to health and the public healthcare system in Brazil. It influenced the disruption of a programme of primary care once the cooperation of Cuban doctors was described as a political plot to divert the programme for ideological purposes. More than that, it encapsulated efforts during the Covid-19 pandemic, with accusations of corruption, involving misuse, embezzlement and bribery in the acquisition of instruments, medicine and vaccines, being the main discourse from actors at both ends of the political spectrum. An adapted discourse that portrays affirmative action for the access of ethnic minorities to publicly funded higher education universities and the job market as a form of deviation of opportunities, or undue privilege for black people, has also been behind some attempts to abrogate or impede initiatives in favour of black people. As we have seen, the indigenist governmental policy was also colonised by the idea of corruption and fraud in the development of land demarcation reports, and so forth.

It is possible to argue that anti-corruption has become a catalysing prism through which many different rights and policies are discussed in Brazil, which represents a democratic decay that goes beyond episodic political intervention as promoted by the anti-corruption advocates. Corruption and anti-corruption have been a dominant dynamo that has trapped Brazilian democracy in an infinite loop that always starts and ends at the same point. The democratic impoverishment experienced in Brazil has also reached human rights regimes, generating historical setbacks in all areas considered in this book. The local, popular and participatory element of democracy was not only infiltrated and distorted by the anti-corruption obsession, but its influence also led to a process of continuous intervention against policies and measures largely supported by the cosmopolitan, universalist and rights-based element of democracy. It is possible to argue that anti-corruption has become the language, the vocabulary of a new cycle of exclusion in Brazil, which reverses the means through which democracy can thrive.

5

The Brazilian Anti-Corruption Push and Democracy Around the World

5.1. Introduction

Multiple authors and movements understand that a strong and well-articulated response to corruption is essential for the triumph of the rule of law and the establishment of democracy.[1] The Brazilian case seems to have made this certainty cloudier. Marona and Kerche assert that the most recent anti-corruption push in Brazil jeopardised Brazilian democracy,[2] Santos and Gallego consider that anti-corruption crusades can be used for anti-democratic purposes,[3] and Prado and Machado suggest that the political use of anti-corruption efforts may undermine democracy.[4]

We argue that the international anti-corruption legal regime, strongly legitimised by the good governance/accountability/transparency semantics, found lower-level judicial and quasi-judicial authorities, enjoying high levels of functional independence, empowered by a myriad of new investigative and prosecutorial methods, techniques and tools, willing to promote an anti-corruption

[1] The positive relationship between the fight against corruption and democracy is found in many 'quality of democracy' arguments, for example Marc Buhlmann et al, 'The Democracy Barometer: A New Instrument to Measure the Quality of Democracy and its Potential for Comparative Research' (2011) 11(4) *European Political Science* 521, Larry Jay Diamond and Leonardo Morlino, 'The Quality of Democracy: An Overview' (2004) 15(4) *Journal of Democracy*, and Guilhermo A O'Donnell, 'Why the rule of law matters' (2004) 15(4) *Journal of Democracy* 36. It is also a paramount basis for the international anti-corruption agenda, eg Transparency International, 'Together Against Corruption: Transparency International Strategy 2020' (TI, 2015), TogetherAgainstCorruption_Strategy2020_EN.pdf (transparencycdn.org), Timothy J Power and Mathew M Taylor, *Corruption and Democracy in Brazil. The Struggle for Accountability* (University of Notre Dame Press, 2011); Mathew M Taylor, 'Corruption, Accountability Reforms, and Democracy in Brazil' in CH Blake and SD Morris (eds), *Corruption and Democracy in Latin America* (University of Pittsburgh Press, 2009).

[2] Marjorie Marona and Fábio Kerche, 'From the Banestado Case to Operation Car Wash: Building an Anti-Corruption Institutional Framework in Brazil' (2021) 64(3) *Dados, Rio de Janeiro* 8, 31.

[3] João Guilherme B dos Santos and Esther Gallego, 'Fighting Corruption, Dismantling Democracy: Antagonism, Communication, and the Political Use of Lava Jato in Brazil' in Sandra Botero, Daniel M Brinks and Ezequiel A Gonzalez-Ocantos (eds), *The Limits of Judicialization: From Progress to Backlash in Latin America* (Cambridge University Press, 2022) 311.

[4] Mariana Mota Prado and Marta R de Assis Machado, 'Uso do Direito Penal para Combater a Corrupção: Potencial, Risos e Limitações da Operação Lava Jato' (2021) 17(2) *Revista Direito GV* 8, 286.

crusade. Following the steps of similar movements in other parts of the world (eg the Italian '*Mani Pulite*' operation), and incentives to promote social awareness against corruption found in the UN Convention against Transnational Organized Crime and the UN Convention against Corruption, those judicial actors acted in cooperation with the media to put forth an unprecedented social mobilisation around zero tolerance against corruption. We have suggested that the interaction between international legal regimes and the local, political community is constitutive of contemporary democracy. In the case of the international anti-corruption regime, that interaction was intentionally manipulated to promote a transition of the anti-corruption discourse from horizontal institutional accountability to a matter of vertical electoral accountability. International anti-corruption norms, protocols, guidelines, reports and indexes were deployed to their full potential, an effort epitomised by the so-called *Car Wash* operation. The combination of cautionary measures and collaboration agreements, all leaked to spectacular media coverage, had an undeniable contribution to the destabilisation of President Dilma Roussef's second term, being an underlying influence for the 2016 impeachment. Moreover, criminal convictions in an environment of strong social uproar led to decisions regarding candidacy registration, and a broader sense of lack of trust in the political spectrum decisive in the outcome of the 2018 elections. The engulfment of the participatory, popular element of democracy by the international anti-corruption rationale generated direct repercussions for core democratic institutions, such as the Presidential term in office, and procedures, with the electoral scenario directly shaken by judicial intervention. Beyond that, we propose that an overspill of the anti-corruption agenda populated the whole Brazilian public sphere, being adopted as the dominant vocabulary to address issues only indirectly related to corruption. The colonisation of the public sphere by the anti-corruption obsession led to setbacks in inclusion, and access to human rights.

In the first section of this last chapter, we will discuss the effects produced by anti-corruption sagas in different parts of the world. The countries examined have a strong link to the developments witnessed in Brazil. Italy was a declared source of inspiration for the Brazilian prosecution and judicial authorities who led the *Car Wash* operation. The outcomes of *Mani Pulite* for Italian society and politics will be discussed, as well as the new cycle of anti-corruption initiatives such as the creation of the National Anti-Corruption Authority (ANAC), the resultant adoption of the National Anti-Corruption Plan, the enactment of some new legislative measures and an analysis of the current state of Italian democracy. Portugal witnessed the '*Marquês Operation*' which culminated in the cinematographic arrest of former Prime Minister, José Sócrates, and had some overlaps with the *Car Wash* investigation. In Latin America, two other countries were directly impacted by the *Car Wash* operation, Ecuador and Peru. We will describe the deployment of many international anti-corruption devices, the main findings, and their repercussions for democracy in these cases.

In the second section, we describe how 'corruption-fighters' envision the latest events in Brazil, articulating their discourse to keep pressuring for more reforms, efficiency, and the punishment of corruption. We will address how their rhetoric moves from an analysis of presumptive defective constitutional arrangements that would facilitate corruption in Brazil, to the adoption of a soft language to describe human rights violations by public prosecutors and judicial authorities, often referring to decisions that overrule those abuses as backlashes from politically compromised superior courts, creating an adversarial contempt of court that was appropriated by authoritarian populists to undermine democracy.

In the same section, we consider our responses to the assessments made by 'anti-corruptioners'. We will see how political fragmentation and 'coalition presidentialism', pointed out as constitutional defects that make the Brazilian constitutional system prone to corruption, have been partially addressed by constitutional reforms. We will also offer an analysis of how the soft language on human rights violations and the theories that strongly critique superior courts' decisions were assimilated in the vocabulary of the most recent anti-democratic upheaval in Brazil.

Lastly, we will address the problems with anti-corruption statistics and causality assumptions and the importance of gauging the success or undesirable side effects of anti-corruption efforts by their results, and not their intentions.

5.2. Anti-Corruption Pushes and Democracy Around the World

5.2.1. Italy

Operation *Mani Pulite* is arguably the first and most well-renowned campaign ever carried out by prosecutors and judicial authorities against influential politicians involved in acts of corruption. The operation occurred in the mid-1990s and implicated in suspicious activities no fewer than six former Prime Ministers, more than 500 members of Parliament, and thousands of local and public administrators, causing a turbulent effect on Italian politics.[5]

The virtuous effect of the implosion of the whole political spectrum produced by the succession of cinematographic arrests that put politicians and businesspersons behind bars seemed to have faded quickly. Vannucci alludes to a 'saturation' effect that generated a sense of indifference toward corruption in most Italians as if it were an unescapable fate. According to him, a decline in media coverage around the subject and the decimation of political parties was followed by the

[5] Alberto Vannucci, 'The Controversial Legacy of "Mani Pulite": A Critical Analysis of Italian Corruption and Anti-Corruption Policies' (2009) 1(2) *Bulletin of Italian Politics* 233.

ascension of centre-right populist and media mogul, Silvio Berlusconi, who won two consecutive elections, in 2001 and 2006, a period in which the clash with judicial authorities ahead of investigations against him became part of the Prime Minister's political agenda.[6]

Berlusconi, who benefited from a cynical response of the electorate to the deterioration of politics produced by the triumph of *Mani Pulite* to reach power, became a critic of the judiciary himself, passing legislation that can be interpreted as setting back the anti-corruption cause, such as Laws No 367/2001, No 61/2002 and No 248/2002.[7] Not without reason, the striking success of an anti-corruption probe such as *Mani Pulite* might have resulted in unchecked corruption in the regime installed right after the political earthquake it caused, with a progressive worsening of Italy's situation in the Transparency International Corrupt Perceptions Index (CPI) from 2001 to 2009.[8] It is perplexing to note that Berlusconi is the Prime Minister who governed Italy for the longest period in the post-war era while being charged in more than 100 investigations, out of which at least 30 concerned his involvement in corruption.

In 2008, the *Banca d'Italia* created the *Unità di informazione finanziaria*, responsible as the financial intelligence unit working with the Financial Action Task Force (FATF). In 2009, the National Anti-Corruption Authority (ANAC) was created to articulate, guide and regulate the prevention of corruption and transparency measures. Law No 190/2012 set forth a National Anti-Corruption Plan, carried out by the ANAC at the national level, and a Plan for Transparency and Prevention of Corruption to be developed every three years by regional authorities. The concurring competencies of the ANAC, the Court of Auditors, and the *Guardia di Finanza* – a branch of the police specialised in financial and economic activity – have contributed to a multi-institutional web of accountability that has renewed the capacity of the State to detect and prosecute corruption.[9] According to Sberna and Vannucci, at the beginning of the 2010 decade, 'a new wave of political scandals for corruption, extortion, misappropriation, and embezzlement crimes hit the Italian party system. Similarly to the Mani Pulite inquiries, high profile representatives of all leading parties were charged.'[10]

The spread of a new wave of anti-corruption inquiries at regional level was coupled with massive media coverage stressing, once again, the multipartisan sources of racketeering, embezzlement and distortion of public funds. The lingering effects of corruption in politics and the financial crisis prompted the resignation of Berlusconi in 2011 and the surge of new political parties with a

[6] Salvatore Sberna and Alberto Vannucci, '"It's the politics, stupid!" The politicization of anti-corruption in Italy' (2013) 60(5) *Crime Law and Social Change* 565–593.

[7] Vannucci (n 5) 254–55.

[8] ibid 239.

[9] Daniel L Feldman, 'The Efficacy of Anti-Corruption Institutions in Italy' (2020) 22(6) *Public Integrity* 590–605.

[10] Sberna and Vannucci (n 6) 580.

strong 'anti-system' and 'outsider' rhetoric, such as the 'Five Star Movement', which achieved 20% of votes in the 2013 general elections,[11] ultimately reaching power five years later.

In 2019, Law No 9 was enacted to establish 'measures to fight crimes against the public administration and on transparency of political parties and movements'. The statute, called the 'bribe-destroyer law', increased penalties for crimes against the public administration, and the duration of restraining measures against legal persons involved in such crimes, such as the suspension of licences, permits and authorisations used in criminal activity, and even suspension of the business itself. Despite its intrinsic connection with OECD and GRECO (Group of States Against Corruption) exigencies, the new legal efficiency in curbing 'the pervasive and persistent lack of perception of corruption as a crime' in Italy is still seen as a challenge to be overcome.[12]

After so many steps taken in the fight against corruption and its impact on democracy over the last 30 years, in September 2022, a political coalition led by the *Fratteli d'Italia* party won the general elections. The right-wing party is also relatively new, reaching power 10 years after its creation, as happened with the populist 'Five Star Movement'. It is considered to represent neo-fascist ideology through ultra-nationalism and conservative agendas and received 26% of votes in an election that also registered the lowest voter turnout in history.

Although a link between the massive success of anti-corruption pushes, the engulfment of Italian political debate by the never-ending fight against corruption and high levels of distrust, disenchantment and disinterest with democracy can be made, it seems beyond doubt that the anti-corruption campaigns were unable to bring about the blooming of a vibrant and inclusionary democracy in Italy.

5.2.2. Portugal

Portugal's system of prevention and combat against corruption has been acknowledged by international authorities on the matter. In a report on best practices to the implementation of Resolution 41/9 of 11 July 2019, adopted by the Human Rights Council on the negative impact of corruption on the enjoyment of human rights, Portugal was considered by the Officer of the High Commissioner on Human Rights as having a 'complete and comprehensive anti-corruption legal framework and policies'.[13] It encompasses the deployment of many e-services by the Public Administration, such as the CITIUS platform, and the SIMPLEX Programme,

[11] ibid.

[12] Paola Maggio, 'A Critical Analysis of Corruption and Anti-Corruption Policies in Italy' (2020) 28(2) *Journal of Financial Crime*.

[13] OHCHR, 'Resolution 41/9 on the Negative Impact of Corruption on the Enjoyment of Human Rights – Challenges Faced and Best Practices Applied – Portugal' (2019), www.ohchr.org/sites/default/files/Documents/Issues/Corruption/Challenges/Portugal.pdf.

which are considered examples of promoting transparency and control. The GRECO 5th evaluation round report recognises that Portugal has an extensive anti-corruption legal and institutional framework, although very reliant on the National Anti-Corruption Mechanism.[14]

Indeed, Portugal has built up its anti-corruption system very much aligned with the International Code of Conduct for Public Officials, the UNCAC, the Criminal Law Convention on Corruption adopted by the European Council, the OECD Convention on Combating Bribery of Foreign Public Officials in International Business Transactions, and the Convention on the fight against corruption involving officials of the European Communities or officials of the Member States of the European Union, tutored by the Council for the Prevention of Corruption (CPC) and materialised in the Plan for the Management of the Risk of Corruption and Connected Infractions (PGRCIC).[15]

This myriad of institutions not just aimed at the prosecution and punishment of the crime of corruption but mainly focused on risk management and planning of anti-corruption initiatives gives that sense of an accountability web, and an integrity system proposed by the anti-corruption cause advocates, resembling the approach found in Brazil and Italy.

Despite such efforts, Portugal also experienced an anti-corruption political thriller. The so-called *Marquês Operation* investigated 28 individuals and legal persons involved in tax evasion, money laundering and corruption schemes, in which €34 million in bribes was circulated between politicians and powerful businesspersons, among whom the prosecutorial authorities found, as a principal, former Prime Minister, José Sócrates.

Amid the collection of evidence phase, mutual legal assistance was undertaken between Portuguese authorities and the *Car Wash* task force as a line of investigation explored the presumable exchange of favours between José Sócrates and former Brazilian President, Luiz Inácio Lula da Silva, in which Sócrates would advocate for Octapharma's interests in Brazil, while Lula would bid for the participation of Odebrecht in infrastructure works in Portugal.[16]

The connections between the two investigatory probes do not stop there. Deploying an arsenal of mechanisms for the search and seizure of assets abroad, also mirrored by *Car Wash*, in November of 2014, Sócrates was arrested at Lisbon International Airport as he was arriving from a trip to Paris. He remained in prison, without any formal charge, for almost nine months, and in April 2021, the examining judge, Ivo Costa, released him from most of the charges, sending him

[14] GRECO, 'Fifth Evaluation Round: Preventing corruption and promoting integrity in central governments (top executive functions) and law enforcement agencies Portugal' (2024), https://rm.coe.int/grecoeval5rep-2022-3-final-eng-evaluation-report-portugal-public/1680ae19a7.

[15] Ricardo Alexandre S Cunha, Sara Alexandra da E Serra, and Maria Manuela O Costa, 'The Fight Against Corruption in Portugal' (2013) *Tourism & Management Studies* 700.

[16] Mamede Filho, 'Como Operação que Levou Ex-Premiê de Portugal à Prisão está Ajudando a Lava Jato', *BBC News Brasil* (2016), www.bbc.com/portuguese/noticias/2016/03/160318_lava_jato_portugal_mdb_mf.

to trial only for the minor offences of money misplacement and document forgery, which had an immediate negative impact on public levels of trust in courts.[17] Magalhães' study also shows that, although not so drastically as in the case of levels of trust in courts, overall confidence in politics has steadily declined over the years in Portugal, in a process of deterioration that was not stopped or diminished by the judicial decision.[18]

In January 2024, the Lisbon Court of Appeal (*Tribunal de Relação de Lisboa*) overturned the decision and reinstating most of the charges against Sócrates, not only for minor offences but for all the corruption crimes listed by the Criminal Prosecution Office. It was another sudden change of direction in the investigations. Coincidently or not, on 10 March, new legislative general elections took place in Portugal. The greatest winner was the far-right Chega party, which quadrupled its representation in Parliament, gaining unprecedented political relevance in presenting, alongside an ultra-nationalist and radical liberal agenda, 'clean Portugal of corruption' as one of its main platforms.

5.2.3. Peru

The *Car Wash* operation revealed a massive corruption scheme at the heart of Peruvian government in 2016. The cooperation between Brazilian prosecutorial authorities and the US Department of Justice revealed that Odebrecht had paid around $29 million in bribes to take hold of three major infrastructure works in Peru, through 64 different bank accounts and more than 50 offshore companies.[19]

The scandal met a Public Prosecutor's Office with high levels of autonomy, significatively enhanced by the enactment of laws regarding the achievement of collaboration agreements, cautionary arrests, restraint orders and the freezing of assets to prevent interference in investigations, jurisdictional privilege to carry out arrests and seizures against high-level officials without Congress approval, and the creation of the Financial Intelligence Unit and an anti-corruption division in the National Police.[20] Furthermore, Peru fully 'engaged in the legal translation of international anti-corruption standards', adopting the UNCAC provisions, especially those related to mutual legal assistance, the criminalisation of bribery, the protection of whistleblowers, and leniency agreements with legal persons involved in the misappropriation or distortion of money.[21]

[17] Pedro Magalhães, 'When Corruption Investigations Come to Nothing: A Natural Experiment on Trust in Courts' (2024) 37 *Governance* 114.

[18] ibid.

[19] Ezequiel A Gonzalez-Ocantos et al, *Prosecutors, Voters, and the Criminalization of Corruption in Latin America: The Case of Lava Jato* (Cambridge University Press, 2023) 74–75.

[20] ibid 81.

[21] ibid 87–88.

This advanced weaponry was deployed in the Peruvian *Car Wash* branch, which 'quickly expanded its original remit, implicating politicians both in and out of power and across all branches of government'.[22] The first reaction to such an overwhelming amount of evidence was the resignation of President Pedro Pablo Kuczynski in March 2018, who was absolutely discredited by the scandal that took over his administration. In October of that year, prosecutors Rafael Vela and José Domingo Pérez requested the detention of Keiko Fujimori, a leader of the opposition, and later, the imprisonment of former Presidents Kuczynski and Alan Garcia, causing an earthquake that shook the whole political spectrum. The case gained even more dramatic tones after, in the face of imminent arrest, former President Garcia committed suicide.

At that point, the chief prosecutors of the task force enjoyed unconditional support from the media, public opinion, and even international organisations. Their dismissal by Chief Prosecutor Chávarry ignited strong a public reaction and even the filing of a request for provisional measures before the Inter-American Commission on Human Rights to secure the autonomy of the investigators.[23]

Not even new President Martin Vizcarra could escape the carrousel of criminal charges, findings and scandals prompted by the *Car Wash* operation, and a leaked tape recording containing evidence that he was involved in bribes when he was Governor of Moquegua precipitated his impeachment in November 2020. After it came to public knowledge, the content of the declarations that implied President Vizcarra's participation in acts of corruption was contested by a journalist, claiming that the deposition against the politician was not spontaneous, but forced by the *Car Wash* prosecution task force members.[24]

The complete dismantlement of the Peruvian political landscape by bold, young, determined, neutral and apolitical prosecution authorities has striking similarities with the way *Car Wash* was carried out in Brazil. The multitude of spectacular cautionary arrests against traditional figures in the political scenario, and the capacity of those judicial actions to produce political influence, removing Presidents from office in sequence, resembles the political instability that preceded Brazil's 2018 general elections.

As Muñoz said after the 2021 general election results:

> Peru is now entering a period of great uncertainty as charges of vote fraud fly and political polarization goes from bad to worse. The legitimacy of the newly elected government has been damaged, and prospects for overcoming the recent political crisis look bleak. Democracy could suffer derailment by authoritarian forces, in the worst case, and even in the best case will have to endure further instability and the loss of yet more legitimacy in the eyes of citizens.[25]

[22] ibid 75.
[23] ibid 109.
[24] ibid 112.
[25] Paula Muñoz, 'Latin America Erupts: Peru Goes Populist' (2021) 32(3) *Journal of Democracy* 48.

Indeed, Pedro Castillo beat Keiko Fujimori by less than a 1% margin of votes, and the losing party challenged the results without any piece of credible evidence, mimicking a dynamic common to Trump in 2020 or Bolsonaro in 2022. The winner did not take it all, though. After three attempts by the Parliament to impeach Castillo under the 'lack of permanent moral capacity' clause, the newly elected and populist President attempted an auto-coup by dissolving Parliament, which ultimately led to his removal on 7 December 2022.

Dina Boluarte then took office and came under severe pressure after a group of 40 law enforcement officials, made up of police and public prosecutors, invaded her house and the Presidential Residence at the end of March 2024 to search for a collection of Rolex watches that could show evidence of illicit enrichment.

Peru, like Brazil, seems to be trapped in an infinite anti-corruption loop in which politics is completely engulfed by discussion about inquiries, arrests, police operations, and the never-ending hunt against the corrupt. The completely shattered political spectrum can hardly get to its feet to defend democracy.

5.2.4. Ecuador

Ecuador underwent a process of incremental enhancement of its constitutional and legal framework for the prevention, detection and prosecution of crimes of corruption and financial illicit acts. Strongly influenced by the Inter-American Convention Against Corruption (IACAC), the UN Convention against Transnational Organized Crime (UNTOC) and the UN Convention against Corruption (UNCAC), the 2008 Constitution had already put in place an autonomous prosecutorial authority and an accusatory system that endows public prosecutors with independence and the legitimacy to conduct investigations without interference from political forces. The creation of the *Unidade de Análisis Financiero y Económico* to work in coordination with the Office of the Comptroller General improved the State's capacity to detect financial illicit activities, reporting to the FATF, as the Financial Intelligence Unit. To all that can be added reform to the criminal code, which occurred in 2014, and criminalised most of the forms of corruption addressed by international instruments, importing the possibility of reward for collaboration agreements and mutual legal assistance with law enforcement authorities abroad.[26]

With such a well-assembled multi-institutional approach to the fight against corruption, the Chief Prosecutor created a specialist unit, under Diana Salazar, to lead all investigations related to the *Car Wash* case. After a 2015 bilateral agreement on Criminal cooperation between Brazil and Ecuador was invoked to boost the mutual legal assistance between prosecutorial authorities in both countries, the Ecuadorian arm of *Car Wash* gained pace. Information shared by Brazilian

[26] Gonzalez-Ocantos et al (n 19) 123.

authorities led to formal charges against Carlos Polit, former Comptroller General, and Jorge Glas, former Vice-President, for receiving bribes from Odebrecht to grant the Brazilian construction giant contracts for major infrastructure projects.[27]

In a bold move, in January 2018, Carlos Baca gave a press conference in which he leaked to the press a recording of a wired telephone call between the sitting President of the Congress, José Serrano, and Carlos Polit, in which they discussed plans to murder the Chief Prosecutor. The scandal ended in the removal of Serrano from office and the dismissal of Carlos Baca, as the tape should not have been presented at a press conference.[28]

That year also recorded a sequence of convictions that reached former Electricity Minister, Carlos Polit, and Pamela Martinez, a former Constitutional Court Justice who confessed to receiving bribes to finance political campaigns, including that of President Rafael Correa. In February 2020, Ecuadorian courts sentenced 18 people to eight-year sentences, including former President Rafael Correa, three of his former ministers, a member of congress and a governor for receiving approximately $8 billion in bribes,[29] which ultimately resulted in the ineligibility of Correa to contest the 2021 elections.

Guillermo Lasso, a right-wing conservative banker, was elected and in the second year of his tenure called a 'constitutional referendum' for the enactment of seven changes to the Ecuadorian Constitution, among which were powers to extradite Ecuadorians to foreign states in cases of international organised crime, reforms to place the Prosecution Office under the remit of the Attorney General, and a massive reduction in the number of the National Assembly seats.

On 5 February 2023, the 'referendum' backfired and all seven proposals were rejected. Lasso was himself facing an inquiry in which he was accused of embezzlement, corruption, and even having links to the Albanian mafia. In April, under growing pressure and social turmoil, Lasso announced a pro-gun decree in an attempt to curb a rising and uncontrollable level of violence.

On 16 May, an impeachment hearing was held by the National Assembly. On the following day, he triggered an emergency constitutional device called *Muerte Cruzada* ('crossed death'), dissolving the National Assembly and scheduling new general elections for Parliament, which ultimately resulted in his impeachment.

The *Car Wash* tornado had made chairs spin again in a succession of events that resembled a police thriller in which the people were willing to participate. In the case of Ecuador, tension levels rose to the point that Fernando Villavicencio was murdered in the streets of Quito on the eve of elections, leading to more public commotion and havoc.

Diana Salazar, once the fierce technocrat head of the anti-corruption unit in the Prosecution Office, was Attorney General under Lasso's administration.

[27] ibid 126.
[28] ibid 128.
[29] ibid 128.

President-elect Daniel Noboa has had to deal with grave social unrest following his inauguration, having resorted to 'emergency state' decrees that curtail civil liberties and the imposition of curfews to try to restore order.

5.3. The Anti-Corruption Crusaders Double-Down the Bet

The evidence collected in the previous section indicates that there is probably no democratic 'promised land' waiting for those who walk the path of faith in the international anti-corruption regime. In Brazil, as well as in Italy, Ecuador and Peru, global governance bodies' guidelines, multinational organisations' toolkits and goals, United Nations Convention investigatory methods and review mechanism reports, transnational NGOs' directives and assessment mechanisms, and their push for societal engagement against corruption found judicial and quasi-judicial actors keen on promoting a social and political 'revolution'. Equipped with the machinery to put forth that agenda, heavily supported by media coverage and enjoying functional immunity to deploy their arsenal, those actors initiated an anti-corruption crusade that surpassed the boundaries of legal discussions to become a way society understands itself and behaves politically. The triumph of the anti-corruption discourse generated serious political/electoral consequences, and its 'misuse of entrusted power for private benefit' rationale has become the vocabulary of anti-democratic forces.

Confronted with these undesirable side effects of the anti-corruption efforts, 'anti-corruption crusaders' have resorted to some arguments to defend the reform packages prescribed by international organisations, and the investigatory probes ignited and fuelled by them. The first argument focuses on the incapacity of prior legislative reform to 'fix' defective constitutional mechanisms that favour the occurrence of systemic and persistent corruption.

In the case of Brazil, Da Ros and Taylor point to three aspects that reflect what they call the 'prevailing elite cartel syndrome'. *Coalition presidentialism* describes a political system in which the President is often constrained to form political coalitions to govern in a very fragmented partisan landscape in which representatives are not ideologically oriented but work according to a rent-seeking logic. The *developmental state* points to a choice of the Brazilian State to be very active in different economic fields, holding some monopolies and raising opportunities for corruption, and a *problematic campaign financing system* refers to the facilitation of donations from large conglomerates as 'loans' to be recovered through overpriced contracts during the winner's tenure in office.[30]

[30] Luciano Da Ros and Matthew M Taylor. *Brazilian Politics on Trial. Corruption and Reform under Democracy* (Lynne Rienner Publishers, 2022) 16–17.

Oliveira and Moisés believe these constitutional arrangements explain, at least partially, 'the scale of corruption practices and their persistence over time'.[31] Vieira also attributes the seismic shock caused by the *Car Wash* operation to the growing independence of prosecution authorities and the fragile political system, hampered by the *coalition presidentialism* model.[32] *Coalition presidentialism* is a term coined by Sergio Abranches to describe the political system put in place in Brazil in which a multi-partisan spectrum is mixed with proportional voting, and an 'imperialist' type of presidentialism, which imposes some difficulties in terms of conflict resolution and tensions between the executive and the legislative, with a tendency to produce a crisis that would typically destabilise the Presidency.[33] His work became a classic in Brazilian political science for its capacity in predicting the ill fate of two Presidential mandates after the 1988 Constitution.

It is interesting to note that this derogatory approach to so-called *coalition presidentialism* is not shared by Abranches himself. Albeit signalling the difficulties it would impose on Brazilian political life, he acknowledges that the peculiar combination of multi-parties, proportional representation, and a strong form of presidentialism belongs to an institutional tradition very much embedded into Brazilian social dynamics, with no evidence that the alternative adoption of parliamentarism, majoritarian vote criteria for seats in parliament or a bi-party system would be better or even viable solutions as a conflict catalyst or in crisis prevention.[34]

Furthermore, according to anti-corruption crusaders, *coalition presidentialism* would be a trigger for corruption as the President would always be pressed by the need to form large coalitions to govern, resorting to unlawful ways to please a multi-party fragmented parliament to obtain the necessary support for their policies. The critique ignores evidence in the sense that the power and influence of the Presidency have largely been able to overcome this hurdle and form the majorities needed to pass legislative initiatives in almost all governments elected after the 1988 Constitution.[35] They also tend to overlook the recent approval of Constitutional Amendment 97, which imposes a performance clause for political parties that will gradually enter into force until 2030 and will likely lead to the extinction of two-thirds of the currently existing political parties.

The defective campaign financing system has also been addressed with a decision laid down by the Brazilian Supreme Court banning donations of private

[31] Emmanuel Nunes de Oliveira and José Álvaro Moisés, 'Corruption in the Perception of Brazilian Society: Persistence and Resilience' (2023) 29(2) *Revista do CESOP* 272.

[32] Oscar Vilhena Vieira, 'Clash of powers: Did Operation Car Wash trigger a constitutional crisis in Brazil?' (2021) 71(1) *University of Toronto Law Journal* 189.

[33] Sérgio HH de Abranches, 'Presidencialismo de Coalizão: o Dilema Institucional Brasileiro' (1988) 31(1) *Revista de Ciências Sociais* 5–34.

[34] ibid 32.

[35] Fernando Limongi, 'A Democracia no Brasil: Presidencialismo, Coalizão Partidária e Processo Decisório' (2006) 76 *Novos Estudos CEBRAP* 23; Marcos André Melo and Carlos Pereira, *Making Brazil Work: Checking the President in a Multiparty System* (Palgrave Macmillan, 2013).

corporations and companies to political parties and electoral campaigns.[36] The decision, celebrated among 'corruption fighters', might have unbalanced the Brazilian electoral system in favour of candidates sponsored by institutions and organisations that deal with large sums of cash daily, better suited to a multitude of small anonymous donations that are impossible to trace back to the donor by the financial monitoring system, namely from neo-Pentecostal churches, drug traffickers and militias.

Coalition presidentialism and the demolition of the political party system have become a 'go-to argument' for those who work with the phenomenon of corruption in Brazil despite the absence of an alternative to that institutional characteristic that would not hyperinflate/diminish the powers of the President, regardless of empirical evidence that shows this has not been a problem in times of economic prosperity and political balance, and the fact that political party fragmentation and campaign financing have been the target of two recent course-altering reforms in Brazilian constitutionalism.

Another characteristic of the *anti-corruptioners*' analysis of the concurrence around the big anti-corruption pushes in countries like Italy, Brazil, Ecuador and Peru is a very mild self-critique in which they describe the setbacks and collateral damage caused by those crusades as a matter of pace in the reforms, using a soft language to downplay human rights violations caused by the anti-corruption prosecutors' authorities.

Da Ros and Taylor, for instance, prefer incremental reforms to 'judicial policy entrepreneurship' big pushes – like *Mensalão* or *Car Wash*.[37] Conversely, Gonzalez-Ocantos et al believe that only anti-corruption crusades can fight big transnational corruption schemes protected by influential political and business interests.[38] Barbabella et al understand that courts must show a 'costly display of commitment' to the fight against corruption to ramp up their credibility before the eyes of public opinion.[39]

Da Ros and Taylor refer to politically motivated actions of the public prosecutors, like the press conference given by the *Car Wash* task force chief after filing formal charges against the former President of the Brazilian Republic, in which a PowerPoint presentation that linked all recent corruption scandals to him referred to 'self-inflicted wounds', missteps, or a lack of attention to unintended side effects. This type of soft language has an undisguisable intention to safeguard the main judicial/quasi-judicial actors from their responsibilities.[40] Likewise, Gonzalez-Ocantos et al comment that in anti-corruption crusades, public prosecutors make moves that are on a 'blurry line' between aggressive investigation

[36] STF [2015] ADI 4.650.

[37] Da Ros and Taylor (n 30).

[38] Gonzalez-Ocantos and others (n 19) 5.

[39] Letícia Barbabella, Miquel Pellicer and Eva Wegner, 'Court Performance and Citizen Attitudes Towards Fighting Corruption' (2022) 35 *Governance*.

[40] Da Ros and Taylor (n 30).

and human rights violations,[41] and also that, when leaking to the press the content of illegal tape recordings, as former Judge Sérgio Moro did with the conversation captured between Dilma Roussef and Luiz Inacio Lula da Silva, or as Peruvian prosecutors did in implicating President Vizcarra in bribes while he was Governor of Monquegua, or as Carlos Baca did with the conversation between José Serrano and Carlos Polit, public prosecutors made controversial choices.[42] As enthusiasts of the anti-corruption crusades, they understand as positive initiatives the 'waves of evidence-gathering activities, often in spectacular fashion', the 'coordination' between courts, police and prosecution offices, and the occurrence of 'eventful repercussions'.[43]

Another look at the same events could classify them differently. The freezing of assets, cautionary arrests, and coercive questioning orders with broad media coverage could be interpreted as an unnecessary 'spetacularisation' of criminal prosecution. The joint venture between prosecutorial authorities and courts could consist of a violation of the accusatory system and even collusion, and both aspects, together, could be described as 'lawfare'. The so-called 'eventful repercussions' are indistinguishable from traumatic political events, with possible dismantling effects on democratic institutions, procedures, and substantial preconditions like human rights.

Even Prado and Machado, who at first proposed to analyse the 'innovative decision techniques' deployed during the *Car Wash* trials, mapping the limitations and risks of some theories 'without picking a side',[44] in a later work acknowledged the abuses committed and the lack of judicial accountability for the dissimulated political aspirations of prosecutorial and judicial authorities ahead of *Car Wash*.[45]

'Anti-corruptioners' also tend to generically describe rulings from high-level courts that overrule decisions laid down during the apex of the task forces as a backlash from politically compromised courts. Commenting on the Supreme Court's stance on the *Car Wash* case, Da Ros and Taylor first address how a well-articulated move between the task force members, media, and public opinion was important to 'force the hand' of the Justices towards a more aggressive approach regarding criminal prosecution as if the Court were an obstacle *Car Wash* had to get around to reach its full potential.[46] Following a similar pattern, they say, after 2017, the Supreme Court systematically overruled *Car Wash* task force initiatives and decisions, building a body of case law that promises to hinder future

[41] Gonzalez-Ocantos et al (n 19) 67.
[42] ibid 69.
[43] ibid 8.
[44] Mariana Mota Prado and Marta R de Assis Machado, 'Uso do Direito Penal para Combater a Corrupção: Potencial, Risos e Limitações da Operação Lava Jato' (2021) 17(2) *Revista Direito GV* 8, 4.
[45] Mariana Mota Prado and Marta R de Assis Machado, 'Turning Corruption Trials into Political Tools in the Name of Transparency: the Lava Jato Case' in S Botero, Daniel M Brinks and Ezequiel A Gonzalez-Ocantos (eds), *The Limits of Judicialization: From Progress to Backlash in Latin America* (Cambridge University Press, 2022) 281.
[46] Da Ros and Taylor (n 30) 137.

anti-corruption efforts.[47] Barbabella strongly criticises this type of swing in the Court's decisions regarding anti-corruption operations, believing it shows an 'insincere institutional commitment' to the fight against corruption that demoralises law enforcement authorities.[48] Gonzalez-Ocantos et al raise the manner of the adversarial environment that arises between courts during anti-corruption crusades, asserting that they are an 'open-ended battle between, on the one hand, a handful of maverick rank-and-file investigators, and on the other, politicians and their allies in senior judicial and prosecutorial roles'.[49]

In the case of Brazil, the idea that the Supreme Court would be a politically packed Court willing to shield corrupt politicians from anti-corruption investigations, while the lower-level members of the Public Prosecutor's office and regional courts are the true heroes of the fight against corruption, is hardly supported by the facts. While in AP 470, the biggest criminal trial ever held by the Supreme Court, most of the defendants faced harsh punishment, reaching former Ministers and the President of the Deputy Chamber, in the *Car Wash* operation, most of the collaborators that confessed to having received astronomic figures in bribes, voluntarily returning large amounts of money to the public treasury, barely served any time in prison, receiving low penalties, often converted to home detention.

Systematic pressure and attacks against courts matter,[50] as shown by the conflicting rulings of the Brazilian Supreme Court on the presumption of innocence guarantee. More importantly, a variation of this very same discourse that throws shade on the credibility of the Supreme Court became a central plank in the far-right authoritarian populism that came to power in Brazil. Contempt for the Court became the preferential discourse of '*Bolsonarism*', in the same way that Berlusconi used to call the judicial authorities in Italy by the nickname 'red robes', alluding to their presumptive undisclosed communist inclinations.

As is well known, the alignment between *Car Wash* prosecutors, judges, and the authoritarian movement that reached power in Brazil after 2018, goes far deeper than only a mere distrust in the Supreme Court. Da Ros and Taylor acknowledge the presence of anti-democratic enthusiasts in public rallies against corruption 'as early as 2015'.[51] Indeed, as Santos and Gallego highlight, 'the punitivist rhetoric of Lava Jato [Car Wash] supporters was therefore part of bolsonarism from the beginning and exists quite comfortably alongside the "internal threat" discourse inherited from the dictatorship'.[52] It is beyond any doubt that the mobilisation of public opinion, strongly pushed forward by members of the *Car Wash* task force in symposiums, summits, churches and public manifestations, has always shared

[47] ibid 174.

[48] Leticia Barbabella, 'Judicial Inconsistency and Citizen Anti-Corruption Demobilization: Evidence from Brazil' (2023) *Government & Opposition* 1–20, 2.

[49] Gonzalez-Ocantos et al (n 19) 11.

[50] Luiz Vilaça, 'A Social Movement Model for Judicial Behavior: Evidence from Brazil's Anti-Corruption Movements' (2024) 103(1) *Social Forces* 223–44.

[51] Da Ros and Taylor (n 30) 204.

[52] Santos and Gallego (n 3) 296.

a platform with protesters demanding 'military intervention', and even for the re-imposition of AI-5, the most authoritarian decree ever issued by the military government during the dictatorship period.

Eduardo Bolsonaro even threatened to suspend the Supreme Court during the electoral campaign in October 2018, and his father, former President Jair Bolsonaro, has always expressed admiration for torturers while being accused of managing a very flagrant system of kickbacks in his office, and his sons' offices, when they were all congressmen or members of State and Municipal chambers of representatives. When Sérgio Moro stepped down as a magistrate to become his Ministry of Justice, he did not take a step in the dark, but he condoned a strong anti-democratic discourse, choosing to turn a blind eye to the corruption scandals that already surrounded the former President even before his candidacy. Not long after, Diana Salazar also jumped from the position of head of the anti-corruption unit in the Public Prosecutor's Office to become Attorney General under Lasso's administration in Ecuador. The 'maverick rank-and-file' law enforcement authorities were not as ideologically neutral, technically sound, and driven as they presented themselves.

Da Ros and Taylor refuse to assess the anti-corruption reforms based on what they call a dependent variable, meaning their success or failure.[53] It seems like a convenient omission, even reckoning for the controversial outcomes of 'judicial policy entrepreneurship' in big pushes against corruption in democracies, not to assess the main features of the reform packages they prescribe. Gonzalez-Ocantos et al say that pessimists tend to focus on the crimes and the difficulties in punishing them when assessing anti-corruption crusades. On the other hand, optimists pinpoint the accomplishments of task forces as reasons for hope in extinguishing corruption, as proposed by Sérgio Moro when he quoted Theodore Roosevelt to say that 'the exposure and punishment of corruption is an honour to a nation, and not a disgrace'.[54]

Anti-corruption crusaders had the opportunity to witness the outcomes of some big anti-corruption campaigns in places like Italy, Ecuador, Peru and, mainly, Brazil, to reassess their motives, rationales and practices. Instead of affirming that there is no fight against corruption worthy of the sacrifice of democracy and human rights, they chose to double down on the bet that the chance to combat corruption would be conducive to democracy, development and the enjoyment of human rights.

This book skews to more critical appraisals like the one presented by David Kennedy, in which he proposes the exact opposite approach to evaluate international reforms and interventions. Kennedy says that humanitarian efforts abroad must 'weigh outcome, not structure'.[55] As Kennedy warns, international reformists

> often mute awareness that their best ideas can have bad consequences. When things do go wrong, rather than facing the darker consequences of humanitarian [anti-corruption,

[53] Da Ros and Taylor (n 30).
[54] Gonzalez-Ocantos et al (n 19) 167.
[55] D Kennedy, *The Dark Sides of Virtue: Reassessing International Humanitarianism* (Princeton University Press, 2004) 350.

> in this instant case] work, we too often simply redouble our efforts and intensify our condemnation of whatever other forces we can find to hold responsible.[56]

If we are to adopt such pragmatism, we must be sure of what the fight against corruption can and cannot do.

5.4. Fighting Corruption for All the Wrong Reasons

As already discussed, one of the most successful moves made by the international anti-corruption movement was to detach corruption from its criminological origins to root it in the human rights, developmental and managerial agendas. Transparency International (TI) reports, World Bank balances, OECD guidelines, and World Economic Forum documents often adopt a reciprocal referencing system to support the need for anti-corruption reforms worldwide. Those references usually address data on the pervasive effects of corruption on development or access to human rights.

A joint report published by TI and the World Economic Forum in 2008 stated that corruption costs $2.6 trillion or 5% of global GDP every year, a figure repeated in a speech given by an IMF director years later. A study carried out by Wathne and Stephenson shows that the last time 5% of global GDP was $2.6 trillion was in 2006, which indicates that the statistics are outdated and unfounded. The authors warn that 'no organisation or advocate should cite this statistic under any circumstances'.[57] The same study disputes the assertion found in World Bank, IMF and OECD reports that 10–30% of publicly funded infrastructure investments are lost to corruption every year, as the source of the statistics is a report of the World Bank's office in Jakarta edited in 1997 and considering infrastructure projects in Indonesia alone that year. This 'generalising strategy' is also found in an article published by Transparency International and the World Economic Forum Partnering Against Corruption Initiative that refers to $455 billion in healthcare spending being diverted each year, 'leading to the death of more than 140,000 children'. The study that underpins such an assertion found a statistically relevant negative correlation between the Corruption Perceptions Index (CPI) and child mortality, adopting a cautious conclusion about the causality between corruption and infant mortality as there could be many uncontrolled variables influencing both indexes. Wathne and Stephenson found the use of the study by international anti-corruption agencies problematic.[58]

The UNDP Global Thematic Programme on Anti-Corruption for Development Effectiveness summarises the consensus on the capacity of anti-corruption

[56] ibid 327.
[57] Cecilie Wathne and Matthew C Stephenson, 'The Credibility of Corruption Statistics' (2021) Anti-Corruption Resource Centre (U4 Issue 2021:4) 13.
[58] ibid 30.

measures to foster development and economic growth and to improve the State's capacity to better invest resources in needy areas. Kahn shows that while developed countries invariably rank higher in indexes that gauge the presence of strong accountability/combat of corruption institutions, the difference in those indices between developing countries that register high economic growth rates and those that have lagged is marginal or irrelevant, which suggests that the purported causality is weak, or might be reversed.[59] In other words, although World Bank reports, Transparency International material and UNDP programmes are filled with syllogistic conclusions in terms of 'since' corruption is efficiently tackled 'then' development and economic growth can happen, empirical evidence in that sense is not as strong, with a more historically accurate hypothesis being that once countries experience sustained development and economic growth, strong accountability/anti-corruption institutions are consolidated.

This is an aspect that deserves further investigation, but some specific cases seem to corroborate Khan's suggestion and replicate effects felt in Brazil. Indeed, the anti-corruption movement has stormed the political sphere in other parts of the globe, which has not exactly been followed by economic growth or development. In South Korea, a sequence of scandals, from trading in influence of a Christian-shamanistic guru to the acceptance of bribery for the approval of a merger between two subsidiaries of the Samsung conglomerate, led to street rallies and, ultimately, to the impeachment of former President Park Geun-hye and her sentencing to 24 years in prison at the turn of 2016 and 2017. Samsung's de facto boss, Lee Jae-Yong, who was also involved in the case, was sentenced to two-and-a-half years in prison in a plot that not only shook South Korean politics but also its most important multinational companies. The Asian country registered a GDP growth rate of 2.8% in 2015, 2.9% in 2016, and 3.2% in 2017. After the anti-corruption intervention, South Korea's economic growth rate fell back to 2.9% in 2018, and 2% in 2019.

In South Africa, in October of 2017, the Constitutional Court upheld a decision to reinstate 783 corruption charges against former President, Jacob Zuma. In December 2017, the High Court of Pretoria decided that the appointment of Shaun Abrahams as National Director of Public Prosecutions (NDPP) was invalid because Zuma had acted in a conflict of interest. The decision led to large street demonstrations for Zuma's resignation, which ultimately came to pass in February of 2018, and to the installation of a Commission of Inquiry into Allegations of State Capture with broad media coverage. South Africa's GDP growth rate was 1.2% in 2015, 0.4% in 2016, and 1.4% in 2017. After the sequence of judicial decisions and public protests that rocked the government and the ANC headquarters, South Africa's growth rate fell to 0.8%, and then to 0.2% in 2019.

[59] Mushtaq Khan, 'Governance and Anti-Corruption Reforms in Developing Countries: Policies, Evidence and Ways Forward' (2006) G-24 Discussion Papers 42, United Nations Conference on Trade and Development.

The positive impact expected from the triumph of the anti-corruption crusades on economic development has also fallen short of those expectations in Brazil. The country was already facing economic decline in 2013 and 2014, with a negative swing in the GDP growth rate of 3% to 0.5%. In 2015 and 2016, when the *Car Wash* operation was at the epicentre of all political developments that culminated in President Dilma Roussef's impeachment and the criminal conviction of many Workers' Party leaders and former government officials, Brazil suffered one of the worst economic depressions in its history, with consecutive falls of -3.5% and -3.3% in the GDP growth rate. Warde points out that big Brazilian contractor companies were severely hit by the investigations, with Camargo Correa, Andrade Gutierrez, Odebrecht, Queiroz Galvao and OAS alone making more than 290,000 redundancies and suffering economic losses of approximately R$187 billion.[60] Brazilian economic performance improved between 2017 and 2019, with GDP growth rates of 1.3%, 1.8% and 1.4% in the three-year span, which is still far from representing a recovery or a scenario of prosperity.

If the correlation between law enforcement institutions' empowerment to fight corruption and economic growth or development seems problematic, the idea that the efficient combating of corruption can be a 'game changer' in terms of public investment in areas of need is also very disputable. In Brazil, for instance, the turbulent year of 2016 ended with the approval of Constitutional Amendment 95, which determined measures to control public debt by establishing expenditure caps on social security, education and healthcare. In healthcare, for instance, Brazil registered a per capita/expenditure of $1,482,26 in 2019, which is below the worst two performing OECD countries (Latvia – $1,991/per capita, and Romania – $1,924/per capita), indicating the need for more investment. Although the nominal value of public expenditure on healthcare increased from R$231 billion in 2015 to R$290 billion in 2019, that investment decreased from 4% of GDP in 2017 to 3.9% in 2019, while the average of OECD countries in the same period spent 6.1% of their GDP on public healthcare.[61] In education, the effects have been more drastic, with a steady nominal reduction of the Ministry of Education budget allocation being observed since 2017, from R$154 billion to R$137 billion in 2020, with an even sharper decrease in expenditure from R$141 billion to R$116 billion in 2020.[62] The lauded success of anti-corruption operations in the mid-2010s did not result in any improvement in the State's capacity to invest in areas of such crucial importance for social development. In fact, to assume that the efficient combating of corruption is key to improving State performance in areas such as education and

[60] Walfrido Warde, *O espetáculo da corrupção: Como um sistema corrupto e o modo de combatê-lo estão destruindo o país* (Leya, 2018) 36–46.

[61] IPEA, 'Contas de saúde na perspectiva da contabilidade internacional: conta SHA para o Brasil, 2015 a 2019' (Instituto de Pesquisa Econômica Aplicada, 2022), www.ipea.gov.br/portal/images/stories/PDFs/livros/livros/220202_livro_contas_de_saude.pdf.

[62] Educação Tp, 'Anuário Brasileiro da Educação Básica' (Todos pela Educação, 2021), https://todospelaeducacao.org.br/wordpress/wp-content/uploads/2021/07/Anuario_21final.pdf.

health is to misplace expectations of what the triumph of anti-corruption efforts can deliver, to say the least. The *Car Wash* operation, which is the most successful anti-corruption operation in Brazilian history in terms of assets and money recovery, currently estimates that, in the most optimistic scenario, it will bring back R$14.7 billion to the public treasury.[63] Those results, already diluted across almost 10 years of investigations, cases, convictions, collaboration agreements and so forth, clearly fall shy of any possibility of reversing the current scenario of disinvestment in the Brazilian welfare system. Even if realised soon, the estimated total of assets and money to be recovered by *Car Wash* will correspond to less than 10% of the Ministry of Education budget for the year of 2019 alone, or approximately 5% of public expenditure on healthcare in that year, before the Covid-19 pandemic. This assertion does not intend to devalue the merits or the efficiency of the mechanisms activated to localize, freeze, seize and recover funds that had been misallocated, deviated, and hidden in tax havens overseas. Its importance is to align expectations toward what the international anti-corruption machinery can realistically achieve. As the recent developments in Brazil and other countries suggest, full compliance with the international anti-corruption regime does not guarantee economic growth and development nor improve public investment in areas that demand greater State intervention.

The type of bond between law enforcement authorities and the media to generate public engagement in the anti-corruption crusade witnessed in Brazil can generate another undesirable side effect. Paradoxically, anti-corruption crusades can generate a favourable environment for corruption. As Vannucci warns when analysing the outcomes of the Italian '*Mani Pulite*', the exposition of corruption can generate a sense of institutional saturation in pushing forward the efforts, leading to high levels of corruption.[64] In Brazil, zero tolerance against corruption was a decisive banner in the 2018 general elections, culminating with the leading lower-level judge in *Car Wash* being appointed as Minister of Justice by the new elected President under the promise of expanding institutional and legal reforms to increment the so-called national integrity system. However, investigations into a scheme of fraudulent personnel recruitment for public office, salary kickbacks and illicit enrichment, and militia financing in Rio de Janeiro, encircling the President and his family, ended with the former judge and Minister of Justice's resignation in April 2020. Even before that, investigatory bodies such as the Federal Prosecution Office, the Brazilian Intelligence Agency (ABIN), the Department of Assets Recovery and International Mutual Legal Assistance of the Ministry of Justice (DRCI), and the Ministry of Justice itself were all packed with the former President's cronies, which had depleted anti-corruption efforts. A conflict of interests of the former Secretary of Communication for being a partner of publicity agencies that had contracts with the government, a former Minister of Environment's involvement with illegal

[63] Ministério Público Federal (MPF), 'Caso Lava Jato', www.mpf.mp.br/grandes-casos/lava-jato.
[64] Vannucci (n 5).

loggers in natural reserves, the former President's son lobbying the Ministry of Regional Development in favour of mining companies, bribery attempts in the public procurement of Covid-19 vaccines in the Ministry of Health during the pandemic, and the distortion of Ministry of Education funds to benefit evangelical pastors and their political allies with promised bribes in gold bars, are some of the cases that have investigations pending, and in some of them, the police officers heading the investigations were fired or removed. Brazil might be a curious case in which the triumph of the anti-corruption movement led to the impunity of corruption. The situation has drawn attention from the international community with the recent adoption of an unprecedented measure by the OECD to install a working group to continuously monitor anti-corruption setbacks in Brazil. The same can be said about the situation in Peru, in which for every new President, commencing with Kuczynski and ending with Boluarte, and throughout Vizcarra's and Castillo's abbreviated terms, there has been an ongoing shadow of corruption.

As highlighted by the United Nations, the UN Convention against Corruption has 186 State Parties, and corruption, in its most varied forms, is considered a crime in almost every corner of the world. Obviously, part of that can be attributed to the success of the international anti-corruption movement. It is important to consider, though, that even before the rise of the international anti-corruption discourse, corruption was a criminal offence in many societies because it is morally wrong. The idea that bribery, cronyism, trafficking in influence, and illicit enrichment are corrupt acts that demand censorship in the form of criminal sanctions is underpinned by the idea that they are threats to or attacks on moral values such as honesty, probity, and equality of opportunities. Moral values that are sensible and dear to societies tend to be protected by law, and that involves the criminalisation of behaviours that menace them. This seems to be enough to justify or legitimise continuous initiatives to investigate, prosecute and punish acts of corruption, without further expectations of positive political, economic and social outcomes. When the fight against corruption is pushed forward for the wrong reasons, it can leave a sense of unfulfilled promises that can, paradoxically, create opportunities for the spread of unchecked corruption.

Conclusion: Closing Pandora's Box without Trapping Hope Inside

Corruption and human rights are defining concepts for understanding Brazilian society's formation and evolution. For a constant thread in Brazil's most influential sociological literature, corruption is the cursed heritage from the colonial period, and the failed attempts at cutting ties with corruption, in family, in business, and mainly, in State management, explain underdevelopment, economic stagnation, and the overall incapacity of Brazil to fulfil its destiny. In a different direction, other equally influential interpreters of Brazilian history point to inequality, racism, systemic prejudice against the poor, the black, and the indigenous, embedded structural social and economic division and deprivation as the core of Brazil's problem.

Although presented as concurring views, the fight against corruption and the promotion of human rights do not necessarily need to be mutually exclusive. On the contrary, as maintained by international anti-corruption supporters, efficient mechanisms of corruption prevention, detection and repression would, ideally, enhance the capacity that governments have to address social and economic challenges. The fight against corruption would be complementary to human rights regimes. That seemed to be the plan of the 1988 Brazilian Constitution, which featured the seminal structure of a multilayered integrity system alongside a comprehensive catalogue of civil, political, social, economic and cultural fundamental rights. Moreover, the 1988 Constitution contained mechanisms for the formal incorporation of international norms and a universalist and cosmopolitan aspiration that created scope, via constitutional jurisdiction, governmental cooperation and integration in supranational organisations, for the penetration of international agendas and discourses legitimised by ideas such as efficiency, good governance, transparency and human rights. The combination of high levels of popular participation and the return of Brazil to the international community is the foundational alloy of Brazilian democracy and the very dynamic through which it has evolved ever since the 1988 Constitution came into force.

In the last 35 years, more people gained citizenship as they came out of extreme poverty to assume a decisive political role as a collective actor able to unbalance electoral results in the recent general elections. Users of the healthcare system started to participate as both rights holders and policy-makers, as local health councils became a source of decision-making and control with which local authorities must now contend. The judiciary has been receptive to claims to hold those authorities accountable to policies decided by peer members of the community.

More black students are present in public university campuses, bringing new insights and perspectives to the academic sphere, and affirmative action has advanced to reach recruitment to important public positions. Indigenous people have become part of society, not only respected in their own way of living and being but also participating in judicial litigation, voting and running in elections for important federal offices. Not all that would happen through electoral participation alone. International human rights treaties, covenants, declarations, protocols and targets were progressively transformed into State policies and decisions through constitutional law procedures. Poverty, healthcare, racism and ethnic diversity became issues discussed on a *right/not right* basis, with a considerable sum of legal debate before judicial or *quasi*-judicial institutions such as constitutional and international courts. To a larger or lesser extent, the dialectic relation between the input from different international human rights regimes and the local, participatory, deliberative component of democracy created a cycle of mutual reinforcement and legitimisation that led to more participation, inclusion, and access to rights. Social change in different areas has been, to some degree, influenced by the penetration of international human rights in the way constitutional rights, promises and guarantees were interpreted and enforced.

A concurrent view to the one presented here would point out that those achievements have nothing to do with citizenship construction and democratic consolidation but were the mere results of economic growth. We would suggest, however, that the economic aspect might not have played such a decisive role. In the early 1970s, for example, Brazil recorded higher economic growth rates than those registered between 2000 and 2010. However, studies demonstrate that the so-called 'Brazilian economic miracle' was also characterised by the concentration of income among the wealthier layers of society, worsening social and economic inequality, with the Gini coefficient, for example, ramping up between 1960 and 1980.[1] Economic growth boosts the State's capacity to carry on social policies, but State actions are destined to produce more social inclusion when there is a pre-commitment to human dignity and democracy, outlined in the 1988 Constitution and strengthened by international human rights regimes.

International anti-corruption regimes can only become repelling to human rights if, and only if, they come to jeopardise democracy itself because there are no human rights without democracy and there is no democracy without human rights.

The fact that some undesirable consequences to democracy and human rights accompanied the triumph of anti-corruption efforts in Brazil is striking evidence that the causality between the adoption of the fight against corruption crusades and democratic enhancement, proposed by their advocates in specialist literature and Transparency International publications, is absent. A simple glance at some

[1] Rosane Silva Pinto de Mendonça and Ricardo Paes de Barros, 'A evolução do bem-estar e da desigualdade no Brasil desde 1960' (1995) 49(2) *Revista Brasileira de Economia – RBE*; R Hoffman, 'Desigualdade e Pobreza no Brasil no Periodo 1979-90' (1995) 49 *Revista Brasileira de Economia – RBE*.

of the most well-known democratic indices is enough to corroborate our claim. After the full deployment of international anti-corruption packages and the major political repercussions they generated in Brazil during the 2010s, some 'quality of democracy' indices show considerable democratic backsliding. Freedom House's Global Freedom Score registers a sustained fall since 2017 – the year that reflected the evaluation for 2016, when the Presidential impeachment occurred – from 79/100 points to 73/100 in 2022.[2] The Economist Intelligence Unit Democracy Index also shows a retraction from 7.38 points in 2014 – the year the *Car Wash* operation started – to 6.86 in 2021, which represents Brazil moving down into the 'flawed democracy' band, approaching the 'hybrid regime' classification (scores below 6.01). International IDEA – Global State of Democracy highlights that 'the countries that have declined the most (measured in terms of the average across all 16 sub attributes of democracy and that were democracies at the start of the decline) in the past 10 years are: Turkey, Nicaragua, Serbia, Poland and Brazil'.[3] The Varieties of Democracy (V-Dem) index records a drop from 0.79 in 2010 to 0.51 in 2020, the fourth worst process of autocratisation in the world in the decade, according to the Swedish institute.

More than just a flawed causality between the adoption of the international anti-corruption agenda and democracy consolidation, it is plausible to argue that, at the very least on a semantic level, some traits that the international anti-corruption discourse possesses make it prone to strategic appropriation and adoption by domestic legal elites and political forces. The focus on societal engagement and the need to educate the population in search of electoral vertical accountability, expressly found in the UN Convention against Corruption, World Bank guidelines and Transparency International publications, certainly draws the attention of judicial/prosecutorial actors and minoritarian political radicals in search of an ethos or a common moral banner under which to disguise their authoritarian interests. The 'econometric' jargon adopted to present corruption as more than just a criminal phenomenon, but as a public management malaise, and a hurdle to democracy and development, attracted those who saw orthodox neoliberal economic and institutional reform prescriptions succumb to the 2008–09 global financial crisis.

Looking at the full picture, it is possible to assert that however present in contemporary democracy since democracy itself became the political consensus around the globe, international legal regimes backed up by cosmopolitan, universalist values such as human rights, development, science, or religion do not always come to the domestic scene to produce more democracy and inclusion. The means by which they are absorbed, the stakeholders directly involved in the process of

[2] Freedom House, 'Freedom in the World 2021' (Freedom House), https://freedomhouse.org/country/brazil/freedom-world/2021.

[3] IDEA, 'The Global State of Democracy 2021: Building Resilience in a Pandemic Era' (International Institute for Democracy and Electoral Assistance, 2021), www.idea.int/democracytracker/sites/default/files/2022-11/GSOD21.pdf, 6.

integration – legislative, judicial, social movements, decentralised administration – and the way they connect with local, political and participatory dynamics, all play a decisive role in their outcomes. In some cases, the two constitutive elements of contemporary democracy couple to produce emancipation, citizenship enhancement, a sense of rights attainment, in sum, inclusion and democratic consolidation. In others, the interaction is conflictual, the hegemonic tendency of the 'we the people' in trying to cast out foreign influence prevails. Conversely, in the case of the fight against corruption, the external element has the tendency to colonise the public sphere and control political debate, policy planning, execution and assessment, monopolising the vocabulary through which problems are discussed and solutions found.

To different extents and through different processes, in the fight against poverty, the right to healthcare, the access of ethnic minorities to higher education, and the protection of indigenous populations, the dialectic relationship between the general will, Supreme Court case law on international human rights, and international courts' decisions, was leaning toward a more inclusive and diverse society. Brazilian democracy thrived as it generated more participation and inclusion in all those areas. This dynamic suffered disruption in the mid-2010s, whose causes are still to be fully explored. It is hard to measure, for instance, the exact contribution the economic crisis experienced in 2015 and 2016 had on the political events that followed. Nevertheless, one factor in that disruption, both on practical and semantic levels, was the triumph of an anti-corruption discourse induced, propelled and rewarded by the international anti-corruption regime. The fight against corruption was one, if not the main, element in a new cycle of alienation and exclusion for which the inflamed masses offered their support.

One way to move forward is to re-confine the fight against corruption to its place, praising the achievements accomplished, strengthening accountability institutions to ensure they can work independently and responsibly, but bearing in mind the pitfalls in the path, and keeping a realistic expectation of what can be achieved through a robust integrity system. A better understanding of the relationship between human rights, corruption, and democracy can certainly help to close Pandora's box, taking special care to not trap hope inside. That is the hope that Brazil can find the correct balance of the elements on which its democracy was founded and can advance to a more equal society. Looking at the challenges of Latin American constitutionalism, Gargarella asks, 'What are the needs of our time? What is the main legal drama of the present time? How could the Constitution react in face of that drama? We maintained that the main drama confronted by the entire region, since its independence, was the drama of inequality.'[4]

Analysing Brazil's recent history, Benvindo explains the current scenario of democratic backsliding in Brazil by the presence of high levels of inequality

[4] Roberto Gargarella, *Latin American Constitutionalism, 1810–2010: the Engine Room of the Constitution* (Oxford University Press, 2013) 196.

and a persistent authoritarian mindset that still informs and shapes Brazilian understanding of the rule of law.[5] We agree with his claim by proposing that the prevailing institutional mindset is authoritarian precisely because it leans toward producing and reproducing inequality and exclusion. Although he acknowledges that 'Operation Car Wash and also other probes before it yielded a tectonic shift in the "institutional equilibrium" that had until then prevailed in the relationship between the political and judicial realms',[6] we believe he overlooks the mechanisms through which the success of anti-corruption efforts made a decisive contribution to reinforcing the authoritarian mindset/inequality that is at the core of his diagnosis of our democratic shortcomings.

Brazilian society has historically struggled to identify its real drama, failing to offer a clear, straightforward response to Gargarella's provocative question. The trouble in recognising our main constitutional challenge can be attributed to an understanding of the rule of law that is essentially authoritarian and that reproduces inequality, as proposed by Benvindo. The social obsession with corruption and misplaced trust in the international anti-corruption regimes, agenda, discourses and correlated domestic initiatives has decisively contributed to making that self-awareness more difficult. The capture of the public sphere by corruption and the fight against corruption has clouded Brazilian society's view of its own problems and tasks ahead. The image in the mirror is nebulous, blurred and distorted. We hope to have generated an innovative breeze that can bring some clarity to the picture.

[5] Juliano Zaiden Benvindo, *The Rule of Law in Brazil: The Legal Construction of Inequality* (Hart Publishing, 2022).
[6] ibid 202.

BIBLIOGRAPHY

de Abranches, SHH, 'Presidencialismo de Coalizão: o Dilema Institucional Brasileiro' (1988) 31(1) *Revista de Ciências Sociais*

ActionAid, 'HungerFree Scorecard 2010: Who's Really Fighting Hunger' (ActionAid, 14 September 2010), https://actionaid.org/publications/2010/whos-really-fighting-hunger

Agência Brasil, 'Presidente eleito diz que programas sociais passarão por auditoria' (Agência Brasil, 24 November 2018), https://agenciabrasil.ebc.com.br/politica/noticia/2018-11/bolsonaro-diz-que-programas-sociais-passarao-por-auditoria> accessed 28 November 2020

Anderson, S and Heywood, PM, 'Anti-corruption as a risk to democracy: on the unintended consequences of international anti-corruption campaigns' in L de Sousa, PJ Larmour and B Hindess (eds), *Governments, NGOs and Anti-Corruption: The New Integrity Warriors* (Routledge, 2008)

de Araújo, FD, 'Corrupção e Novas Concepções de Direito Punitivo: Rumo a um Direito de Intervenção Anticorrupção?' (2011) 8(2) *Brazilian Journal of International Law* 205

——, 'Uma análise da Estratégia Nacional contra a Corrupção e a Lavagem de Dinheiro (ENCCLA) por suas diretrizes' (2012) 2 *Revista Brasileira de Políticas Públicas* 53

Bailey, J, 'Corruption and Democratic Governability' in CH Blake and SD Morris (eds), *Corruption and Democracy in Latin America* (University of Pittsburgh Press, 2009)

Bailey, SR, Fialho, F and Peria, M, 'Support for race-targeted affirmative action in Brazil' (2018) 18(6) *Ethnicities* 765

Baptista, TWdeF, Machado, CV and de Lima, LD, 'State responsibility and right to health in Brazil: A balance of the Branches' actions' (2009) 14(3) *Ciência & Saude Coletiva* 829

Barbabella, L, Pellicer, M and Wegner, E, 'Court Performance and Citizen Attitudes Towards Fighting Corruption' (2022) *Governance* 35

——, 'Judicial Inconsistency and Citizen Anti-Corruption Demobilization: Evidence from Brazil' (2023) *Government & Opposition* 1–20

Barbarela, E and Bachini, N, 'Lava Jato e a Mídia' in JF Júnior and F Kerche (eds), *Operação Lava Jato e a democracia brasileira* (Contracorrente, 2018)

Barbosa, LAA, *História constitucional brasileira: mudança constitucional, autoritarismo e democracia no Brasil pós-1964* (Centro de Documentação e Informação, Edições Câmara, 2012)

Barreto, LP, 'A Enccla e o Combate ao Crime no Âmbito Doméstico e Internacional' in *Enccla: Estratégia Nacional de Combate à Corrupção e à Lavagem de Dinheiro: 10 anos de Organização do Estado Brasileiro Contra o Crime Organizado* (Ministério da Justiça, 2012), http://enccla.camara.leg.br/quem-somos/enccla-10-anos

Barrientos, A and Hulme, D, 'Social Protection for the Poor and Poorest in Developing Countries: Reflections on a Quiet Revolution: Commentary' (2009) 37(4) *Oxford Development Studies* 439

—— and Villa, JM, 'Economic and Political Inclusion in Human Development Conditional Income Transfer Programmes in Latin America' (2016) 15 *Social Policy and Society* 421

Barroso, LR, *Curso de Direito Constitucional Contemporâneo* (Saraiva, 2019)

Basta, PC and de Souza Hacon, S, 'Avaliação da exposição ambiental ao mercúrio proveniente de atividade garimpeira de ouro na Terra Indígena Yanomami' (Fiocruz, PUC-RJ, Instituto Socioambiental Hutukara, Associação Yanomami, and Associação do Povo Ye'kwana do Brasil, 2016)

Beetham, D, *Democracy and Human Rights* (Wiley, 1999)

——, *Democracy: A Beginner's Guide* (Oneworld Publications, 2012)

Benvindo, JZ, *The Rule of Law in Brazil: The Legal Construction of Inequality* (Hart Publishing, 2022)

Besson, S, 'Human rights as transnational constitutional law' in AF Lang and A Wiener (eds), *Handbook on Global Constitutionalism* (Edward Elgar Publishing, 2017)

Blake, CH, 'Public Attitudes toward Corruption' in CH Blake and SD Morris (eds), *Corruption and Democracy in Latin America* (University of Pittsburgh Press, 2009)

Bobbio, N, *The Future of Democracy: A Defence of the Rules of the Game* (University of Minnesota Press, 1987)

Bohn, SR, 'Social policy and vote in Brazil: Bolsa Família and the Shifts in Lula's Electoral Base' (2011) 46(1) *Latin American Research Review* 54

Bolsonaro, JM, 'Após Cuba irresponsavelmente retirar-se do Mais Médicos por não aceitar dar liberdade e salário integral aos seus cidadãos, quase 100% das vagas já foram preenchidas por brasileiros. Está claro que o acordo do PT era pretexto para financiar a ditadura membro do foro de São Paulo.' (Twitter, 27 November 2018), https://twitter.com/jairbolsonaro/status/1067495309431980033

——, 'Live de Quinta-feira - 19:00' (Facebook, 29 August 2019), https://pt-br.facebook.com/jairmessias.bolsonaro/videos/-live-de-quinta-feira-1900-29082019-fatos-da-semana-link-no-youtube-httpsyoutube/481394389360908/

Bonavides, P, *Curso de Direito Constitucional*, 15th edn (Malheiros, 2004)

Bresser Pereira, LC, *A reforma do estado dos anos 90: lógica e mecanismos de controle* (Ministério da Administração Federal e Reforma do Estado, 1997)

Brown, E and Cloke, J, 'Neoliberal Reform, Governance and Corruption in the South: Assessing the International Anti-Corruption Crusade' (2004) 36(2) *Antipode* 272

Brown, GW, 'Cosmopolitanism and global constitutionalism' in A Lang and A Wiener (eds), *Handbook on Global Constitutionalism* (Edward Elgar Publishing, 2017)

Brunkhorst, H, *Critical Theory, Legal Theory, and the Evolution of Contemporary Society* (Continuum, 2012)

Buhlmann, M et al, 'The Democracy Barometer: A New Instrument to Measure the Quality of Democracy and its Potential for Comparative Research' (2011) 11(4) *European Political Science* 519

Calleros-Alarcón, JC, *The Unfinished Transition to Democracy in Latin America* (Routledge, 2007)

Campbell, DFJ, *Global Quality of Democracy as Innovation Enabler: Measuring Democracy for Success* (Springer International Publishing, 2019)

Campello, T and Neri, MC, *Bolsa Família Program: a decade of social inclusion in Brazil* (Ipea, 2014)

Canotilho, JJG, *Direito constitucional e teoria da constituição* (Almedina, 2013)

Carothers, T, 'Democracy and Human Rights: Policy Allies or Rivals?' (1994) 17(3) *The Washington Quarterly* 109

Carson, L and Prado, MM, 'Mapping Corruption and its Institutional Determinants in Brazil' (2014) *SSRN Electronic Journal*, https://papers.ssrn.com/sol3/papers.cfm?abstract_id=2497935

——, 'Brazilian Anti-Corruption Legislation and Its Enforcement: Potential Lessons for Institutional Design' (2014) *SSRN Electronic Journal*, https://ssrn.com/abstract=2497936

Castro, MC et al, 'Brazil's unified health system: the first 30 years and prospects for the future' (2019) 394(10195) *The Lancet* (British edition) 345

Cavalcanti, ABVR, 'Brazil in comparative perspective: the legacy of the founding, and the future of constitutional development' (2019) 6(1) *Revista de Investigações Constitucionais*

Chaikin, DA, 'Controlling corruption by heads of government and political élites' in P Larmour and N Wolanin (eds), *Corruption and Anti-Corruption* (ANU Press, 2013)

Chieffi, AL, Barradas, RDCB and Golbaum, M, 'Legal access to medications: a threat to Brazil's public health system?' (2017) 17 *BMC Health Services Research*, https://link.gale.com/apps/doc/A511292175/AONE?u=jrycal5&sid=bookmarkAONE&xid=8254978e

Childs, P and Stromquist, NP, 'Academic and diversity consequences of affirmative action in Brazil' (2015) 45(5) *Compare* 792

CNI, 'Pesquisa CNI-Ibope: Problemas e Prioridades do Brasil para 2014' (Confederação Nacional da Indústria, 2014)

——, 'Retratos da Sociedade Brasileira: problemas e prioridades' (Confederação Nacional da Indústria, 2015)

——, 'Retratos da Sociedade Brasileira: problemas e prioridades para 2016' (Confederação Nacional da Indústria, 2016)
——, 'Retratos da Sociedade Brasileira: problemas e prioridades' (Confederação Nacional da Indústria, 2017)
——, 'Retratos da Sociedade Brasileira' (Confederação Nacional da Indústria, 2018)
CNJ, 'O Poder Judiciário na aplicação da Lei Maria da Penha' (Conselho Nacional de Justiça, 2018), www.cnj.jus.br/wpcontent/uploads/conteudo/arquivo/2018/06/2df3ba3e13e95bf17e33a9c10e60a5a1.pdf
——, 'Justice in Figures' (2021), https://paineis.cnj.jus.br/QvAJAXZfc/opendoc.htm?document=qvw_l%2FPainelCNJ.qvw&host=QVS%40neodimio03&anonymous=true&sheet=shResumoDespFT
Co, EEA, 'Challenges to the Philippine Culture of Corruption' in S Bracking (ed), *Corruption and Development: The Anti-Corruption Campaigns* (Palgrave Macmillan, 2007)
Cordini, N, 'The internationalization of criminal law: Transnational criminal law, basis for a regional legal theory of criminal law' (2018) 8(1) *Revista Brasileira de Políticas Públicas* 261
Cornwall, A and Shankland, A, 'Engaging citizens: Lessons from building Brazil's national health system' (2008) 66(10) *Social Science & Medicine* 2173
Cruz-Martínez, G, 'Going beyond aggregated measures in the conditional cash transfer programs: The effective coverage of benefits and beneficiaries' (2015) 14(27) *Cadernos PROLAM/USP* 102
Cunha, RAS, Serra, SAdaE, and Costa, MMO, 'The Fight Against Corruption in Portugal' (2013) *Tourism & Management Studies* 700
Dahl, M, 'How do International Organizations Scrutinize Transforming States? The Case of Transparency International and the Baltic States' in L de Sousa, PJ Larmour and B Hindess, (eds), *Governments, NGOs and Anti-Corruption: The New Integrity Warriors* (Routledge, 2009)
Dahl, RA, and Shapiro, I, *On Democracy* (Yale University Press, 1998)
Da Ros, L and Taylor, MM, *Brazilian Politics on Trial. Corruption and Reform under Democracy* (Lynne Rienner Publishers, 2022)
Diamond, LJ and Morlino, L, 'The Quality of Democracy: An Overview' (2004) 15(4) *Journal of Democracy* 20
Dissenha, RC and Junior, PRI, 'A internacionalização do poder punitivo: riscos normativos e políticos da demanda por leis penais universais' (2018) 147 *Revista Brasileira de Ciências Criminais* 813
Dunoff, JL, 'The multifaceted relationship between functionalism and global constitutionalism' in A Lang and A Wiener (eds), *Handbook on Global Constitutionalism* (Edward Elgar Publishing, 2017)
Economist, The, 'The Economist Intelligence Unit's Index of Democracy 2008', https://graphics.eiu.com/pdf/democracy%20index%202008.pdf
Editorial, 'Moro é tratado como herói em manifestação em Brasília' (Estado de Minas, 13 March 2016), www.em.com.br/app/noticia/politica/2016/03/13/interna_politica,743045/moro-e-tratado-como-heroi-em-manifestacao-em-brasilia.shtml
Educação Tp, 'Anuário Brasileiro da Educação Básica' (Todos pela Educação, 2021), https://todospelaeducacao.org.br/wordpress/wpcontent/uploads/2021/07/Anuario_21final.pdf
Eiró, F, 'Anti-poverty Programs and Vote-Buying Strategies: Lessons from Northeast Brazil' in I Kubbe and A Engelbert (eds), *Corruption and Norms: Why Informal Rules Matter* (Springer International Publishing, 2017)
——, 'The Vicious Cycle in the Bolsa Família Program's Implementation: Discretionality and the Challenge of Social Rights Consolidation in Brazil' (2019) 42(3) *Qualitative Sociology* 385
Engel, CL, 'A Violência Contra a Mulher' (IPEA – Instituto de Pesquisa Economica Aplicada 2019), www.ipea.gov.br/retrato/pdf/190215_tema_d_a_violenca_contra_mulher.pdf> accessed 2 November 2021
Engelmann, F, 'The "Fight against Corruption" in Brazil from the 2000s: A Political Crusade through Judicial Activism' (2020) 47 *Journal of Law and Society* S74
Faoro, R, *Os Donos do Poder: Formação do Patronato Político Brasileiro*, 5th edn (Globo, 2012)

Fassbender, B, *The United Nations Charter as the Constitution of the International Community* (Martinus Nijhoff Publishers, 2009)
Feldman, DL, 'The Efficacy of Anti-Corruption Institutions in Italy' (2020) 22(6) *Public Integrity*
Fernandes, FA and Gomes, AC, 'Acerca da experiência brasileira com o Instituto da Delação Premiada, expectativas político-criminais transmudadas em Políticas Públicas Criminais' 83 *Revista Jurídica Lex* 359
Fernandes, F, *Brasil em Compasso de Espera* (Editora Hucitec, 1980)
——, *A Revolução Burguesa no Brasil*, 3rd edn (Editora Guanabara, 1987)
Fernandes, T, 'Bolsonaro diz que há fraude em 30% do Bolsa Família', *Folha de São Paulo* (8 October 2018), www1.folha.uol.com.br/poder/2018/10/bolsonaro-diz-que-ha-fraude-em-30-do-bolsa-familia.shtml
Filho, AdN, 'Brazil: a long journey towards a universal healthcare system' in JM Zuniga, SP Marks and LO Gostin, *Advancing the Human Right to Health* (Oxford University Press, 2013)
Filho, M, 'Como Operação que Levou Ex-Premiê de Portugal à Prisão está Ajudando a Lava Jato', *BBC News Brasil* (2016), www.bbc.com/portuguese/noticias/2016/03/160318_lava_jato_portugal_mdb_mf
Filho, MGF, *Curso de Direito Constitucional* (Saraiva, 2012)
Fleury, S et al, 'Local governance in the decentralized health care system in Brazil' (2010) 28(6) *Revista panamericana de salud pública* 446
Fontainha, F and de Lima AEC, 'Judiciário e Crise Política no Brasil Hoje: Do Mensalão a Lava Jato' in F Kerche and JF Junior, *Operação Lava Jato e a democracia brasileira* (Contracorrente, 2018)
Freedom House, *Freedom in the World 2019: the annual survey of political rights and civil liberties* (Rowman & Littlefield Publishers, 2020)
——, 'Freedom in the World 2021' (Freedom House), https://freedomhouse.org/country/brazil/freedom-world/2021
Freixo, Ad and Machado, RP, *Brasil em transe: Bolsonarismo, nova direita e desdemocratização* (Oficina Raquel, 2019)
Freyre, G, *Casa Grande e Senzala: Formação da Família Brasileira sob o Regime da Economia Patriarcal*, 51st edn (Global Editora, 2006)
Gargarella, R, *Latin American Constitutionalism, 1810–2010: the Engine Room of the Constitution* (Oxford University Press, 2013)
Geissel, B, Kneuer, M and Lauth, H-J, 'Measuring the Quality of Democracy: Introduction' (2016) 37(5) *International Political Science Review* 571
Gilbert, J-A and Sharman, JC, 'Turning a Blind Eye to Bribery: Explaining Failures to Comply with the International Anti-corruption Regime' (2016) 64(1) *Political Studies* 74
Giraut, C, 'From privileges to rights: changing perceptions of racial quotas in Brazil' (2023) *Ethnic and Racial Studies* 1–24
Gonzalez-Ocantos, EA et al, *Prosecutors, Voters, and the Criminalization of Corruption in Latin America: the Case of Lava Jato* (Cambridge University Press, 2023)
Governo Federal, 'Mais Médicos Resultado para o País' (Governo Federal, 2018) http://maismedicos.gov.br/resultados-para-o-pais
GRECO, 'Fifth Evaluation Round: Preventing corruption and promoting integrity in central governments (top executive functions) and law enforcement agencies Portugal' (2024), https://rm.coe.int/grecoeval5rep-2022-3-final-eng-evaluation-report-portugal-public/1680ae19a7
Guilhot, N, *The Democracy Makers: Human Rights and International Order* (Columbia University Press, 2005)
Gutterman, E and Lohaus, M, 'What is the "Anti-corruption" Norm in Global Politics?' in I Kubbe and A Engelbert, (eds), *Corruption and Norms. Political Corruption and Governance* (Palgrave Macmillan, 2018)
Hall, A, 'The Last Shall be First: Political Dimensions of Conditional Cash Transfers in Brazil' (2012) 11 *Journal of Policy Practice* 25

Hasselmann, J, *Sérgio Moro – A história do homem por trás da operação que mudou o Brasil* (Universo dos Livros Editora, 2016)

Havercroft, J et al, 'Editorial: Donald Trump as global constitutional breaching experiment' (2018) 7(1) *Global Constitutionalism* 1

Held, D, *Models of Democracy*, 3rd edn (Polity, 2006)

Hevia, FJ, 'Society-State relationships, citizen participation and political clientelism inside programs that combat poverty. the case of Bolsa Familia in Brazil' (2011) 57 *América Latina Hoy* 205

Hindess, B, 'Good government and corruption' in P Larmour and N Wolanin (eds), *Corruption and Anti-Corruption* (ANU Press, 2013)

Hoffman, R, 'Desigualdade e Pobreza no Brasil no Periodo 1979–90' (1995) 49 *Revista Brasileira de Economia – RBE*

de Holanda, SB, *Raízes do Brasil*, 27th edn (Companhia das Letras, 2014)

Huber, E, Rueschemeyer, D and Stephens, JD, 'The Paradoxes of Contemporary Democracy: Formal, Participatory, and Social Dimensions' (1997) 29(3) *Comparative Politics* 323

Hunter, W and Sugiyama, NB, 'Assessing the Bolsa Família Successes, Shortcomings, and Unknowns' in PR Kingstone and TJ Power (eds), *Democratic Brazil Divided* (University of Pittsburgh Press, 2017)

Huntington, SP, *The Third Wave: Democratization in the Late Twentieth Century* (University of Oklahoma Press, 1993)

IBGE, 'Síntese de Indicadores Sociais' (Instituto Brasileiro de Geografia e Estatística (IBGE) 2012–2020), www.ibge.gov.br/estatisticas/multidominio/condicoes-de-vidadesigualdade-e-pobreza/9221-sintese-de-indicadores-sociais.html?=&t=resultados

——, 'Síntese de indicadores sociais: uma análise das condições de vida da população brasileira' (Instituto Brasileiro de Geografia e Estatística (IBGE), 2016), https://biblioteca.ibge.gov.br/visualizacao/livros/liv98965.pdf

——, 'Indígenas: Gráficos e Tabelas' (Instituto Brasileiro de Geografia e Estatística), https://indigenas.ibge.gov.br/graficos-e-tabelas-2.html

——, 'Síntese de Indicadores Sociais: uma análise das condições de vida da população brasileira' (Instituto Brasileiro de Geografia e Estatística (IBGE), 2021), https://biblioteca.ibge.gov.br/visualizacao/livros/liv101760.pdf

IDEA, 'The Global State of Democracy 2021: Building Resilience in a Pandemic Era' (International Institute for Democracy and Electoral Assistance, 2021), www.idea.int/democracytracker/sites/default/files/2022-11/GSOD21.pdf

IPEA, 'Contas de saúde na perspectiva da contabilidade internacional: conta SHA para o Brasil, 2015 a 2019' (Instituto de Pesquisa Econômica Aplicada, 2022), www.ipea.gov.br/portal/images/stories/PDFs/livros/livros/220202_livro_contas_de_saude.pdf

Insper, 'Judicialização da Saúde no Brasil: Perfil das demandas, causas e propostas de solução' (Conselho Nacional de Justiça, 2019)

International Council on Human Rights Policy, 'Corruption and Human Rights: Making the Connection' (ICHRP, 2009), https://ssrn.com/abstract=1551222

——, 'Integrating Human Rights in the Anti-Corruption Agenda: Challenges, Possibilities and Opportunities' (ICHRP, 2010), https://ssrn.com/abstract=1705396

Ivanov, KS, 'The Limits of a Global Campaign against Corruption' in S Bracking (ed), *Corruption and Development: The Anti-Corruption Campaigns* (Palgrave Macmillan, 2007)

Jakobi, AP, 'Global Anti-Corruption Norms' in AP Jakobi (ed), *Common Good and Evils? The Formation of Global Crime Governance* (Oxford University Press, 2013)

Júnior, JF and Kerche, F, *Operação Lava Jato e a democracia brasileira* (Contracorrente, 2018)

Karl, TL, 'Latin America: Virtuous or Perverse Cycle' in G O'Donnell, JV Cullell and OM Iazzetta (eds), *The Quality of Democracy* (University of Notre Dame Press, 2004)

Kelley, T, 'Beyond the Washington Consensus and new institutionalism: what is the future of law and development? (2010) 35(3) *North Carolina Journal of International Law and Commercial Regulation* 539

Kennedy, D, *The Dark Sides of Virtue: Reassessing International Humanitarianism* (Princeton University Press, 2004)

Kerbauy, MTM, 'Os programas de transferência de renda e o voto regional nas eleições presidenciais de 2010' (2011) 17(2) *Opinião pública: publicaçao do CESOP* 477

Khan, M, 'Governance and Anti-Corruption Reforms in Developing Countries: Policies, Evidence and Ways Forward' (2006) G-24 Discussion Papers 42, United Nations Conference on Trade and Development

King, M and Thornhill, CJ, *Niklas Luhmann's Theory of Politics and Law* (Palgrave Macmillan, 2003)

Klitgaard, RE, *Controlling Corruption* (University of California Press, 1988)

Koechlin, L and Carmona, MS, 'Corruption and Human Rights: Exploring the Connection' in RI Rotberg (ed), *Corruption, Global Security, and World Order* (Brookings Institution Press, 2009)

Koskenniemi, M, 'Constitutionalism as Mindset: Reflections on Kantian Themes About International Law and Globalization' (2006) 8(1) *Theoretical Inquiries in Law* 2

——, *The Politics of International Law* (Hart, 2011)

——, 'Hegemonic Regimes' in MA Young (ed), *Regime Interaction in International Law: Facing Fragmentation* (Cambridge University Press, 2012)

Krisch, N, *Beyond Constitutionalism: The Pluralist Structure of Postnational Law* (Oxford University Press, 2010)

Kumm, M, 'The Cosmopolitan Turn in Constitutionalism: On the Relationship between Constitutionalism in and beyond the State' in J Dunoff and J Trachtman (eds), *Ruling the World? Constitutionalism, International Law, and Global Governance* (Cambridge University Press, 2009)

——, Havercroft, J, Dunoff, J and Wiener, A, 'Editorial: The end of 'the West' and the future of global constitutionalism' (2017) 6(1) *Global Constitutionalism* 1

Lang, AF and Wiener, A, 'A constitutionalising global order: an introduction' in A Lang and A Wiener (eds), *Handbook on Global Constitutionalism* (Edward Elgar Publishing, 2017)

Larmour, P and Wolanin, N, 'Introduction' in P Larmour and N Wolanin (eds), *Corruption and Anti-Corruption* (ANU Press, 2013)

Lauth, H-J, *The Matrix of Democracy: A Three-Dimensional Approach to Measuring the Quality of Democracy and Regime Transformations* (2015)

——, 'The internal relationships of the dimensions of democracy: The relevance of trade-offs for measuring the quality of democracy' (2016) 37(5) *International Political Science Review* 606

Layton, ML et al, 'Does Welfare Provision Promote Democratic State Legitimacy? Evidence from Brazil's Bolsa Família Program' (2017) 59(4) *Latin American Politics and Society* 99

Lechner, N, 'On the Imaginary of the Citizenry' in G O'Donnell, JV Cullell and OM Iazzetta (eds), *The Quality of Democracy* (University of Notre Dame Press, 2004)

Leubolt, B, 'Institutions, discourse and welfare: Brazil as a distributional regime' (2013) 13(1) *Global Social Policy* 66

Levine, DH and Molina, JE, *The Quality of Democracy in Latin America* (Lynne Rienner, 2011)

de Lima, RK and Mouzinho, GMP, 'Produção e reprodução da tradição inquisitorial no Brasil: Entre delações e confissões premiadas' (2016) 9(3) *Dilemas – Revista de Estudos de Conflito e Controle Social* 505

Limongi, F, 'A Democracia no Brasil: Presidencialismo, Coalizão Partidária e Processo Decisório' (2006) 76 *Novos Estudos CEBRAP* 23

Limongi, F and O'Neil, EP, 'Democracy in Brazil: presidentialism, party coalitions and the decision-making process' (2007) 3 *Novos Estudos CEBRAP*

Lindner, J and Weterman, D, 'Mais Médicos formava "núcleos de guerrilha", diz Bolsonaro', *Terra News Web Portal* (1 August 2019), www.terra.com.br/vida-e-estilo/saude/bolsonaro-diz-que-mais-medicos-tinha-objetivo-de-formar-nucleos-de-guerrilha,7ed4229d8ed1383a3fd685880d2b0998mqcwe5cr.html

Luhmann, N, *O direito da sociedade* (Martins Fontes Selo Martins, 2017)

Magalhães, P, 'When Corruption Investigations Come to Nothing: A Natural Experiment on Trust in Courts' (2024) *Governance* 37

Maggio, P, 'A Critical Analysis of Corruption and Anti-Corruption Policies in Italy' (2020) 28(2) *Journal of Financial Crime*

Manzetti, L and Wilson, CJ, 'Why Do Corrupt Governments Maintain Public Support?' (2007) 40(8) *Comparative Political Studies* 949

Marks, S, *The Riddle of All Constitutions: International Law, Democracy and the Critique of Ideology* (Oxford University Press, 2000)

Marona, M and Kerche, F, 'From the Banestado Case to Operation Car Wash: Building an Anti-Corruption Institutional Framework in Brazil' (2021) 64(3) *Dados, Rio de Janeiro*

Martins, CZ, Martins, VTZ and Valim, R, *Lawfare: uma introdução* (Editora Contracorrente, 2019)

Martins, D, 'Comercial Johnnie Walker O Gigante Acordou Rio de Janeiro Brasil', *YouTube* (1 July 2013), www.youtube.com/watch?v=Ja2CP0W3E6c

McFarlane, J, 'Transnational crime corruption, crony capitalism and nepotism in the twenty-first century' in P Larmour and N Wolanin (eds), *Corruption and Anti-Corruption* (ANU Press, 2013)

Melo, MA and Pereira, C, *Making Brazil Work: Checking the President in a Multiparty System* (Palgrave Macmillan, 2013)

de Mendonça RSP and de Barros RP, 'A evolução do bem-estar e da desigualdade no Brasil desde 1960' (1995) 49(2) *Revista Brasileira de Economia – RBE*

Meyer, EPN, 'Judges and Courts Destabilizing Constitutionalism: The Brazilian Judiciary Branch's Political and Authoritarian Character' (2018) 19(4) *German Law Journal* 727

Ministério da Cidadania, 'Programa Bolsa Família – quantidade de famílias e valores (até outubro/2021)' (Secretaria de Avaliação e Gestão da Informação), https://aplicacoes.mds.gov.br/sagi/vis/data3/v.php

Ministério do Desenvolvimento Social e Combate à Fome, 'Fome Zero: Uma História Brasileira', vol 3 (MDS, 2010), www.mds.gov.br/webarquivos/publicacao/Fome%20Zero%20Vol1.pdf

Ministério da Justiça e Segurança Pública (MJSP), 'Polícia Federal completa mais de 100 operações contra fraudes relacionadas às ações de enfrentamento à pandemia' (*Polícia Federal Website*, 2021), www.gov.br/pf/pt-br/assuntos/noticias/2021/07/policia-federal-completa-mais-de-100-operacoes-contra-fraudes-relacionadas-as-acoes-de-enfrentamento-a-pandemia

Ministério Público Federal (MPF), 'Caso Lava Jato', www.mpf.mp.br/grandes-casos/lava-jato

Mohallem, MF and Ragazzo, CEJ, 'Diagnóstico institucional: primeiros passos para um plano nacional anticorrupção' (Fundação Getúlio Vargas-Rio, 2017), https://bibliotecadigital.fgv.br/dspace/handle/10438/18167

—— et al, 'Novas medidas contra a corrupção' (Fundação Getúlio Vargas-Rio, 2018), https://static.poder360.com.br/2019/05/Novas_Medidas_pacote_completo.pdf

Moreira, MR and Escorel, S, 'Municipal health councils of Brazil: A debate on the democratization of health in the twenty years of the UHS' (2009) 14(3) *Ciência & Saude Coletiva* 795

Moro, SF, 'Considerações sobre a operação mani pulite' (2004) 26 *Revista do Centro de Estudos Judiciários (CEJ)* 6

Morris, SD and Blake, CH, 'Introduction: Political and Analytical Challenges of Corruption in Latin America' in SD Morris and CH Blake (eds), *Corruption and Democracy in Latin America* (University of Pittsburgh Press, 2009)

Munck, GL, 'What is democracy? A reconceptualization of the quality of democracy' (2016) 23(1) *Democratization* 1–26, www.tandfonline.com/doi/abs/10.1080/13510347.2014.918104?journalCode=fdem20

Muñoz, P, 'Latin America Erupts: Peru Goes Populist' (2021) 32(3) *Journal of Democracy*

Neri, M, *Mapa da Nova Pobreza* (Fundação Getúlio Vargas (FGV), 2022)

Neto, CPS and Sarmento, D, *Direito Constitucional* (Fórum, 2012)

Netto, V, *Lava Jato: O juiz Sergio Moro e os bastidores da operação que abalou o Brasil* (Primeira Pessoa, 2016)

Neves, RTS and Resque, JDD, 'Diálogo judicial transnacional: a Recepção dos Tratados Internacionais na Jurisprudência do Supremo Tribunal Federal sobre Territórios Indígenas' in AMDA Lopes and MM'AB Lima (eds), *A Internalizacao de Direitos Internacionais de Direitos Humanos na America do Sul* (Livraria do Advogado, 2017)

O'Donnell, GA, Vargas Cullel, J and Iazzetta, OM, *The Quality of Democracy: Theory and Applications* (University of Notre Dame Press, 2004)

——, 'Why the rule of law matters' (2004) 15(4) *Journal of Democracy* 32

Okojie, P and Momoh, A, 'Corruption and Reform in Nigeria' in S Bracking (ed), *Corruption and Development: The Anti-Corruption Campaigns* (Palgrave Macmillan, 2007)

de Oliveira, EN and Moisés, JA, 'Corruption in the Perception of Brazilian Society: Persistence and Resilience' (2023) 29(2) *Revista do CESOP*

Organization of American States, 'Mechanism for Follow-Up on the Implementation of the Inter-American Convention Against Corruption' (OAS, 2011), www.oas.org/en/sla/dlc/mesicic/docs/mesicic3_bra_en.pdf

Paes-Sousa, R and Vaitsman, J, 'The Zero Hunger and Brazil without Extreme Poverty programs: a step forward in Brazilian social protection policy' (2014) 19(11) *Ciência & Saude Coletiva* 4351

Pan American Health Organization, 'Relatório 30 anos de SUS, que SUS para 2030?' (PAHO, 2018), https://iris.paho.org/handle/10665.2/52517

Paixão, C, 'Direito, política, autoritarismo e democracia no Brasil: da Revolução de 30 à promulgação da Constituição da República de 1988' (2011) 13(26) *Araucaria*, https://revistascientificas.us.es/index.php/araucaria/article/view/1379

Pereira, LM, 'A Aplicação do Direito Internacional no Combate à Corrupção no Brasil: A Cooperação Jurídica Internacional e a Atuação do Ministério Público Federal na "Operação Lava Jato"' in W Menezes (ed), *Direito Internacional em Expansão*, vol VII (Arraes Editora, 2016)

Peters, A, 'Corruption as a violation of international human rights' (2018) 29(4) *European Journal of International Law* 1251

Pilau, L and Azevedo, R, 'Os impactos da Operação Lava Jato na Polícia Federal brasileira' in JF Júnior and F Kerche (eds), *Operação Lava Jato e a democracia brasileira* (Contracorrente, 2018)

Piovesan, F, *Direitos Humanos e o Direito Constitucional Internacional* (Saraiva Educação SA, 2018)

Power, TJ and Taylor, MM, *Corruption and Democracy in Brazil The Struggle for Accountability* (University of Notre Dame Press, 2011)

Prado Jr, C, *Formação do Brasil Contemporâneo: colônia* (Livraria Martins Editora, 2011)

Prado, MM and Machado, MRdA, 'Uso do Direito Penal para Combater a Corrupção: Potencial, Risos e Limitações da Operação Lava Jato' (2021) 17(2) *Revista Direito GV*

——, 'Turning Corruption Trials into Political Tools in the Name of Transparency: The Lava Jato Case' in S Botero, DM Brinks and EA Gonzalez-Ocantos (eds), *The Limits of Judicialization: From Progress to Backlash in Latin America* (Cambridge University Press, 2022)

Przeworski, A, 'Minimalist Conception of Democracy: A Defense' in I Shapiro and C Hacker-Cordon (eds), *Democracy's Value* (Cambridge University Press, 1999)

——, *Crisis of Democracy* (Cambridge University Press, 2019)

Rehren, A, 'The Crisis of The Democratic State' in CH Blake and SD Morris (eds), *Corruption and Democracy in Latin America* (University of Pittsburgh Press, 2009)

Ribeiro, D, *O Povo Brasileiro: Formação e Sentido do Brasil*, 3rd edn (Global Editora, 2015)

Ricupero, B, *Sete Lições sobre as Interpretações do Brasil*, 2nd edn (Alameda, 2011)

Ritchie, H et al, 'Coronavirus Pandemic (COVID-19)' (OurWorldinData.org, 2020), https://ourworldindata.org/coronavirus

da Rocha, RCB, 'Programas condicionais de transferência de renda e fecundidade: Evidências do bolsa família' (2018) 22(3) *Economia Aplicada* 175

Roda Viva, 'O Roda Viva recebe o candidato à Presidência da República pelo Partido Social Liberal (PSL), Jair Bolsonaro, que fala sobre seus planos para a presidência, caso venha a ser eleito', *YouTube* (31 July 2018), www.youtube.com/watch?v=lDL59dkeTi0&t=1s

Rodrigues, MGM, 'Indigenous Rights in Democratic Brazil' (2002) 24(2) *Human Rights Quarterly* 487

Rodriguez-Garavito, C, 'Toward a Sociology of the Global Rule of Law Field: Neoliberalism, Neoconstitutionalism, and the Struggle over Judicial Reform in Latin America' in B Garth and Y Dezalay (eds), *Lawyers and the Rule of Law in an Era of Globalization* (Routledge, 2011)

Rose-Ackerman, S, *Corruption and Government: Causes, Consequences, and Reform* (Cambridge Unversity Press, 1999)

—— and Palifka, BJ, 'Corruption, Organized Crime, and Money Laundering' in K Basu and T Cordella (eds), *Institutions, Governance and the Control of Corruption. International Economic Association Series* (Palgrave Macmillan, 2018)

Rosenfeld, M, 'Is global constitutionalism meaningful or desirable?' (2014) 25(1) *European Journal of International Law* 177

Rueschemeyer, D, 'The Quality of Democracy: Addressing Inequality' (2004) 15(4) *Journal of Democracy* 76

Sarlet, IW and Figueiredo, MF, 'Algumas considerações sobre o direito fundamental à proteção e promoção da saúde aos 20 anos da Constituição federal de 1988' (2008) 17 *Revista de Direito do Consumidor* 47

Sampson, S, 'The anti-corruption industry: from movement to institution' (2010) 11(2) *Global Crime* 261

——, 'Anti-corruption: Who Cares?' in S Arvidsson (ed), *Challenges in Managing Sustainable Business* (Palgrave Macmillan, 2018)

Sánchez-Ancochea, D and Mattei, L, 'Bolsa Família, poverty and inequality: Political and economic effects in the short and long run' (2011) 11(2–3) *Global Social Policy* 299

Santiso, C, 'Economic reform and judicial governance in Brazil: Balancing independence with accountability' (2003) 10(4) *Democratization* 161, www.tandfonline.com/action/showCitFormats?doi=10.1080%2F13510340312331294077> accessed 11 December 2021

dos Santos AP and Diana, GM, 'O perfil racial nos quadros da administração pública no Brasil: um primeiro balanço dos efeitos da reserva de vagas para negros em uma organização de segurança pública' (2018) 69(4) *Revista do Serviço Público* 951

dos Santos JGB and Gallego, E, 'Fighting Corruption, Dismantling Democracy: Antagonism, Communication, and the Political Use of Lava Jato in Brazil' in S Botero, DM Brinks and EA Gonzalez-Ocantos (eds), *The Limits of Judicialization: From Progress to Backlash in Latin America* (Cambridge University Press, 2022)

dos Santos, SA, 'Affirmative Action and Political Dispute in Today's Brazilian Academe' (2014) 41(5) *Latin American Perspectives* 141

Sartori, G, *The Theory of Democracy Revisited* (Chatham House Publishers, 1987)

Sberna, S and Vannucci, A, '"It's the politics, stupid!" The politicization of anti-corruption in Italy' (2013) 60 *Crime Law and Social Change* 565–93

Schertel Mendes, F, *Leniency Policies in the Prosecution of Economic Crimes and Corruption* (Nomos Verlagsgesellschaft mbH & Co KG, 2021)

Sen, A, *Development as Freedom* (Oxford University Press, 2001)

Senkevics, AS and Mello, UM, 'O perfil discente das universidades federais mudou pós-Lei de Cotas?' (2021) 49(172) *Cadernos de Pesquisa* 184

Sewall, RG, 'Conditional Cash Transfer Programs in Latin America' (2008) 28(2) *The SAIS Review of International Affairs* 175

Shapiro, I, *The State of Democracy Theory* (Princeton University Press, 2003)

Simon, J, *Governing Through Crime: How the War on Crime Transformed American Democracy and Created a Culture of Fear* (Oxford University Press, 2007)

da Silva CT, 'A homologação da terra indígena Raposa/Serra do Sol e seus efeitos: Uma análise performativa das 19 condicionantes do STF' (2018) 33(98) *Revista Brasileira de Ciências Sociais* 1

Silva, GM, Daflon, VT and Giraut, C, 'Seeing race like a state: higher education affirmative action verification commissions in Brazil' (2024) 66(1) *Latin American Politics and Society*

Silva, JA, *Curso de Direito Constitucional Positivo*, 25th edn (Malheiros, 2005)

da Silva MR, 'A colaboração premiada como terceira via do direito penal no enfrentamento à corrupção administrativa organizada' (2017) 3 *Revista Brasileira de Direito Processual Penal* 285

Silva, TD, *Ação Afirmativa e População Negra na Educação Superior: Acesso e Perfil Discente* (Instituto de Pesquisa Econômica Aplicada – Ipea, 2020)

Soares, F and Recuero, R, 'A Argumentação dos Deputados na Votação do Processo de Impeachment de Dilma Rousseff' (2018) 1 *Estudos em Comunicação* 69

Soares, S, 'The efficiency and effectiveness of social protection against poverty and inequality in Brazil' in J Midgley and D Piachaud (eds), *Social Protection, Economic Growth and Social Change* (Edward Elgar Publishing, 2013)

Souza, J, *A elite do atraso: Da escravidão à Lava Jato* (Leya, 2017)

——, *A Classe Média no Espelho: Sua História, Seus Sonhos e Ilusões, sua Realidade* (Estação Brasil, 2018)

de Sousa, L, Larmour, PJ and Hindess, B, *Governments, NGOs and Anti-corruption: The New Integrity Warriors* (Routledge, 2009)

Sundaram, JK, 'Good Governance, Anti-Corruption, and Economic Development' in RI Rotberg RI (ed), *Corruption, Global Security, and World Order* (Brookings Institution Press, 2009)

Tavares, LA and de Campos, CH, 'A Convenção Interamericana para prevenir, punir e erradicar a Violência contra a Mulher, "Convenção de Belém do Pará", e a Lei Maria da Penha' (2018) 6(3) *Interfaces Científicas – Humanas e Sociais* 9

Taylor, MM, 'Corruption, Accountability Reforms, and Democracy in Brazil' in CH Blake and SD Morris (eds), *Corruption and Democracy in Latin America* (University of Pittsburgh Press, 2009)

Teubner, G, *Constitutional Fragments: Societal Constitutionalism and Globalization* (Oxford University Press, 2012), https://doi.org/10.1093/acprof:oso/9780199644674.001.0001

——, 'Quod omnes tangit: Transnational Constitutions Without Democracy?' (2018) 45(S1) *Journal of Law and Society* S5

Teorell, J, Coppedge, M, Lindberg, S and Skaaning, S-E, 'Measuring Polyarchy Across the Globe, 1900–2017' (2018) 54(1) *Studies in Comparative International Development* 71

Thornhill, CJ, 'The Enlightenment and global constitutionalism' in A Lang and A Wiener (eds), *Handbook on Global Constitutionalism* (Edward Elgar Publishing, 2017)

——, *The Sociology of Law and the Global Transformation of Democracy* (Cambridge University Press, 2018)

Tibaldo, G and Roberto, W, 'Bolsonaro diz que vai usar Revalida para "expulsar" médicos cubanos do Brasil', *G1 News Web Site* (22 August 2018), https://g1.globo.com/sp/presidente-prudente-regiao/noticia/2018/08/22/bolsonaro-diz-que-vai-usar-revalida-para-expulsar-medicos-cubanos-do-brasil.ghtml

Tocqueville, A and Reeve, H, *Democracy in America* (Saunders & Otley, 1835)

Tourinho, M, 'Brazil in the global anticorruption regime' (2018) 61 *Revista Brasileira de Política Internacional*

Transparency International, 'The Americas: Economies grow, democracies shrink. What does corruption have to do with it?' (TI, 5 December 2012), https://blog.transparency.org/2012/12/05/the-americas-economies-grow-democracies-shrink-what-does-corruption-have-to-do-with-it/index.html> accessed 08 August 2022

——, 'Together Against Corruption: Transparency International Strategy 2020' (TI, 2015), TogetherAgainstCorruption_Strategy2020_EN.pdf (transparencycdn.org)

——, 'The Conviction of Former Brazilian President Lula for Corruption Shows the Strength of the Judiciary' (TI, 13 July 2017), www.transparency.org/en/press/the-conviction-of-former-brazilian-president-lula-for-corruption-shows-the

Tribunal Superior Eleitoral, *Estatísticas do eleitorado* (TSE, 2020), www.tse.jus.br/eleitor/estatisticas-de-eleitorado/estatistica-do-eleitorado-por-sexo-e-grau-de-instrucao

Trindade, A, 'Dilemas e desafios da Proteção Internacional dos Direitos Humanos no limiar do século XXI' (1997) 40 *Revista Brasileira De Política Internacional*

Trubek, DM and Santos, A, *The New Law and Economic Development: A Critical Appraisal* (Cambridge University Press, 2006)

Tully J, 'The Imperialism of Modern Constitutional Democracy' in M Loughlin and N Walker (eds), *The Paradox of Constitutionalism: Constituent Power and Constitutional Form* (Oxford University Press, 2008)

United Nations Development Programme, 'Corruption and Good Governance' (UNDP, 1997), https://digitallibrary.un.org/record/1491472

——, 'Human Development Report 2015' (UNDP, 2015), http://report2015.archive.s3-website-us-east-1.amazonaws.com/

United Nations Office on Drugs and Crime, 'Anti-Corruption Toolkit' (UNODC, 2004), www.unodc.org/documents/treaties/corruption/toolkit/toolkitv5_foreword.pdf

——, 'Technical Guide to the United Nations Convention Against Corruption' (UNODC, 2009), www.unodc.org/documents/treaties/UNCAC/Publications/TechnicalGuide/0984395_Ebook.pdf

——, 'Review by Haiti and Mexico of the Implementation by Brazil of articles 15–42 of Chapter III. "Criminalization and law enforcement" and articles 44–50 of Chapter IV. "International cooperation" of the United Nations Convention against Corruption for the review cycle 2010–2015' (UNODC, 2016), www.unodc.org/documents/treaties/UNCAC/CountryVisitFinalReports/2017_01_19_Brazil_Final_Country_Report.pdf

—— and Ministério da Justiça e Segurança Pública, 'Relatório Nacional sobre Tráfico de Pessoas: Dados 2017 a 2020' (MJSP, 2021), www.unodc.org/documents/lpo-brazil/Topics_TIP/Publicacoes/relatorio-de-dados-2017-2020.pdf

Vaitsman, J, Borges de Andrade, GR and Otavio Farias, L, 'Proteção social no Brasil: o que mudou na assistência social após a Constituição de 1988' (2009) 14(3) *Ciência & Saúde Coletiva* 731

Vannucci, AP, 'The Controversial Legacy of "Mani Pulite": A Critical Analysis of Italian Corruption and Anti-Corruption Policies' (2009) 1(2) *Bulletin of Italian Politics* 233

Vieira, ACA and Quack, S, 'Trajectories of transnational mobilization for indigenous rights in Brazil' 56/4 *RAE* 380, www.scielo.br/j/rae/a/FJdGRJhmQsHCjKJK9BHytCH/?lang=en#

Vieira, OV, 'Clash of powers: Did operation car wash trigger a constitutional crisis in Brazil?' (2021) 71(1) *University of Toronto Law Journal* 174

Vilaça, L, 'A Social Movement Model for Judicial Behavior: Evidence from Brazil's Anti-Corruption Movements' (2024) 103(1) *Social Forces*

Villeneuve, J-P, Mugellini, G and Heide, M, 'International Anti-Corruption Initiatives: A Classification of Policy Interventions' (2019) 26(4) *European Journal On Criminal Policy And Research* 431

Walker, N, 'Post-Constituent Constitutionalism? The Case of the European Union' in M Loughlin and N Walker (eds), *The Paradox of Constitutionalism: Constituent Power and Constitutional Form* (Oxford University Press, 2008)

Wang, DWL, 'Courts and health care rationing: the case of the Brazilian Federal Supreme Court' (2013) 8(1) *Health Economics, Policy and Law* 75

Warde, W, *O espetáculo da corrupção: Como um sistema corrupto e o modo de combatê-lo estão destruindo o país* (Leya, 2018)

Warf, B, *Global Corruption from a Geographic Perspective* (Springer, 2019)

Wathne, C and Stephenson, MC, 'The Credibility of Corruption Statistics' (2021) U4 Anti-Corruption Resource Centre, UF Issue 2021:4

Whelan, DJ and Donnelly, J, 'The West, Economic and Social Rights, and the Global Human Rights Regime: Setting the Record Straight' (2007) 29(4) *Human Rights Quarterly* 908

Wikileaks, 'Brazil: Illicit Finance Conference Uses the T Word, Successfully' (30 October 2009), https://wikileaks.org/plusd/cables/09BRASILIA1282_a.html

Wolf, ML, 'The World Needs an International Anti-Corruption Court' (2018) 147(3) *Daedalus* 144

World Bank Group, 'Helping Countries Combat Corruption: The Role of the World Bank' (WB, 1997), http://documents.worldbank.org/curated/en/799831538245192753/Helping-countries-combat-corruption-the-role-of-the-World-Bank

——, 'Strengthening World Bank Group engagement on governance and anticorruption: Main Report' (WB, 2007), https://documents.worldbank.org/pt/publication/documents-reports/documentdetail/426381468340863478/main-report

World Health Organization, 'The world health report: health systems financing: the path to universal coverage' (WHO, 2010), https://apps.who.int/iris/handle/10665/44371

——, 'Brazil: The mais médicos programme' (WHO, 2018), https://apps.who.int/iris/bitstream/handle/10665/326084/WHO-HIS-SDS-2018.19-eng.pdf

INDEX

www.ingramcontent.com/pod-product-compliance
Ingram Content Group UK Ltd.
Pitfield, Milton Keynes, MK11 3LW, UK
UKHW020816290926
15470UKWH00003B/1192

9 781509 981977